THOMAS MCMAHON'S

Search for Fame

MAX QUANCHI

Published in Australia by Sid Harta Books & Print Pty Ltd,
ABN: 34632585293
23 Stirling Crescent, Glen Waverley, Victoria 3150 Australia
Telephone: +61 3 9560 9920, Facsimile: +61 3 9545 1742
E-mail: author@sidharta.com.au

First published in Australia 2025
This edition published 2025
Copyright © Max Quanchi 2025
Cover design, typesetting: WorkingType (www.workingtype.com.au)

ISBN: 978-1-922958-94-5

About the author

Max Quanchi has taught Pacific History at Queensland University of Technology, University of Papua New Guinea and University of South Pacific. His research is on the history of photography in the Pacific.

He was a founding member of the Executive of the PHA and AAAPS and is on the Editorial Boards of *Journal of Pacific History* (2007) and the *Journal of New Zealand and Pacific Studies*.

He was guest editor for special issues on photography for *Pacific Studies* (1997), the *Journal of Pacific History* (2007) and the *Journal of New Zealand and Pacific Studies* (2020), and since 1996, he has convened panels on photography at the biannual Pacific History Association conferences. In 2007, his monograph, *Photographing Papua*, focused on the colonial frontier in Papua New Guinea.

His recent books include *Postcards from Oceania; Plantations, Pirogues and Port Towns* with Max Shekleton (2015), *Postcards from Colonial Fiji* with Max Shekleton (2019), *Tales from the Sak sak: Doing Nasho in New Guinea (2020)* and *Glorious Company; The Polynesia Company in Fiji and Melbourne* (2022).

Articles since the 1990s on the history of photography appear in the following journals: *History of Photography, History Focus, Pacific Arts, Journal of Pacific Studies, Agora, Australian Historical Studies, Journal of Australian Studies, Journal of New Zealand and Pacific Studies, Journal of Pacific History, The Oxford Companion to the Photograph* (2005), *Berg Encyclopaedia of Fashion and Dress* (2009), and *Coast to Coast* (2010).

He was born in rural Victoria in 1945 and studied at Frankston Teachers College, Monash University and the University of Queensland. He retired to Brisbane and now does some casual teaching, barracks for AFL Brisbane Lions, enjoys Mali blues music, red wine and art-house movies and does guest speaker trips on P&O cruises in the Pacific.

*This book is dedicated to my mother and father, Grace Quanchi
and Harry Quanchi, who gave up so much so their third son
could finish high school, matriculate and go on to tertiary studies.*

*They had passed on before I began gathering material on Thomas
McMahon, but they would have been proud, as descendants of
mid-18th century Scot and Swiss-Italian immigrants,
to see their son's name on a book about an Australian
pioneering photojournalist.*

Contents

Illustrations

List of Tables

Acronyms

ANA	Australian Natives Association
ANC	Armed Native Constabulary
ANU	Australian National University
BSIP	British Solomon Islands Protectorate
FRGS	Fellow of the Royal Geographical Society
GEIC	Gilbert and Ellis Islands Colony
GNC	German New Guinea Company
GT	*Geografisk Tidskrift* (Danish Journal of Geography)
HMSO	Her Majesty's Stationery Office, Britain
HSANZ	*Historical Studies of Australia and New Zealand*
JASO	*Journal of the Anthropological Society of Oxford*
JNZPS	*Journal of New Zealand and Pacific Studies*
JPH	*Journal of Pacific History*
LMS	London Missionary Society
NSW	New South Wales

NT	Northern Territory
PIM	*Pacific Islands Monthly*
POM	Port Moresby
Qld	Queensland
RGS	Royal Geographical Society
TI	Thursday Island
TSI	Torres Strait Islands
UH	University of Hawaii
WPHC	Western Pacific High Commission
WPHG	*Handels-und Plantagen-Gesellschaft der Südsee-Inseln zu Hamburg*

Acknowledgements

In the 1990s, I came across TJ McMahon during research for my doctorate on early photography in Papua, as a visit to Papua had been his initial foray into published photography. I then discovered he had travelled widely in the Pacific Islands, and I kept finding his published photographs, some unattributed, when I moved on to the study of illustrated serialised encyclopedias, the illustrated weekend editions of metropolitan newspapers and postcards. It seemed that, no matter which topic I pursued in the broader field of early photography in the Pacific, I could always refer to one or more of McMahon's photographs.

I thank those editors who published my work on these topics and who tolerated these diversions. Thanks go to curators and librarians who facilitated my search for his published photographs in Australia, Britain, the US and especially at the Royal Geographical Society (Queensland). A huge thank you goes to the brilliant concept and platform we all know simply as Trove. Thanks also to Queensland University of Technology for offering Undergraduate Summer Research Scholarships that enabled Hannah Perkins, Samantha Rose, Emma Francis and Jessica Collins to compile catalogues of published photographs from *The Sydney Mail, Northern Herald, The Queenslander, Otago Times* and *Auckland Weekly News*. The digital copying service of the State Library of Queensland located many photographs – thanks.

Thanks also to Brian Hoepper, who read the manuscript and made many useful comments on structure, content and expression.

Thanks go mostly to TJ (Tom) McMahon, a brilliant photographer who lives on today through Trove and on the bookshelves of libraries that hold serial collections of magazines, illustrated newspapers and serial encyclopedias, and whose photography certainly needs to be more well-known.

Timeline

1864   Born on Mount Abundance pastoral property, west of Roma, Queensland

?   Tutor to children on rural properties, Upper Burnett region, Queensland

1914   Farmer at Malanda near Cairns, Queensland

1915   Sept: 'special correspondent', publishes reports on Innisfail and Ingham; visits Papua and German New Guinea

Nov: reports on Cairns' hinterland

Dec: speaks on New Guinea at Chamber of Commerce and Royal Geographical Society in Brisbane

1916   Tours outback, Northern Territory and Torres Strait for *The Cairns Post* and *Northern Herald*

1917   Jan–May: publishes on Northern Territory and Torres Strait Islands

May: gives lectures in Melbourne for the ANA and in Cairns for the Red Cross

July–Aug: visits German New Guinea

Sept: reports on Eacham, Atherton and Ravenshoe Agricultural Shows

Oct–Nov: visits Solomon Islands

1918   May: exhibits photographs and gives talk at Kodak Gallery, Sydney; takes Burns Philp's 'islands run' to Nauru, Banaba, Gilbert Islands and Marshall Islands

1919   Visits England

1920	June: speaks in Adelaide and Melbourne on return passage; speaks at the Millions Club, Sydney, on the topic of Japan in the Pacific
	Sept: visits New Hebrides, Norfolk Island and Lord Howe Island; photographs on the Pacific published in pictorial serial encyclopedias throughout the 1920s
1921	May: short visit to Papua
	Aug: visits Fiji for three months
1922	Travels to China, Japan and Borneo; contributes full-page collage to annual Christmas issue of *The Sydney Mail*
1923	Publishes seven Pacific Island albums with McCarron Publishers in Sydney; publishes an illustrated series, 'The North', in *The Telegraph* (Brisbane)
Nov:	talks at Royal Colonial Institute, Sydney, on Queensland's economic potential; becomes reporter and photographer on rural Queensland, taking photographs and sending in reports for *The Brisbane Courier* and *The Queenslander*
1925	Full-page collage, 'Through Queensland', in Christmas Annual of the *Weekly Times* (Melbourne)
1926	His book, *The Orient I Found,* published in London
1928	Begins visits to Cairns, Malanda Agricultural Show, Atherton, Daintree, Mossman and Evelyn; reports on numerous outback towns and districts and on Brisbane's suburban hinterland
1933	Dies in Brisbane

Photographer, journalist, patriot

In 1915, Thomas McMahon changed careers at the age of fifty-one and began a personal quest to become famous as an expert on the nearby Pacific Islands as a photographer and a journalist. This was quite a change from his previous life as a tutor on outback pastoral properties, briefly as a farmer at Malanda near Cairns and later as a back-country photographer for Cairns and Townsville newspapers.

Between 1915 and 1922, he took self-funded voyages and photographed eleven Pacific Island colonies and territories, amassing a small collection of negatives and prints, modest by today's standards but a significant commitment considering the weight and size of cameras, plates, chemicals and developing equipment that needed to be carried along at that time. These photographs were then captioned and sent to editors, usually accompanied by a small column. Many appeared in full-page collage arrangements, then a new publishing format, with six to eight captioned photographs per page. Some of McMahon's photographs appeared in a dozen or more publications at the same time, which suggests he was not only ambitious but a hardworking letter writer and student of publishing practices worldwide. McMahon clearly thought there was a career and worldwide acclaim to be gained from espousing the opportunities

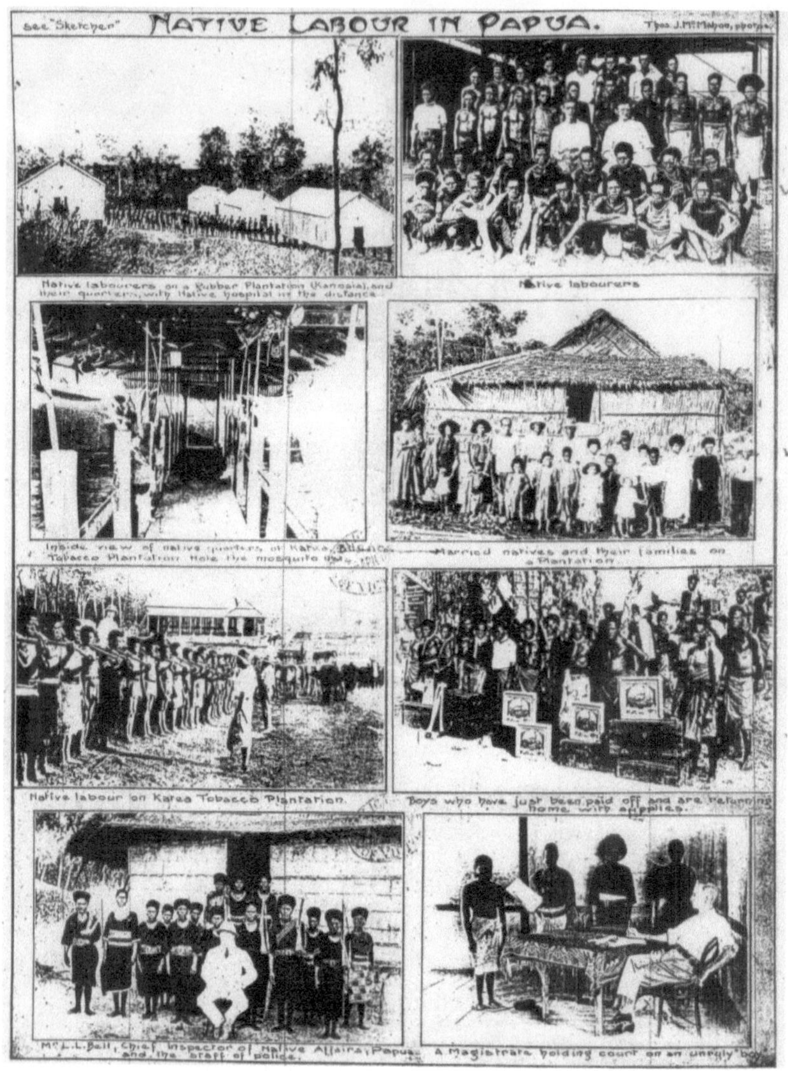

Fig. 1 McMahon, 'Native labour in Papua', 1916

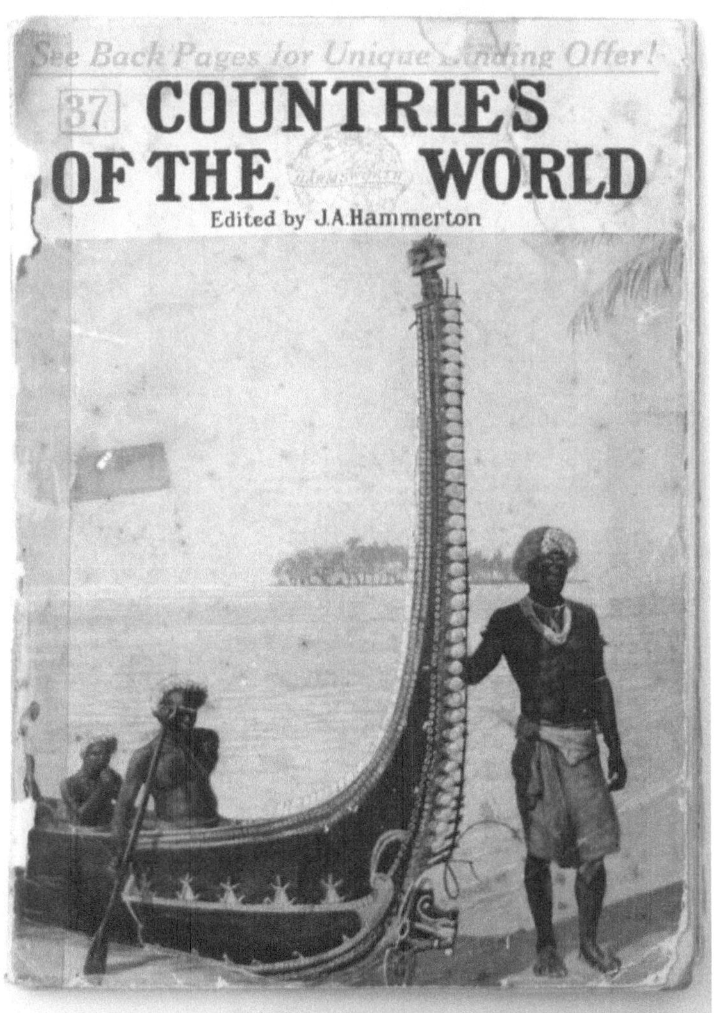

Fig. 2 Solomon Islands canoe, coloured, 1923

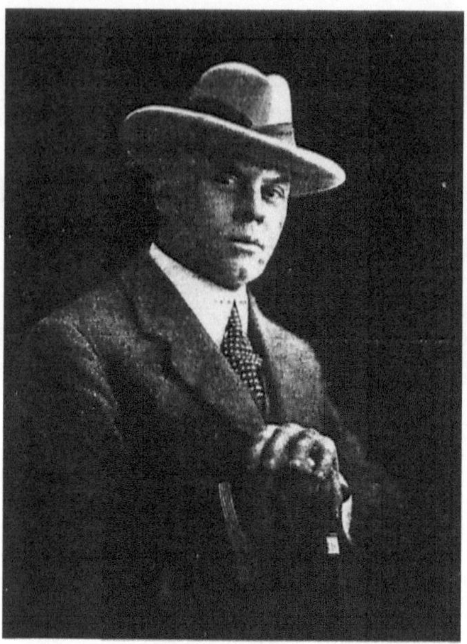

Fig. 3 Portrait of TJ McMahon, 1920

and profits on offer from Australian trade and commercial expansion and sub-empire in the 'Islands'. This possibility had arisen with the outbreak of World War I and Australia's immediate military expeditions to Nauru and New Guinea, and the eventual defeat of Germany. His self-promoted role as an Islands expert and imperialist promoter as the world was being reshaped means his publications and journalism offer insights into publishing generally and specifically the worldwide popularity of photographically illustrated newspaper features, magazines, books and encyclopedias.

In 1919, TJ McMahon visited Britain briefly in an attempt to further his career as a photographer, journalist and expert commentator on the Pacific Islands. His hometown newspaper in Roma, Queensland, declared that 'the eyes of the world were on the Pacific, which would become the amphitheatre of international interest before long'. This would have pleased McMahon greatly as for the previous six years, he had been travelling through the Pacific Islands, then publishing his photographs in newspapers and magazines in Australia and across the world. McMahon's career as a published photographer and journalist was brief. After giving up on a career as a Pacific expert in 1922, he took a paid job as a back-country photographer and journalist for *The Brisbane Courier* and *The Queenslander*. In the following decade, he published hundreds of articles and thousands of photographs of outback Queensland. He died suddenly in 1933. We know little of his life before he changed careers as a fifty-one-year-old and headed to Port Moresby. In the adventures detailed here, you will find that McMahon – often given the by-line 'Thos' but known as Tom to friends – was a photographer, a journalist and a patriot boosting both British rule in the region and the possible expansion of Australian settlement, commerce and trade in the Pacific Islands.

McMahon was a patriot with firsthand information and one of Australia's earliest photojournalists, despite tagging himself as a geographer and nursing an ambition to be awarded a Fellowship of the Royal Geographical Society (RGS) in London. McMahon became a member of the Queensland branch of the RGS in May 1917 and in 1920 was still listed as a paid-up Fellow. He cheekily used the impressive letters 'FRGS' for several years, despite not being a member, let alone a Fellow, of the London-based society. This drew a reprimand and admonition from London to cease using its acronym, which he reluctantly obeyed. He never called himself or was called a photojournalist, although he was described as being 'well known for his photography and journalist work'.[1]

McMahon was born in 1864, the fourth son of a family of

---

1   *Northern Herald*, 13.2.1917, p. 4; *Adelaide Register*, 25.6.1920.

workers at Mount Abundance Station in the Roma district and died aged sixty-nine in 1933. Nothing is known of his earlier occupations, private life, family, friendships or other pursuits. How Thomas McMahon made the transition from tutoring children on a pastoral property in the Upper Burnett in the 1890s to landing in Port Moresby in 1915 as a photographer, patriot and newspaperman remains obscure. It was certainly a late career change when he headed to the Islands. He first appeared in the public domain after a Port Moresby newspaper listed him as a passenger arriving on the shipping run between Townsville and Port Moresby, the capital of the recently acquired former British colony renamed the Australian Territory of Papua. He was identified as a photographer and special correspondent of *The Cairns Post* and the *Northern Herald*.

We only know of his life after that visit through his published images and articles. Even the magnificent online resources of Trove do not reveal any personal details of his life. Personally, he remains a mystery, despite his Pacific Islands photographs appearing all over the world. In 1922, he changed careers again, becoming a photojournalist for *The Brisbane Courier* and *The Queenslander* in Brisbane. He was now a salaried employee, photographing outback Queensland, the Torres Strait and the Northern Territory as a 'back-country' reporter.

The world being reimagined

The Great War provided an opportune moment for Australia to step up and claim a pre-eminent position as the agent of the British Empire in the south Pacific. When the war broke out, Japan occupied the Caroline and Marshall Islands, the former German possessions in the north Pacific. Australia quickly took Nauru and the former German New Guinea, and New Zealand occupied Western Samoa. After the war, these were to be formalised as mandates under the newly formed League of Nations and there was a possibility that Australia might take a more controlling role in the New Hebrides, replacing Britain in the jointly administered condominium of France and Great Britain. Britain also had colonies in Fiji, the Gilbert Islands and the Solomon Islands. The French were in New Caledonia, Wallis and Futuna, Tahiti and the Tuamotu, Marquesas and Austral Islands, but while these were important for shipping, trade and tourism, they were out of bounds with regard to possible colonial control by Australia.

Through fiction, published photography, art, colonial exhibitions and travelogues, Australians knew about Pacific Island cultures and peoples but were not overly familiar with the problems of colonial administration or the economic potential of planting, mining and trading. There had been at times close connections between Australia and Fiji, with settlers 'rushing' to Fiji in the 1860s and to the New Hebrides in the early 1900s, and in eastern New Guinea there had been a gold rush to Sudest, Misima and later the Woodlark Islands.[2] Burns Philp, the large Australian shipping and trading company, ran, among other routes, a long mail and supply route through the islands to Nauru, Ocean Island (now Banaba), Gilbert Islands (now Kiribati) and on to the former German but then Japanese-controlled Marshall Islands.[3] Thomas McMahon later took this 'islands run', amassing a folio of glass plates in each island group, which he then printed and posted to editors around the world. McMahon also visited Lord Howe Island and Norfolk Island, home to the descendants of the *Bounty* mutineers and administered by the state of New South Wales.

McMahon was not the only Australian writer, photographer or

---

2   The gold rush is brilliantly covered in Nelson, Hank. *Black, White and Gold: Goldmining in Papua New Guinea 1878–1930*, Canberra, ANU Press, 1976.

3   Buckley, K. and Klugman, K. *The Australian presence in the Pacific: Burns Philp 1914–16*, Sydney, George Allen and Unwin, 1983.

aspiring political player interested in the islands. Roger Thompson detailed these connections thoroughly in his two-volume study of Australia's engagement with the Pacific at the turn of the century[4], and Nic Halter has pointed out there was a strong literary tradition of using island tropes and motifs for novels that focused on the Islands, inspired by the allure of the tropical Pacific, but adding to and benefitting from the introduction of cruising.[5] For example, the artist Norman Hardy and the well-known political, mining and literacy figure Randolph Bedford made an 'Islands' trip resulting in books, illustrated columns, articles and private albums. Jack McLaren was also publishing books and serialised stories in newspapers.[6] Frances Steel's study of New Zealand shipping in the Islands is equally valuable in tracing the relationship between Australia and New Zealand with the Pacific, a historical connection that John Young had named the Pacific Frontier.[7]

The term 'booster' was not used at the time and is rarely applied today, but before and after the federation of the Australian colonies, there were writers and speakers who promoted expansion, dreamt up settlement schemes, praised investment opportunities and generally applauded a sense of colonial expansion, nationalism and development in commerce and trade. These journalists and literary figures were patriots, imperialists, schemers and seekers of personal fame, and they had a large audience as Australia sought

---

4   Thompson, R. *Australian imperialism in the Pacific: the expansionist era 1820–1920*, Melbourne, Melbourne University Press, 1980.

5   Halter, N. *Australian travellers in the South Seas*, Canberra, ANU Press, 2021.

6   Quanchi, M. '"Recording of my journeys in the Coral Sea": Randolph Bedford's 1906 album of the Solomon Islands"' *Journal of New Zealand and Pacific Studies*, Vol. 8, no. 1, 2020, pp. 39–56; Quanchi, Alan M. '*Norman H. Hardy: Book Illustrator and Artist*'. *The Journal of Pacific History*, Vol. 49, no. 2, 2014, pp. 214–233.

7   Young, JMR. 'Australia's Pacific frontier', *HSANZ*, Vol. 12, 1966, p. 47; Young, JMR, ed. *Australia's Pacific Frontier: Economic and cultural expansion into the Pacific 1795–1885*, Melbourne, Cassell, 1968; Steel, F. *Oceania Under Steam: Sea transport and the cultures of colonialism, c.1870–1914*, Manchester, Manchester University Press, 2016.

to establish itself as a nation – albeit a British offshoot in the Pacific. These public figures and literary lions were enthusiastic and vocal advocates who 'boosted' Australian commercial and trade expansion opportunities and called for policies that engaged Australia in global affairs. They were mostly self-promoting and were using public appearances and publishing opportunities to improve their own reputations. McMahon was a booster in all these meanings of the term. (This Australia–Pacific role in McMahon's career is covered in chapters 5 and 12.)

His role as an imperial booster became more noticeable towards the end of World War I when McMahon visited German New Guinea, now under Australian military control, in 1917. It led to an onslaught of articles and photography published around the world. McMahon was certainly alert to imperial negotiations and post-war realignments and wrote almost the same article, with and without illustrations, in a range of publications.[8] In *The Mid-Pacific*, a travel and tourism bulletin of the Pan-Pacific Union in Honolulu, he declared Germany's presence in north-eastern New Guinea to be shameful.[9] He declared in classic boosterism language that the Australian takeover of New Guinea was a 'notable and remarkable fact that brings forward the eminence of Australia in Imperial affairs'.[10] For Australia's popular magazine, *The Lone Hand*, he rephrased this as 'the prominence of Australia in British Empire affairs'.[11] He also published an article when in London in 1919, stressing the value of the Islands to the British,

---

8   For example, McMahon, TJ. 'German New Guinea', *The Bulletin*, 17.1.1918, p. 7; Ibid., 'The South Pacific Islands', *Empire Review*, Aug. 1919, Vol. 33, pp. 249–51; Ibid., 'The South Pacific Islands Trade', *Empire Review*, May 1921, Vol. 35, pp. 154–67.

9   McMahon, TJ. 'Australia's Heritage: German New Guinea', *The Mid-Pacific*, 17.5.1919, p. 433.

10   McMahon, TJ. 'The German menace in the Pacific', *World's Work*, December 1918, p. 479.

11   McMahon, TJ. 'German New Guinea', *The Lone Hand*, 1.3.1918, p. 159.

claiming in London's *Daily Telegraph* that, 'to the young and energetic man, the investor with small capital, there is not more attractive field than the British South Pacific possessions'.[12] For American readers of the popular *Munsey's Magazine*, in a long article on New Guinea with twelve photographs, he stressed the future of these 'magnificent islands' and their 'great commercial possibilities'.[13] He had headlined an article in *Life* magazine, 'Who shall own German New Guinea after the war?'[14] He declared the Australian military administration of the former German New Guinea, 'though its powers are limited … has certainly not been a failure'.[15] He noted for readers of the London publication, *The Wide World*, that he travelled with 'a letter of authority from the Prime Minister of the Commonwealth of Australia'.[16] These articles on German New Guinea were accompanied by fifty-four photographs, proving to readers in an 'I was there' fashion that the views being expressed were supported by visual evidence. In the 1920s, after Australia had been given a League of Nations mandate over the former German territory in north-eastern New Guinea, he continued to send away photographs to publications such as *The Far Eastern Review*, *The London Times* (Illustrated Supplement), *Travel* and *Mid-Pacific Magazine*.[17] The boosting,

---

12   *Daily Telegraph* (London), 1.2.1919, p. 13.

13   McMahon, T.J. 'Germany in the Pacific', *Munsey's Magazine*, Dec. 1918, Vol. 65, pp. 481.

14   McMahon, T.J. 'Australia in the Pacific: Who shall own German New Guinea after the War?', *Life*, 1.6.1918, Vol. 29, pp. 396–98.

15   McMahon, T.J. 'Germany's dream of a Pacific Empire', *The Sydney Mail*, 16.1.1919, p. 18. This by-line sat above a full, two-page spread of eight of McMahon's photographs. *The Sydney Mail* was the weekend illustrated paper for rural areas, published by the *Sydney Morning Herald*.

16   McMahon, T.J. 'The Gordon of the Pacific: My visit to Germany's South Sea Possessions', *The Wide World*, Mar. 1919, p. 349.

17   McMahon, T.J. 'German New Guinea: Australia's new task', *The Far Eastern Review*, June 1921, pp. 378; Ibid., 'Australia's mandate in the Pacific', *Travel*, Dec. 1921, Vol. 38, pp. 27–29, 37; Ibid., 'Australia's new task' *Mid-Pacific Magazine*, Oct. 1922, Vol. 24, pp. 375–380.

expansionary message was repeated – Australia could reap a huge reward once the war was over and could reap economic benefits as well as earn imperial prestige. His publications on German New Guinea demonstrate McMahon's skill in sending much the same article to editors in the US, London and several Australian cities, slightly reworded and given new by-lines but using different photographs.

McMahon's knowledge of the Pacific before making his first trip to Papua in 1915 is not known. He rarely cited any books or works by other authors. However, there was no shortage of material to read. He may have seen Beatrice Grimshaw's series of articles in *Life* magazine in 1909, illustrated by seventeen photographs, with headlines like those later used by McMahon. Grimshaw's three-part article was titled:

THE BEAUTIES AND POSSIBILITIES OF PAPUA (PART 1) AUSTRALIA; HOW TO MAKE MONEY IN PAPUA (PART 2) WHAT LIFE IS LIKE IN PAPUA (PART 3)

She offered a patriotic, boosting, expansionary narrative, the same as used later by McMahon. He may also have seen other publications that were popular at the turn of the century, extolling the progress and prosperity of the Australian colonies such as *Victoria and its Metropolis* (two volumes, 1888), *Picturesque Atlas of Australasia* (three volumes, 1888), [18] *Queensland 1900: A narrative of her past* (1900) and *Australia Unlimited* (1918). These were all heavily illustrated with photographs and full of panegyric, laudatory phrasing. *Australia Unlimited* also included a short chapter on 'British New Guinea (Papua)' with nine photographs

---

18   For a brilliant analysis, see Hughes-D'Aeth, Tony. *Paper nation: the story of the Picturesque Atlas of Australia 1886–1888*, MUP, Melbourne, 2001.

that have a noticeable similarity to those later published by McMahon.

He was not a particularly gifted writer and the columns published alongside his photographs from Papua, Solomon Islands, Nauru, Marshall Islands and elsewhere can be more accurately described as jingoistic, gung-ho polemical reiterations of anecdotal accounts gathered over dinner or drinks in missions, on plantations or ship's decks, and in port-town bars. His language was littered with catchphrases, popular rather than scholarly or editorial prose and always stressed that 'I was there'.

The patriot

McMahon was a patriot. He would have been pleased when he was quoted in 1919 in an article in the popular magazine, *The Lone Hand*, on 'The problem of the Pacific: Australia's entry into international affairs'; it noted he was making 'an investigation into the condition of the Pacific islands'.[19] *The Lone Hand* regularly published essays on Australia and the Pacific, and McMahon shared its goal of keeping this topic in the news.[20] In 1920, in the magazine, *Trade Promoter of Australia and New Zealand*, he was described as 'a noted authority on South Pacific questions',[21] and in *Stewart's Handbook of the Pacific Islands*, an invaluable reference work at the time, he was often cited in regard to the New Hebrides, Norfolk Island, Nauru, Papua, Torres Strait and Fiji.[22] When he sailed to the Orient in 1922, he was described

---

19   Anon., 'The problem of the Pacific: Australia's entry into international affairs', *The Lone Hand*, 16.9.1919. p. 9. The two photographs used in the article were by McMahon.

20   For mandates, see *The Lone Hand*, 16.9.1919; 25.11.1919; 1.4.1920; 1.1.1921.

21   *Trade Promoter of Australia and New Zealand*, 1920, p. 38.

22   Stewart's *Handbook of the Pacific Islands* came out in numerous editions between 1908 and 1921.

as 'the well-known writer and traveller … a keen observer and an enthusiastic worker in Australia's trade interests abroad'.[23] When *The Sydney Mail* reported on an exhibition and talk by McMahon, illustrated with lantern slides at the Kodak Gallery in Sydney, it stressed the same theme, noting that 'it cannot be doubted that Mr McMahon is doing a national service in keeping watch and ward over developments in the Pacific'.[24] It is clear from his choice of images, the phrasing of his captions, and the text of his columns that he wanted to be known as an expert on the Islands.

He spoke in the federal parliament about issues in the New Hebrides and gave public lectures at the Lyceum in Sydney, the Royal Geographical Society in Brisbane and the Melbourne Chamber of Commerce. In 1917, he spoke in Cairns for a Red Cross fundraising function, giving two lectures, 'In the central Mountains of Papua' and 'Life in the Never-Never land of the Northern Territory'. The *Northern Herald* reported that his 'long series of lantern slides proved a revelation for most of the people present'.[25] His paper, with a lantern slide show, given to the Royal Geographical Society (Queensland) on his return from his second visit to New Guinea, was also published, without photographs, in its journal in 1917.[26]

McMahon had quickly established his credentials, and armed with a lantern slide show to support his talks, he was in popular demand in all states. He would have been pleased, despite having moved away from a career in the Pacific, to see his name listed in 1925 among 'authorities on Pacific subjects' when Frank Coffee

---

23   In the personal columns of *Sea Land Air*, 1.9.1922, p. 419.

24   *The Sydney Mail*, 29.5.1918, p. 21. The presence of the Governor of New South Wales was also noted.

25   *Northern Herald*, 12.5.1917, p. 4.

26   McMahon, T.J. '*Papua (British New Guinea)*', Queensland Geographical Journal, Vol. 32, 1916–18, pp. 81–88.

published *Forty Years on the Pacific*.[27] This means we can label him self-proclaimed, but he was also publicly recognised. He was an imperialist, or sub-imperialist, a booster of an expansionary regional role for Australia and for the economic and political potential of the islands. This boosting was not jingoism – the populist advancement of military conquests and expansion – but a proselytising of the economic potential of trade and commercial opportunities and the income to be earned by Australians migrating and planting copra, sisal and rubber under, of course, the British flag. Australia had only recently federated at this time and foreign policy and external affairs were still under British imperial control.[28]

As well as carefully chosen photographs on specific islands and specific industries, McMahon sent articles to editors on more general south Pacific topics, with accompanying photographs, always referring to the British presence and Australia's future role. For example, in 1919, 'The islands of the South Pacific' was published in the American business magazine, *Dun's Review*, with seven of McMahon's photographs of the copra, tobacco, sisal and rubber industries that were 'splendid opportunities for capital and enterprise ... to be seized by the trading nations of the world'. This is an example of McMahon tailoring his approach to suit the journal's readership. In a draft of this article for another publication, McMahon removed 'America' and scribbled 'now the Japanese are making a try'. In 1922, after eight years trying to claim fame as an Islands expert, he was still pushing the bountiful Pacific in the *International Importer and Exporter Magazine of*

---

27   Coffee, F. *Forty Years on the Pacific*, Sydney, Oceanic Publishing Company, 1925, p. xii.

28   See Hudson, WJ. *New Guinea Empire. Australia's Colonial Experience*, Melbourne, Cassell, 1974; Ward, S. *Australia and the British Embrace: The Demise of the Imperial Ideal*, Melbourne, Terra Australis, 2001; Schreuder, DM. and Ward, S, eds. *Australia's Empire: The Oxford History of the British Empire*, Melbourne, OUP, 2008.

Australia, arguing that the 'South Pacific is now to be rightly considered the zone of trade rivalries, numerous and keen'. To emphasise the opportunities awaiting Australia, he included ten photographs of sisal hemp, cotton, rice, rubber, copra, gold mining, harbours, schools, local transport and labour lines.[29]

Like other Australians seeking fame in academic and literary circles, McMahon made a trip to Britain, hoping to win the favour of the RGS in London and to further his credentials as an expert on the Islands. He was unsuccessful, despite finding more outlets to publish his photography and attracting invitations to speak at the Chamber of Commerce in London in October, the Royal Colonial Institute, the Royal Photographic Society and Leeds University. Back in Australia, the *Australasian Photo-Review* reported on his photography exhibition in London at the Royal Photographic Society, noting he had presented on four evenings and had received a letter from the king regarding attending the exhibition.[30] The visit to London allowed him to expand his publishing away from weekend illustrated newspapers in Australia, the initial focus of his attention. This led to British publications including the *Illustrated London News, The Times Trade Supplement, The Morning Post* (London), *The Times* (London), *The Observer* (London), *The Blue Peter* (the magazine of the P&O shipping line) and *Empire Review*. McMahon was unsuccessful in gaining a fellowship at the Royal Geographical Society in London, but it did accept as a donation several black-and-white prints. On the way home from Europe, he gave public addresses in Adelaide and Melbourne promoting

---

29 McMahon, TJ. 'The islands of the South Pacific', *Dun's Review*, 26.3.1918, p. 8; Ibid., 'South Pacific islands: Value to the British', *The Daily Telegraph* (London), 16.10.1919; Ibid., 'The South Pacific Islands', *International Importer and Exporter Magazine of Australia*, 24.6.1922. pp. 56–58.

30 *Australasian Photo-Review*, 15.1.1920, p. 52; *The Sydney Mail*, 14.1.1920, p. 10.

the importance of the Pacific to Australia's growth and place in the Empire.

New Zealand

McMahon realised that New Zealand offered a similar market for his photographs and articles as it also had several city-based illustrated weekend newspapers, and like Australia, an interest in the neighbouring Pacific Islands. McMahon contributed extensively to the *Auckland Weekly News* and the Dunedin-based *Otago Witness*, the illustrated weekend publications of New Zealand's two major city daily newspapers. He contributed 203 photographs, or roughly thirty per cent, of their Pacific Islands coverage over a four-year period from 1919 to 1922. For example, the cover of the *Auckland Weekly News* on 6 June 1918, comprised two half-page photographs, often used by McMahon, of a coastal village scene at Hanuabada, Port Moresby, and a mounted overseer and Papuan labourer in a rubber plantation.[31] In a photomontage on 2 May 1919, he used ten photographs under the headline, 'Life in the British Solomon Islands', that visualised the colonial presence through scenes at a mission school, copra, cattle being used to add double value to a plantation, labour lines, cotton growing and ethnographic portraits of Solomon Islanders, reed musical instruments and elaborately decorated dancers at a traditional coconut 'festival'.[32] This was a typical arrangement for McMahon, primarily extolling the economic potential but as a diversion, titillating audiences with strange customs and the dress and appearance of 'natives'.

In the *Auckland Weekly News* in 1922, he used forty-one

---

31   McMahon, TJ. 'Picturesque scene in British New Guinea', *Auckland Weekly News*, 6.6.1918. This was a rare instance of the use of the term 'picturesque' by McMahon.

32   McMahon, TJ. 'Life in the British Solomon Islands', *Auckland Weekly News*, 2.5.1918, p. 33.

photographs of Fiji in four single-page and double-page collages. Nearly half of McMahon's coverage of Fiji in this example was devoted to banana, sugar and cattle production, the associated transport by road, railway and river craft and the availability of Indians as labour, even though the *Girmit* or indentured Indian labour scheme had ended in 1916 and closed finally in 1920. Just over half of the illustrations were ethnographic, related to Fijian housing, dancing, *kava* ceremonies, pottery villages and domestic agriculture. There was only one view that might be categorised as picturesque. Only two photographs depicted a British colonial presence, with officials being served *kava* in a village.

In the *Otago Witness* in Dunedin, McMahon featured the same material used for the Auckland publication. In July 1920, the *Otago Witness* featured a double-page collage of fourteen photographs of Ocean Island (Banaba) and Nauru's phosphate mining operations, railways, machinery, diggings and shipping. Two photographs focused on posed settings of Nauruan women dancers and there was one scenic view of Nauru's *buada* (central lagoon). Four years later, two photographs appeared as half-page plates on the cover of the *Otago Witness,* with villagers sun-drying copra prior to bagging and export and four Fijians posing on the deck of their bamboo raft.[33] His choice of images for publication acknowledged New Zealand's interest in Banaban phosphate imports, a missionary presence in the New Hebrides and its long-standing connections with Fiji,[34] and demonstrates McMahon's awareness of New Zealand readers' interest in both the economic potential of the islands and a human interest fascination with Pacific Island cultures and customs. His published photography in New Zealand was a little skewed towards the ethnographic,

---

33   *Otago Witness*, 29.7.1920, pp. 37–38; 28.1.1924, p.1.

34   New Zealanders had 'rushed' to Fiji in the 1860–1870s cotton boom. Banks, shipping companies and several trade stores were linked directly to New Zealand.

recognising perhaps that New Zealand already had colonial possessions in the Pacific (Cook Islands, Niue, Tokelau and Western Samoa) and New Zealanders were less interested than Australian readers in imperial posturing and further annexations.

Islands commentator

McMahon's tendency to repeat unverified criticisms, grumbles and outright rumours – now called scuttlebutt – that he collected while travelling around the colonies and territories attracted a critical response, especially his reporting of the Australian administration of Papua. In an article in *The Argus* in Melbourne in May 1921, he called for an inquiry and for Papua to be removed from Australian control and returned to British administration. The next day, *The Argus* reported that the Commonwealth's Acting Minister for Territories, George Wise, had replied that McMahon's criticism was 'quite unsupported by facts ... vague references to conditions of which no details are given'. In a second, long reply, Wise rejected McMahon's claims that the administration was unsympathetic to the economic plight of planters and declared there were no grounds for an inquiry.[35] A week later, the Minister for Territories, Alexander Poynton, wrote to *The Argus* reiterating there were no grounds for an inquiry into the treatment of 'natives'. Poynton accused McMahon of hardly leaving Port Moresby during his visit, of having gone only twenty-five kilometres inland and of relying solely on discussions with one disgruntled trading company. The same day, Poynton presented to the Federal Cabinet a report on Papua as the result of his recent trip. McMahon responded the following day, declaring Poynton's response as 'absurd', and highlighting that Poynton had admitted his own visit was at best a 'birds-eye view of the place'.

---

35   *The Argus* (Melbourne), 13.5.1921; 14.5.1921.

McMahon could have defended himself and silenced Wise and Poynton by listing the places he had visited outside of Port Moresby – Sudest, Misima, Panesesa, Woodlark and Yule Islands, Rabaul, Milne Bay, Laloki, Samarai, and Mafula Mission – perhaps not exhaustive but enough to give McMahon a reasonable grasp of development and economic growth of Papua, on which he had written extensively and published photographs about over the previous five years. He could have also pointed out that he had been writing about Papua in *The Argus* in Melbourne for most of 1918, and that in 1920 he had written letters to the editor over the policies and actions of the Expropriation Board in German New Guinea.[36] The list of topics on which McMahon had published in *The Argus,* and its weekend illustrated newspaper, *The Leader,* suggests he had a broad understanding of what was going on in Papua and German New Guinea, and while perhaps not rigorous in verifying his facts and opinions from informants, he was Australia's best-informed journalist of the day regarding Island affairs.

Here is the list of article headings, which he wrote about and published photographs within *The Argus* and *The Leader* in June–July 1918:

- Value of South Seas to Germany
- Britain's Pacific Islands: Native loyalty
- Our Pacific heritage: the German penetration
- Germany in the Pacific: Berlin policy
- Progress of Papua: Part I
- Progress of Papua: Part II
- Papua customs: Habits of the Kuffa tribe
- Revenues
- On Misima gold mine
- Future of German possessions in the Pacific

---

36   *The Argus,* 29.10.1920, p. 7; 30.10.1920, p. 21; 2.11.1920, p. 7.

- Planters and finances
- Judge Murray's views
- Oil fields

  The photograph of 'bales for export' was used in 1922 in *Trans-Pacific* and *International Importer and Exporter Journal of Australia.*

- Prospects: Possible industries.

The Minister and Acting Minister queried McMahon's expertise as an accurate and on-the-spot reporter, but readers of *The Argus* and *The Leader* had been viewing his photographs and reading his accompanying captions and short feature articles for the previous five years, and despite the politicians' criticisms, probably judged McMahon to indeed be an expert on the islands with 'I was there' experience.

He also attracted criticism after his trip to the Solomon Islands. District Officer WR Bell wrote to the Resident Commissioner in the Solomon Islands, CRM Workman, that McMahon's article in *The Queenslander* in May 1918 was a 'libellous epistle'. McMahon had claimed that there were both poor administration and a confusing array of regulations in the BSIP. In an extremely long and detailed letter, Bell alleged that McMahon's article showed how 'absolutely unreliable are his observations and that he must have exercised no care when gathering his information'.[37] Bell declared that McMahon 'has not the moral courage to write what exactly is in his mind', suggesting that he had merely repeated what other people had told him about the BSIP policies.

In 1922, McMahon abandoned his dream to become an Islands expert and be awarded as an FRGS and took a six-month cruise to North Borneo, Manila, Japan and China, seeking fame as an expert observer and author on China as it emerged from the

---

37   WR Bell to CRM Workman, 29.5.1918, Resident Commissioner, BSIP, 33/1918.

warlord period and nationalist struggles. His book, *The Orient I Found*, was poorly received.[38] An anonymous reviewer in *The Sydney Mail* thought McMahon's comments 'through Australian eyes' on China were apt and useful, considering the internecine quarrels that were ravaging China, but added that McMahon had modestly prefaced his book by saying he did not claim any special merits and had written it merely to 'stimulate interest in the present-day conditions of the Orient'.[39]

After his return from Asia, he took a job in Brisbane as a rural reporter and photographer with a Brisbane newspaper *The Brisbane Courier* and its weekend edition, *The Queenslander*, and became well-liked and well-known among Queensland readers. This role involved trips to rural districts, often for their annual agricultural shows or a local development of interest and publishing a short column in *The Brisbane Courier* and a collage of photographs in the weekend illustrated edition, *The Queenslander*. This was a role he had played part-time with the *Northern Herald* and *The Cairns Post* from 1915 to 1922 alongside his travel and photography in the Islands (covered in chapter 13).

A life, a career, a legacy

The journal articles and book chapters that I have written on McMahon's photography form the core of this book-length treatment.[40] His photographic legacy in newspapers and magazines after 1915 can be traced through Trove, Australia's digitised newspaper platform. His presence continues today through the occasional publishing of his photographs, but he has never attracted enough attention to be listed in the *Australian*

---

38   McMahon, TJ. *The Orient I Found.* New York, D. Appleton & Co., 1926.

39   *The Sydney Mail*, 26.10.1926, p. 13.

40   Listed in Appendix 4.

Dictionary of Biography, and brief entries in *Wikipedia* and *The Encyclopedia of the Pacific Islands* are quite recent.[41]

The quality of the photographs reproduced here is variable, as nearly all are copies taken from now-fading newspapers and magazines published between 1915 and 1933 and printed on newsprint paper. A couple are colourised photographs printed on clay-based pages in encyclopedias and therefore reproduced better than newsprint images, and some are copies of prints held by the Royal Geographical Society (Qld) in Brisbane which inherited a hundred of his photographic prints and some of his journalistic drafts, letters and press clippings, along with a few lantern slides.[42] Sadly no sets of lantern slides, or the accompanying lecture notes, have survived.

McMahon's obituary in *The Brisbane Courier* noted he had a kindly personality, was known as 'Tom' and that the large crowd at his funeral in Toowong Cemetery was 'testimony to his great personal worth and the affection and esteem with which he was regarded'. *The Queenslander* noted he had a genial personality and a wide circle of friends, and *The Australasian* in Melbourne noted he was well-known in southern capitals and that everywhere he went, the late Mr McMahon made friends.[43] In central New South Wales where his work was often reprinted, the *Forbes Advocate* noted 'the late Mr McMahon was a bachelor and had no relations'.[44] Both *The Brisbane Courier* and *The Queenslander* noted he had no known relatives, which at the time was a coded

---

41   Lal, BV. and Fortune, K., eds, *The Encyclopedia of the Pacific Islands*, Honolulu, University of Hawaii Press, 2. The McMahon entry was written by Max Quanchi. The Wikipedia entry was written by Peter Lloyd, who tracked down McMahon's will, death certificate and burial plot.

42   McMahon Papers, 9038, 9053, Box 4, Royal Geographical Society (Qld), Brisbane.

43   *The Australasian* (Melbourne), 26.8.1933, p. 9.

44   *Forbes Advocate*, (NSW), 20.10.1933, p. 4. He was wrongly listed as being sixty-one years of age.

phrase for gay men,[45] a preference suggested by his demeanour in self-portraits and the phrasing of his obituaries. In several photographs, McMahon is shown with either his hand resting on the shoulder or leg of a Pacific Islander or with a Pacific Islander resting his hand on McMahon's shoulder,[46] but his preference for male company is unable to be tested due to lack of evidence on McMahon's personal life. In McMahon's case, assertions of a relationship between gender, sexual preference and subject matter when photographing other cultures remain unresolved.

He passed away from a stroke at home during a lunch break from his work at *The Brisbane Courier* in August 1933. He was buried in Brisbane Cemetery in Toowong with a large gathering from the Tattersalls Club, Kodak and friends and representatives of the newspapers where he had worked.[47] He left a modest estate equivalent to AUD$68,700 in today's value, asking for his papers to be burned and donating some photographs to a WWI veterans library in Melbourne. No trace can be now found of that donation. The mass of negatives and prints he amassed have disappeared. Three hundred of his glass plate negatives eventually went to auction, purchased by a private collector, and the State Library of New South Wales has several hundred images from his central Pacific trip in 1919, but they are wrongly accessioned to 'Maslyn Williams', an author who possibly purchased them in the 1950s while co-authoring a book on Burns Philp and the phosphate industry.[48]

This book is arranged in a sequence following McMahon's trips

---

45 *The Brisbane Courier*, 14.8.1933, p. 10; *The Queenslander*, 17.8.1933, p. 9.

46 For example, see *The Sydney Mail*, 19.4.1916, p. 20; *The Australasian*, 21.4.1917, p. 5; *The Wide World*, Mar. 1919, p. 350; *Sea Land Air*, Feb. 1919, p. 658; *World Today*, 1928, p. 304.

47 Obituary, *The Brisbane Courier*, 15.8.1933, p. 15.

48 McMahon's 270-plus photographs of the central Pacific are in Mitchell Library of the State Library of NSW; PXB293 Vols. 2–5.

into the Pacific. The chapters take readers first to Papua, which he visited in 1915, then in turn to the former German New Guinea, the Solomon Islands, New Hebrides (now Vanuatu), Nauru, Ocean Island (now Banaba), the Gilbert Islands (now Kiribati), Marshall Islands and Fiji, Lord Howe Island and Norfolk Island and his other photography in rural Queensland, the Northern Territory and the Torres Strait.

Chapter 1

A photography archive: evidence, interpretation and meaning

I n 1915, it was an opportune time for McMahon to leave his job tutoring children on pastoral properties and to seek out a new career. Newspapers, thanks to the introduction of the photogravure process in the late 1890s, had changed their illustration format from artist's depictions to photographs, and editors were looking for more and more photographs to publish, especially due to the exceptional popularity of the weekend news summary and heavily illustrated editions being published by most major metropolitan newspapers in Australia, New Zealand, Britain and elsewhere.[49] As double- or single-page photomontages became popular in the weekend illustrated issues of daily newspapers, editors were constantly on the search for material.

The use of photographs in publishing had swept the world and editors had to constantly find photographs of faraway places, colonies and 'native' peoples who were subjects of the British Empire, or if not, then potentially people and lands ready to be

---

49 Quanchi, M. 'Power of Pictures; Learning by Looking at Papua in Illustrated Newspapers and Magazines', *Australian Historical Studies*, Vol. 35, no. 123, 2004, pp. 37–53; Quanchi, M. 'The imaging of Samoa in illustrated magazines and serial encyclopedia in the early 20th century', *Journal of Pacific History*, Vol. 41, no. 2, 2006, pp. 207–217. See also Dowling, P. 'Destined not to survive: The illustrated newspapers of colonial Australia,' Vol. 3, nos. 1–2, 1995, pp. 85–98.

annexed and ruled by Britain or its loyal dominion, Australia. The photographs may appear mundane today but a scene with a European overseer managing skilled 'native' workers in a sisal hemp processing factory at Bomana or rubber labourers outside their quarters at Kanosia plantation, both in Papua, had popular appeal. They suggested to Australian investors, and any potential settler seeking life as a planter in the Islands, that Papua already had established export industries, that skilled labour was plentiful and that profit margins were high.[50] For example, these two photographs were used twelve times by McMahon between 1916 and 1919 in an impressive array of publications worldwide – *Dun's Review, World's Work, Town and Country Journal*, the illustrated newspapers, the *Australasian, Northern Herald, Sunday Times* (Sydney) and *The Queenslander* and in New Zealand's illustrated weekend newspapers, the *Otago Witness* and the *Auckland Weekly News*.

The photographer

We do not know when or how McMahon developed his interest and skills in photography, but it must have been well before his first visit to Papua in 1915, as he arrived with seven hundred plates, only losing fifteen, or two per cent. He never referred to his activities as a photographer other than a few references to being with assistants or by appearing in a few, staged photographs of himself with a camera or with expatriates and Pacific Islanders.

Illustrated books, illustrated newspapers and magazines would have provided him with plenty of examples to replicate. He had probably studied the weekend editions of *The Queenslander*, which circulated widely in rural Queensland, and which had

---

50   The Bomana and Kanosia photographs were taken during his visit to Papua, October–
      November 1915.

previously published full-page photography features. In 1899 and 1901, he may have seen *The Wide World*, a popular British magazine circulating in rural districts, which included articles by Basil Thompson and CW Abel, with twenty-seven and twenty photographs respectively of the Islands.[51] In an intriguing coincidence, twenty years later, McMahon contributed ten of the photographs Thompson used in his huge essay, 'Island life in the South Seas' in *Peoples of All Nations*, with seventy-nine pages and ninety-three photographs. McMahon's association with Thompson continued, and he later provided five colour plates and thirteen black-and-white photographs for Thompson's entry, 'Palm-fringed Edens of Oceania', in the serial encyclopedia, *Countries of the World*.[52]

He probably also saw the heavily illustrated London Missionary Society magazine, *The Chronicle*. Australia also had a vibrant display culture and on trips to Brisbane, he may have seen installations in galleries or special exhibitions.[53] There were also thousands of postcards of the Islands circulating prior to 1915, from which he could have borrowed ideas. A budding photographer therefore had an array of photography in a wide range of formats, cheaply circulating, even in rural Queensland where McMahon worked as a tutor, that could be replicated and become an inspiration for a new career.

McMahon was a good photographer but did not create a new genre or trope, and there is an element of familiarity, replication and

---

51   Thompson, B. 'Curiosities of the South Seas' (in two parts), *The Wide World*, Sept. 1899, pp. 323–76 and Oct. 1899, pp. 509–516; Abel, CW. 'A missionary in New Guinea', *The Wide World*, Jan. 1910, pp. 395–402.

52   Thompson, B. 'Island life in the strange South Seas', *Peoples of All Nations*, Vol. 2, 1922, pp. 897–975; Thompson, B. on 'South Sea Islands; Palm fringed Edens of Oceania', *Countries of the World*, Vol. 6, no. 37, 1923, pp. 3769–3789.

53   For installations and photographic exhibitions, see Palmer, D. and Jolly, M. *Installation View: Photography exhibitions in Australia 1848–2020*, Melbourne, Perimeter Editions, 2021.

copying between pre-1915 published photography of the Islands and McMahon's published photography after 1915. McMahon rarely mentioned in his articles the reason he took specific photographs, or the difficulties faced when photographing in the islands, and he published only two articles on the practice of photography. In the *Australasian Photo-Review* in 1916 and 1919.[54] These noted that picturesque natives were keen to be photographed in Papua but said little about camera technique or photography as a craft. His article in 1919 blended an account of his visit to Nauru, Banaba and the Marshall Islands with notes about plates, highlighting several times that he was using 'anti-therm plates' and that he saw many albums of photographs by Japanese photographers who were resident in the Islands and were sending photographs to Japan for the postcard trade. The single photograph in this article was of a Marshallese 'queen' nursing her baby. McMahon stressed in the caption that his photograph was a negative made from *Austral anti-therm* plates, tank developed'. He noted that in the Marshall Islands, 'in every nook and cranny there seemed sure to be an enthusiastic photographer' and that 'everyone there possessed a camera of some sort',[55] a reflection of the enormous popularity and spread of photography across the Pacific, and indeed all colonies worldwide. McMahon concluded that photography was a 'direct aid to the spread of ... commerce',[56] and this certainly became his motif in the ensuing years. There are a few self-portraits that show his camera, but he never mentioned the type or make of camera being used. Other than a few comments in the two articles just mentioned, we have no record of his difficulties and joys in the field, his camera choice, subject preferences or if

---

54   McMahon, TJ. 1919, 'Photography in Papua and German (?) New Guinea',
      Australasian Photo-Review, 15.5.1916, pp. 263–64; 'The Central Pacific', *Australasian
      Photo-Review*, 15.3.1919, pp. 212–14.

55   *Australasian Photo-Review*, 15.3.1919, p. 212.

56   Ibid.

he borrowed openly from the style and composition of other photographers. He does not seem to have belonged to any of the photography clubs or amateur circles popular in his time.

It remains problematic whether McMahon asked Pacific Island people for permission to take their photograph. This probably was not required on plantations, mines and commercial sites because the host European owners or managers would have welcomed his presence. Photographing machinery and labour 'lines' on sisal plantations, phosphate mining railways, well-stocked trade stores on Samarai Island and the tapping of rubber trees would have been accessed easily because hosts were aware of the use of photography for commercial and investment propaganda. The presence of 'othering', racism or exploitation are accusations often made about colonial photographers, but there is little evidence indexically inside the frame of his photographs that might suggest McMahon was influenced by these negative views. There are a few self-portraits of McMahon in the company of Islanders, but these are posed, frozen compositions and do not reveal anything of the personal relationship McMahon may or may not have had with the subjects. His intimate portraits of Islanders are empathetic studies of individuals and groups that were merely passing acquaintances, or arranged as sitters by his hosts at plantations, wharves, mines and missions. The fact that he took virtually no photographs of a sexually exploitive nature, setting aside the three borrowed photographs of partially dressed Papuan belles that he published after his first visit to Papua, suggests that accusations of an exploitive voyeuristic 'colonial gaze' found in other photographer's oeuvre do not apply to McMahon.

The viewer today of McMahon's central Pacific photography seeking agency in the lives of Island peoples will be disappointed. His photography is a record of colonialism and exposes the motivations of the photographer and his distant audiences more than of the motivations of the people in the frame. Nauruans and Banabans and other unnamed Islanders caught in the background might equally be agents or victims. There is nothing to suggest exploitation, injury, injustice, lingering hostility, protest, dissent or nascent struggles for independence. Labourers are mute. Families are stoic. Chiefs are taken up with fancy clothes and fashions. Clam divers and young and muscular policemen play sport and ride bicycles. Women are busy at their sewing machines. Much of this was determined by the limitations of the camera and the care taken to avoid blurring. Yet we also know from histories of the wider Pacific that labourers were not mute and, despite McMahon's observations, that Japan was not universally loved by the Marshallese, that kimonos disappeared soon after the end of Japanese rule and that Panama hats never made it to the top as an export trade. McMahon's photographs instead offered readers an island world characterised by neatness, order, regimentation and benevolent colonial administrations. His photographs offered little access to the actual lived experiences of Pacific peoples.

By comparing his photography of Nauru and Ocean Island against that taken in the Gilberts and Marshalls, a noticeable distinction is obvious. In the former, McMahon offered viewers primarily an industrial Pacific. For the Gilberts and Marshalls, where there was no mining and commercial infrastructure was limited, he focused on aspects of Pacific Island life and customs. But for distant readers, there was no hint of the vastly divergent lives lived by industrial workers on Banaba and Nauru compared to traditional village and community life in the Gilberts and Marshalls.

McMahon often used the popular compositional format of a 'line-up', applied worldwide in colonies to depict authority, the availability and subservience of labour, police and assistants, or to emphasise the extent of conversions if the setting was a mission. There was also an element of boosting in that a line-up of strong-bodied young men suggested the easy recruitment of healthy and willing indigenous labour. McMahon's use of the line-up involved all these motivations. The line-up composition was facilitated usually with the connivance and agreement of planters, missionaries and officials and guaranteed a large assemblage, and with instructions to remain still, images would not be blurred. The artefacts, adornment or clothing in the frame do not indicate the home village or district of the men, their age and marital status, nor whether they lived regimentally in the barracks or maintained their family life freely in homes of local design. In the line-up, the individual was obscured and by definition and practice, the line-up was static, lifeless and dehumanising. The line-up of plantation labour was a routine ritual on plantations and took place either daily in the morning before the labourers marched off to fulfil their day's duties or in the evening when they were dismissed at the end of the working day. The men were depicted barefoot and carrying their tools. They are dressed in regulation *laplap* (sarong) and belt. Later photographs of labour were carefully constructed, with labourers dressed in European trousers and shirts. But in 1915, when McMahon was reporting on new industries like sisal, rubber and tobacco, labourers had not yet switched to European working attire. In 1915, a line-up of labour in Papua, for example, was probably a surprise to some Australian readers, especially those conditioned to think that New Guinea was the 'last unknown' and a frontier of tribes, missionaries and rugged interiors. The framing of the line-up was McMahon demonstrating his best journalistic practice, reporting with photograph and text, on events that were taking place a few months prior to publication, and on events which revealed a world different to most readers' expectations.

A global presence

Between 1915 and 1922, McMahon visited most of Australia's island neighbours and amassed a considerable number of good quality images. The popularity of photography as a means of depicting 'natives', customs and cultures on the other side of the world, and its use as propaganda for colonising ventures, investment and settlement schemes, means that McMahon's career overlaps with photography's use in anthropology, exploration and travel.[57] For example, a collage sent in by McMahon to *The Sydney Mail* in 1919 offered readers an intimate portrait of four phosphate workers on Banaba Island, a gathering of thirty Solomon Islands men about to perform a ceremony and a Banaban man in full dance attire. Later that year, he sent the *Illustrated London News* enough material for two double-page spreads offering fifteen portraits from Papua, Nauru, Banaba and German New Guinea. His output was prodigious. In 1919 alone, he published over two hundred and fifty photographs in thirty-four separate publications. Some were major city, illustrated weekend newspapers, while others were small magazines or journals like *The Week* in Brisbane and the English magazine, *Penny Pictorial*.[58] Some were major international publications like *Life* and *The Wide World*. McMahon also published an illustrated

---

57   See, Ryan, JR. *Picturing Empire; Photography and the Visualization of the British Empire*, Chicago, University of Chicago Press, 1997; Pinney, C. *Photography and Anthropology*, London, Reaktion, 2011; Ryan, JR. *Photography and Exploration*, London, Reaktion, 2013; Smith, G. *Photography and Travel*, London, Reaktion, 2013.

58   *The Week* described itself as 'A Journal of Commerce, Farming, Mining & General Information & Amusement'. It ceased publication in 1934. *Penny Pictorial* was published in England from 1899 to 1922.

article in *The Quiver*, a monthly British temperance and biblical magazine, on 'The South Sea myth'.[59]

In 1922, eleven McMahon photographs appeared in the serial encyclopedia, *The New World of Today*, edited by AR Hope. In 1929, an entry probably written by Basil Thompson for *Lands and Peoples* repeated six of McMahon's photographs previously published in *Countries of the World*, including two full-page colour plates, two half-page colour plates and two half-page black-and-white photographs. This was half of all the photographic illustration for the segments on Melanesia and Micronesia in three of the best-selling serialised pictorial encyclopedias of that era. He was alert to audiences' interests and must have spent a considerable sum on developing and printing, and on domestic and international postage. It had been a rapid rise to the world stage and acknowledgement.

Interpretation

McMahon's photography can be analysed and applied by historians of colonial expansion, plantations, mining, tourism, missions, maritime history, gender, labour and port towns as well as the more well-traversed path of ethnographic study of Islands cultures and peoples. Although McMahon's photographs are now only to be found in published formats, in illustrated newspapers, magazines, illustrated encyclopedia and a few postcards and pamphlets, it raises the question of how historians might use this archive of black-and-white photographs from the early 1900s.

The first historical use made of 'old' photographs was as supporting illustrations to prove the existence of an incident or the participation of certain historical actors, such as proof

---

59   McMahon, TJ. 'The South Sea myth; And the reality behind it', *The Quiver*, Jan. 1920, pp. 247–50. *The Quiver* (1861–1956) was a weekly magazine on 'defence and promotion of biblical truth and the advance of religion in the homes of the people'.

that a particular governor or resident magistrate held office. Later uses as evidence were to reveal curiosities: policemen in Fiji wearing skirts (*sulu*), the Nauruan custom of training frigate birds or tree trucks hollowed out as slit-gong drums in the New Hebrides (now Vanuatu). Old photographs could also be used to suggest change over time and new developments such as railway lines on Banaba or bicycle riding in Nauru. The most common use was to illustrate cultural practices such as house architecture or the artwork and craftsmanship on Solomon Island canoes. Later, historians started to use old black-and-white photographs to reveal hidden nuances or previously unknown aspects of life in the Pacific, and this meant that photographs could be used to bring attention to previously overlooked aspects of history, such as Japanese dental teams touring the Marshall Islands, overseers on Milne Bay sisal plantations who carried whips or the awarding of medals to indigenous heroes who averted a shipping disaster. This more recent interrogation of photographs meant that aspects of life in the Islands that had been marginalised or ignored in colonial histories could now be highlighted. These two uses of photographs – as evidence to support known facts and for revealing new interpretations – can be found in the uses made of McMahon's photographs long after his death.

I have argued elsewhere that McMahon's photographs appeared regularly in serialised illustrated encyclopedias, and this become a third category of use historically. McMahon's prodigious output certainly added to the contribution of photography to entertainment and self-education, when photographs acted as a 'learning-by-looking' format, a trope underlying serialised illustrated encyclopedias.[60] Historians have also looked at how

---

60   Quanchi, M. 'Learning by looking, for example, at *Peoples of All Nations*: European education and serial encyclopedia', *Pacific Geographies*, Vol. 45, Jan–Feb. 2016, pp. 11–16.

photographs captured reality for indigenous subjects, but this is limited to the few instances when indigenous peoples were able to see the images created by Euro-American photographers. This approach is best illustrated by Christopher Wright's study of photography on Roviana Island in the Solomon Islands,[61] Joshua Bell's study of repatriation and the manner in which returned photographs were received by the descendants of people captured in early photographs[62] and Lara Lamb and Christopher Lee who took back Frank Hurley's colonial era photographs to the descendants of the Kerewo and Urama peoples in the Kikori River delta a hundred years after they were taken.[63]

Scholars have tackled the use of colonial photography in Europe such as Marieke Bloembergen's study of Indonesian photography in Dutch exhibitions 1880–1930[64] and the oeuvre of individual photographers such as Mark Rice's study of Dean Worchester and Otto van den Muijzenberg's study of Meerkamp van Embden's photography respectively in the Philippines.[65] There

---

61   Wright, C. *The echo of things: The lives of photographs in the Solomon Islands*, Durham, Duke University Press, 2013.

62   Antsapouva, T. and Maidment, E. 'Pacific focus: Bringing knowledge about Photographic Collections in Australia to Pacific Communities', in *Hunting the collectors: Pacific collections in Australian Museums, Art Galleries and Archives*, edited by Cochrane, Susan and Quanchi, Max, Cambridge, Cambridge Scholars Publishing, 2011, pp. 377–394; Bell, J. 'Sugar Plant Hunting by Airplane in New Guinea: A Cinematic Narrative of Scientific Triumph and Discovery in the "Remote Jungles"', *Journal of Pacific History*, Vol. 45, no. 1, **2010**, pp. 37–56.

63   Lamb, L. and Lee, C. *Repatriation, Exchange, and Colonial Legacies in the Gulf of Papua: Moving Pictures*, London, Palgrave, 2022.

64   Bloembergen, M. *Colonial Spectacles: The Netherlands and the Dutch East Indies at the World Exhibitions 1810–1930*, Singapore, Singapore University Press, 2006; See also, Maxwell, A. *Colonial photography and exhibitions*, London, Leicester University Press, 1999.

65   Rice, M. *Dean Worchester's fantasy islands: Photography, film and the colonial Philippines*, Ann Arbor, University of Michigan Press, 2017; van den Muijzenberg, Odo. *The Philippines through European eyes: late Nineteenth century photographs from the Meerkamp van Embden Collection*, Manila, Ateneo de Manila University Press, 2008.

have been several studies of photography in Asia.[66] With regard to Asia's colonial photography and colonised people, in 2007, David Oda noted that the early emphasis was on European photographic practice and the Euro-American photographer's 'colonial gaze'. Oda highlighted how this biographical, historized approach gave way to new research which saw photographs as a product of specific, localised conditions and contexts. This created the study of photography that was 'moving away from Euro-American models of photographic diffusion'.[67] I have followed that trend by saying less about McMahon the person, his camera and influences on his practice and more about the local contexts he was confronted with, the topics he chose to valorise, the message he wanted to get across to Euro-American and Australasian audiences and his published photography in the public domain.

Photographers in the Pacific such as Frank Hurley, JW Lindt, Ernest Usher, Margaret Mead, the Burton brothers and Thomas Andrew in New Zealand attracted researchers' attention quite early.[68] A study of Robert Louis Stevenson's imaging was followed

---

66   For example, Newton, Gael. *Garden of the East: Photography in Indonesia 1850s–1940s*, Canberra, National Gallery of Australia, 2014; Newton, Gael. *Picturing paradise: Asia-Pacific photography 1840s–1940s*, Canberra, National Gallery of Australia, 2008; Morris, RC., ed. *Photographies East: The camera and its histories in East and Southeast Asia*, Durham, Duke University Press, 2009.

67   Oda. D. 'Asia's colonial photographs' in *IIAS International Study for Asian Studies Newsletter*, Vol. 44, Summer, 2007, p. 3.

68   Specht, Jim, and Fields, John. *Frank Hurley in Papua; Photographs of the 1920–1923 expeditions*, Bathurst, NSW, Robert Brown, 1984; Quartermaine, Peter. 'Johannes Lindt: Photographer of Australia and New Guinea' in *Representing Others: White views of Indigenous people*, edited by Gidley, M. Exeter, Exeter University Press, 1992; Craig, Barry. 'The Papuan photographs of Ernest Sterne Usher', *Pacific Arts*, Vols. 19–20, 1999, pp. 27–37; Hammond, Joan. 'Telling a tale: Margaret Mead's photographic portraits of Fa'amotu, a Samoan Tāupou', *Visual Anthropology*, Vol. 16, 2003, pp. 341–374; Knight, H. *Burton Brothers: Photographers*, Dunedin, 1980; McIndoe, John, and Knight, Hardwicke. 'Burton, Alfred 'Henry', *Dictionary of New Zealand Biography/Te Ara – the Encyclopedia of New Zealand*, https://teara.govt.nz/en/biographies/2b51/burton-alfred-henry (accessed 10 May 2021); Mataia-Milo, Saui'a Louise, 'Picturing Sāmoa: photographs by Thomas Andrew', *The Journal of Pacific History*, Vol. 49, no. 3, 2014, pp. 354–356.

soon after by another book on the same topic.[69] Several researchers have followed Specht and Field's study of Frank Hurley.[70] John Watt Beattie is another to have attracted considerable attention.[71] Thanks to Elsie Stephenson's research, the output of early professional photographers in Fiji such as JW Waters and many others is now recognised.[72] Another photographer to attract researchers' attention was Lucien Gauthier, a newly arrived twenty-nine-year-old in Papeete in the Society Islands who took up photography and created a new genre or photographic icon, the '*Vahine*' or Polynesian beauty. Gauthier left behind a priceless archive of 800 photographs.[73] The Hawaiian photography of Caroline Gurrey has also attracted attention.[74] Missionary photography has been well covered by Richard Eves, Prue

---

69   Colley, AC. *Robert Louis Stevenson and the colonial imagination*, London, Routledge, 2004; Manfredi, Carla, *Robert Louis Stevenson's Pacific impressions: Photography and travel writing*, Basingstoke, Palgrave Macmillan, 2018.

70   Miller, David P. *From snowdrift to shellfire: Captain James Francis (Frank) Hurley 1885–1962*, Sydney, David Ell, 1984; Ennis, Helen. *Man with a camera: Frank Hurley overseas*, Canberra, National Library of Australia, 2002; McGregor, Adrian. *Frank Hurley: A photographer's life*, Sydney, Viking/Penguin, 2004; Dixon, Robert, *Prosthetic God; Travel, representation and colonial governance*, St Lucia, Qld, University of Queensland Press, 2001.

71   Tassell, Margaret, and Wood, David. *Tasmanian Photographer: From the John Watt Beattie Collection*. Melbourne, Macmillan, 1981; Roe, Michael. 'Beattie, John Watt (1859–1930)', *Australian Dictionary of Biography*, http://adb.anu.edu.au/biography/beattie-john-watt-5171; Brown, Terry. 'Transcending the colonial gaze: Empathy, agency and understanding in the South Pacific photography of John Watt Beattie, *JNZPS*, Vol. 8, no. 1, 2021, pp. 151–170.

72   Stephenson, Elsie, *Fiji's past on picture postcards*, Suva, Caines Janiff, 1997.

73   Tréhin, Jean-Eves. *Tahiti: L'Eden à l'épreuve de la photographie, une histoire de la photographie à Tahiti et dans les Îles*, Paris, Gaillimard, 2003; Kakou, Serge. *Tahitian Beauties: Lucien Gauthier, Photographer*, T Adler Books, Santa Barbara, 2009.

74   Maxwell, Anne. 'Beautiful Hybrids: Caroline Gurrey's Photographs of Hawai'i's mixed-race children', *History of Photography*, *Vol. 36, no. 2, 2012, pp. 184–198;* Waldroup, Heather. 'Ethnographic pictorialism; Caroline Gurrey's Hawaiian types at the Alaska–Yukon–Pacific Exposition', *History of Photography*, Vol. 36, no. 2, 2012, pp. 172–83; Maxwell, Anne. 'Celebrating racial hybridity: Caroline Gurrey's portraits of Hawai'ian children', in Maxwell, Anne. *Women photographers in the Pacific world 1857–1930*, London, Routledge, 2023, pp. 173–192.

Ahrens and others.[75] Considerable attention has been given to the photography of anthropologists such as Diamond Jenness, Bronislaw Malinowski, John Layard and Michael Rockefeller.[76] In a small body of work on USA photography in World War II, the photography of Arthur Lavine and Elmer J Williams in New Caledonia has recently been published.[77] The most recent research on Tonga has brought the work of JW Burton, Henry Adams, Randolph Bedford, Edmund Zacher, Wilhelm Knappe and several others to our attention.[78] This book length study of McMahon's photography now adds his name to this ensemble of photographers of the Pacific.

75   Eves, R. 'Colonialism, Corporeality and Character: Methodist Missions and the Refashioning of Bodies in the Pacific', *History and Anthropology*, Vol. 10, no. 1, 1996, pp. 85–138; Eves, R. 'Commentary: Missionary or Collector? The Case of George Brown', *Museum Anthropology*, Vol. 22, no. 1, 1998, pp. 49–60; Ahrens, P. 'Reading Reverend George Brown's Samoan photographs', *History of Photography*, Vol. 27, no. 2, 2003, pp. 188–191; Ahrens, P. 'From darkness to light: The story of conversion in the Reverend George Brown's photographs', *Continuum: Journal of Media & Cultural Studies*, Vol. 19, no. 2, 2005, pp. 279–284; Ahrens, P. 'Colonizing with Christianity? The case of George Brown, missionary photographer', *Third Text*, Vol. 19, no. 3, 2005, pp. 259–267; Ahrens, P., ed. *Tour of paradise: An American soldier in the South Pacific*, Carlton Nth, Victoria, The Vulgar Press, 2006; Ahrens, P. 'Missionary positions: George Brown's bodies', in Cochrane, Susan and Quanchi, Max, eds. *Hunting the collectors: Pacific collections in Australian Museums, Art Galleries and Archives*, Newcastle, UK, Cambridge Scholars Publishing, 2007, pp. 131–149; Waldroup, H. 'Indigenous Modernities: Missionary Photography and Photographic Gaps in Nauru', *Journal of Pacific History*, Vol. 52, no. 4, 2017, pp. 459–481.

76   Goin, CM. 'Malinowski's ethnographic photography: Image, text and authority', *History of Photography*, 21.1.1997, pp. 67–72; Wright, T. 'The Fieldwork photographs of Jenness and Malinowski and the beginnings of modern anthropology', *JASO*, 22.1.1991, pp. 41–58; Young, MW. *Malinowski's Kiriwina: Fieldwork Photography 1915–1918, Chicago, University of Chicago Press*, 1998; Bubriski, K. *Michael Rockefeller: New Guinea photographs 1961*, Harvard, Peabody Museum Press, 2006; Geismer, H. and Herle, A., *Moving images; John Layard, fieldwork and photography on Malakula since 1914*, Honolulu, University of Hawaii Press, 2010.

77   Ahrens, P. ed. *Tour of paradise: An American soldier in the South Pacific*, The Vulgar Press, 2006; Cayrol-Baudrillart, F. *Arthur Lavine's Pacific Inspiration; Early photographs of New Caledonia*, Noumea, Éditions de musée de Nouvelle-Calédonie, 2008; See also Lindstrom, L .and White, G. *Island encounters: Black and white Memories of the Pacific War, Washington, Smithsonian, 1990*.

78   For JW Burton, Henry Adams, Randolph Bedford, Edmund Zacher, Wilhelm Knappe and several early photographers in Tonga, see special double issue on 'History of early photography in the Pacific', *JNZPS*, Vols. 8.1 (2020) and 8.2 (2021).

McMahon's photographs often appear today excised from the full-page photomontage format he had perfected between 1915 and 1922. Researchers do this so they can deconstruct an individual image, but this means it is now divorced from the accompanying images in the original photomontage. McMahon's photographs in illustrated newspapers and magazines, the main medium by which his images entered the public domain, were laid out in a carefully chosen pattern, deliberately educating readers in a sequence of messages.[79] The order of the photographs as they spread out across a full- or double-page photomontage was as important as the accompanying caption or text. Visually, the full array of images was a powerful influence on readers 'knowing' or learning-by-looking at, for example, Nauruans, Banabans, Gilbertese and Marshallese. Although each photograph had the potential to be a separate and stand-alone window 'from real life' (as often claimed for photographs in this period) the full-page gallery or photomontage was equally as persuasive. Separating an image today from its published surroundings and format blocks the opportunity to see the Pacific as audiences did from 1919 to 1922.

What readers/viewers thought of McMahon's photography remains a puzzle. Globally, how audiences 'read' photographs is an unresolved quandary in analysing and making historical use of old photographs, and this debate has attracted a sizeable body of literature.[80] This means that we have a considerable theoretical

---

79   Images were also mediated by captions, banner headlines and a supporting text of anecdotes, reminiscences, recycled facts, tales and assertions.

80   Mackenzie, J. *Propaganda and Empire; the manipulation of British public opinion 1880–1960*, Manchester, Manchester University Press, 1986; Ryan, James. *Picturing empire: Photography and the visualisation of the British Empire*, Chicago, University of Chicago Press, 1997; Hight, EM. and Sampson, GD., eds. *Colonialist photography: imag(in)ing race and place*, London, Routledge, 2002; Pinney, C. and Thomas, N., eds. *Photography's other histories*, Durham, Duke University Press, 2003; Ryan, James. *Picturing Place: Photography and the Geographical Imagination*, London, Bloomsbury, 2003; van den Muijzenberg, O. *The Philippines through European lenses: late nineteenth century photographs from the Meerkamp van Embden Collection*, Manila, Ateneo de Manila University Press, 2008.

platform upon which to draw conclusions on readership but still no definite answers based on archival evidence of how a person, persons or whole nations might have read McMahon's photographs.

The ambivalence and contradictory meanings within a photograph's frame can be illustrated by the example of a scene McMahon arranged in Makin Meang (Little Makin), a coral island just north of Butaritari Atoll, in the far north of the Gilbert chain (see Fig. 19). In this photograph, a crowd seems to be randomly arranged across a cleared space (which has the appearance of a street). From the roof of the trader's store in the background, children wave at the camera. Did children usually climb on the roof of the trader's store? Is the building a store or a house? Is the person leaning out the window a trusted male employee, a lover, relative, not from Little Makin, or perhaps forced to remain on duty and guard the stores while others congregate out on the thoroughfare for the taking of the photograph? Were the loincloths which appear de-rigueur donned for the occasion to replace the more common shirts and trousers? Why does the picket fence dividing the building from the thoroughfare seem to have no influence over the crowd who scatter all over the roof, verandah, and yard and roadway? Why are there no women? Where are the middle-aged and older Gilbertese? How widespread in 1918 was the use of imported corrugated iron? Were local employees relocated to live in local material houses in the yard beside their employer's trade store? The point made by this list of mostly unanswerable questions is that photographs suggest a great many questions but provide few answers.

Published photography

The photographer was not always identified in the avalanche of early twentieth-century published illustrative material across the globe, and although McMahon's photographs appeared worldwide during his lifetime and afterwards, he was often not attributed. For example, his photograph of a New Ireland copra plantation appeared unattributed in the first issue of *Pacific Islands Monthly*,[81] and a much repeated image of the 'bell-topper' headgear of unmarried boys from Buka Island appeared without attribution in the serialised encyclopedia, *Secret Museum of Mankind* published in 1935, despite the exact copying of the photograph and caption from an earlier encyclopedia, *People of All Nations* (see Fig. 4).[82] This was one of McMahon's most circulated images and appeared in *The Wide World, The Sydney Mail*, in McMahon's 'New Guinea' album published by McCarron in 1923 and elsewhere. Not being attributed was no doubt disappointing for photographers, and it remains unknown if McMahon was paid for the images that were published without proper attribution.

McMahon sent his photographs to an enormous range of publishing outlets. For example, he sent photographs on the sugar industry in Fiji to the *International Sugar Journal* in 1922[83] and at the same time wrote about 'a sparkling jewel in the crown of British Administration' in an article on 'The Lepers of the Lonely Isle' (Mokogai Island, Fiji) in *Dental Science Journal of Australia*.[84] A photograph of an unusual food storage technique on Vella Lavala Island in the Solomon Islands appeared over a six-year period

---

81   *Pacific Islands Monthly*, 16.8.1930. p. 8. The same photograph was used on the cover of *PIM*, 17.1.1931.

82   It was captioned, 'Observance of strange rite among youths of Buka Island', in *Peoples of All Nations*, Vol. 2, 1922, p. 928. The *Secret Museum* had no author or credits, no copyright, no date, no page numbers, no index. It copied photographs from previously published encyclopedia and other sources. Vol. 5 was devoted to Oceania. It included twelve McMahon photographs, unattributed.

83   McMahon, TJ, 'The sugar industry of the Crown Colony of Fiji', *International Sugar Journal*, Vol. 24, 1922, pp. 240–43.

84   McMahon, TJ. 'The lepers of the lonely isle', *Dental Science Journal of Australia*, Oct. 1922, pp. 470–73.

in *The Queenslander* (1918), *Sydney Morning Herald* (1919), *Illustrated London News* (1919), *The Wide World* (1921), and then in McCarron's album on the *Solomon Islands* in 1923, indicating again that McMahon was always on the lookout for new outlets in which to publish.

Acknowledgement globally came when his photographs started appearing in a number of serialised illustrated encyclopedia, a booming format in the 1920s. For example, Basil Thompson, in his entry on 'South Sea Islands' in *Countries of the World* in 1923, used fifteen McMahon photographs and then in 'Island life in the strange South Seas' in *People of All Nations*, Thompson used eleven more photographs by McMahon.[85] In the serialised encyclopedia, *Lands and People* (1929–1932), *The World of Today* (1922) and *Peoples of All Nations* (1922–23) ten per cent of all photographs on the Pacific Islands were by McMahon.

His photographs were used widely by short story writers often publishing in the same magazines as McMahon, such as Jack McLaren in *The Lone Hand*.[86] In 1906, McMahon's photographs were used in advertisements, presumably for a fee, in the *Northern Herald*, for example, for banks, Burns Philp, trading companies, stores, hotels and cordial mixtures. McMahon's photographs also appeared in CAW Monckton's 'New Guinea: The island of mysterious Forest' in *Countries of the World* (Volume 4, 1923), SS McKenzie's *The official Australian History of WWI: The Australians at* Reboul; *Volume 10* (1927), in JE Hildebrand's 'The

---

85   Thompson's entry *in Peoples of All Nations* was an extraordinary seventy-nine pages in length with ninety-three illustrations.

86   A McMahon photograph illustrated each episode of Jack McLaren's serialised story. See 'On the fringe of the law', *The Sydney Mail*, 2.2.1921, p. 26; 2.3.1921, p. 26; 9.3.1921, p. 26; 16.3.1921, p. 26; 23.3.1921, p. 26. McLaren's tale went for twenty-five episodes, with thirty-two photographs, starting in November 1920. It was also published as a book. See Quanchi, M. 'The power of pictures; learning-by-looking at Papua in illustrated newspapers and magazines' *Australian Historical Studies*, 35, 123, 2004, pp. 37–53.

Columbus of the Pacific' in *National Geographic* (January 1927) and in Albert Ellis' *Ocean Island and Nauru* in 1935.[87]

A problem occurred when editors added incorrect captions or mismatched photographs and captions sent in by contributors. For example, McCarron in Sydney, the publishers of McMahon's seven small albums (in a booklet or pamphlet format) on the Solomons, Norfolk, Gilberts, Ocean and Marshalls Islands, New Guinea and the Torres Strait, printed a Nauruan on the cover of McMahon's Solomon Island album and a Fijian on the cover of the New Guinea edition.[88]

McMahon rarely included scenery or photographs popularly categorised at the time as picturesque. One of the few instances is a photograph of the 'flowerpot' or 'beehive' in the Duke of York Islands, a small, wave-cut rock outcrop with luxuriant growth ten metres above the water line. It appeared in Australian, New York and London publications.[89] His focus was the economic, imperial and commercial, and pleasant views were not on his list of photographs to be taken when visiting Pacific colonies and territories.

Journalism and photography

McMahon supplemented his images with a text constructed from casual conversations and overheard, often misconstrued tall tales and rumour. This means that, in McMahon's reportage, there were four elements: the banner headline, the framed image, its caption and the associated text. These four elements did not necessarily corroborate each other and indeed the banner headline,

---

87   Three McMahon photographs were attributed by Ellis. Thirty-four photographs by McMahon and others were not attributed.

88   Each album/pamphlet contained eight to thirteen captioned, full-page photographs in black-and-white.

89   *The Sydney Mail*, 16.1.1918, p. 7; *Munsey's Magazine*, Dec. 1918, p. 486; *Illustrated London News*, 15.2.1919, p. 778; *The Telegraph* (Sydney) 24.11.1917.

caption and text often formed a narrative that contradicted the visual indexical evidence. The image McMahon framed as the lens closed, whether in Anibare Bay, Jaliut, Butaritari Atoll or Uma village on Banaba, was often cropped, giving the image a new meaning. The audience's reading of an image was also affected by an editor's addition of a new caption. McMahon's motivations at the time of positioning his tripod were therefore sometimes different to the messages offered to readers a year later in different continents for different audiences.

McMahon was well-published, with hundreds of illustrated articles and photo-essays in Australia, New Zealand, Europe and America, and in his own mind, a potential Gold Medallist and deserving Fellow with the Royal Geographical Society. To add legitimacy to his claim as an 'I was there' commentator and booster of empire, he needed text to accompany his photographs, so he spent time in clubs, on planters' verandahs, on wharves and decks collecting anecdotes, opinions, facts and personal histories. He was both a photographer and a journalist using these borrowed commentaries and scuttlebutt to enhance his photography and in practical terms making the package he sent to editors carry greater topical interest and therefore attracting a higher fee. These elements of photography, journalism and editorial awareness can be seen clearly in all his Pacific photography. Along with the uneasy relationship between image and text, it is important to note that browsers of his illustrated articles in waiting rooms and public libraries may not have read the text at all, preferring to take a longer glance over the photographs in a learning-by-looking manner while searching for the exotic and unusual. As we have little to no archival evidence of reader/viewer reactions to published images, we can only surmise that readers, revisiting their favourite magazines, probably took in both image and text.

Christraud Geary lamented in 1988 that, 'Numerous books have presented photographs of North American Indians as well as photographs from China, Japan, India, and other parts of the world. Yet photographs taken in Africa, a continent that has captured the western imagination since antiquity, remain largely unexplored'.[90] Great steps have been taken by Geary and others to address this gap regarding Africa and elsewhere, and slowly the study of the Pacific is catching up. Geary's statement in the 1980s could easily have been repeated for the study of photography in the Pacific Islands.[91] For example, the link between photography, colonialism and tourism in the Pacific had been noted in the 1980s but not followed.[92] Ngaire Douglas's *They came for savages* in 1996 was an exception, but in Graeme Smith's *Photography and travel* in 2013, the Pacific was overlooked.[93] On a brighter note, new studies of women photographers, on repatriation of Frank Hurley's photography, and on the link between landscape photography and colonial settlement have appeared during 2022–2023.[94] A study of

---

90   Geary, C. *Images from Banum; German colonial photography at the court of King Njoya, Cameroon, West Africa 1902–1915*, Washington, Smithsonian, 1988, p. 10. See also; Haney, E. Photography and Africa, London, Reaktion, 2010.

91   See, Quanchi, M. 'Pacific Island Photography; Knowledge and history in the public domain', *Spectator*, 23.1.2003, pp. 13–26; Quanchi, M. 'Visual histories and photographic evidence', *Journal of Pacific History* 41, 2, 2006, pp. 165–74.

92   Quanchi, M. 'Researching early photography of the Pacific islands; An Overview', *JNZPS*, 8.1, 2021 pp. 269–81. See also, Albers, P. and James, WR. 'Travel photography; a methodological approach', *Annals of Tourism Research*, 15, 1988, pp. 134–58; Hayes, M. 'Photography and the emergence of the Pacific cruise' in *Colonialist Photography: Imag(in)ing race and place*, edited by Hight, EM., and Sampson, GD. London, Routledge, 2002, pp. 172–87.

93   Douglas, Norman. *They came for savages; 100 years of tourism in Melanesia*, Astonville, Southern Cross University Press, 1996; Smith, G. *Photography and travel*, London, Reaktion, 2013.

94   Maxwell, Anne, *Women photographers in the Pacific world 1857–1930*, London, Routledge, 2023; Lamb, L. and Lee, C. *Moving Pictures; Repatriation, Exchange, and Colonial Legacies in the Gulf of Papua*, London, Palgrave, 2022; Hore, J. *Visions of nature; How landscape photography shaped settler colonialism*, Oakland, University of California Press, 2022.

McMahon's photography is offered here in the hope that readers will engage with the multifaceted links between Pacific Island and Australian photography, tourism, colonialism and illustrated journalism and publications. Thanks to Trove, McMahon's large body of Pacific and Queensland photography is accessible, and perhaps this book will inspire researchers to delve deeper into the manner in which published photography informed and entertained and now constitutes an important record of the early decades of the century.

The next chapter focuses on the Australian Territory of Papua, McMahon's first visit to the Islands and the start of his new career.

Chapter 2

Papua: a very comprehensive series of descriptive photographs

McMahon's images of Papua spread fast across a wide domain after his two-month tour in 1915. His departure from Cairns was noted in *The Cairns Post,* which also highlighted his back-country reporting role:

> Mr TJ McMahon, representative of the 'Post' and 'Herald,' has just concluded a very successful tour of the Innisfail and Ingham districts and will leave on the 6th instant for a three-week business tour of New Guinea, visiting Port Moresby, Samarai and Rabaul. Later on, he will travel the Cairns back country in the Interests of the two papers.[95]

Reporting on McMahon's arrival, the *Papuan Times* in Port Moresby announced that 'all Papuan articles appearing in the *Northern Herald* will be profusely illustrated' and 'will be watched with great interest'.[96] McMahon stayed for two months and visited several plantations in Port Moresby, Samarai, Milne Bay, Rabaul and the eastern archipelago, and went on patrol to Yule Island and inland to Mafula. His photographs of Papua appeared in the *Northern Herald* and *The Cairns Post* (one hundred and

---

95   *The Cairns Post,* 3.9.1915, p. 4.

96   *Papuan Times,* 6.10.1915; 3.11.1915.

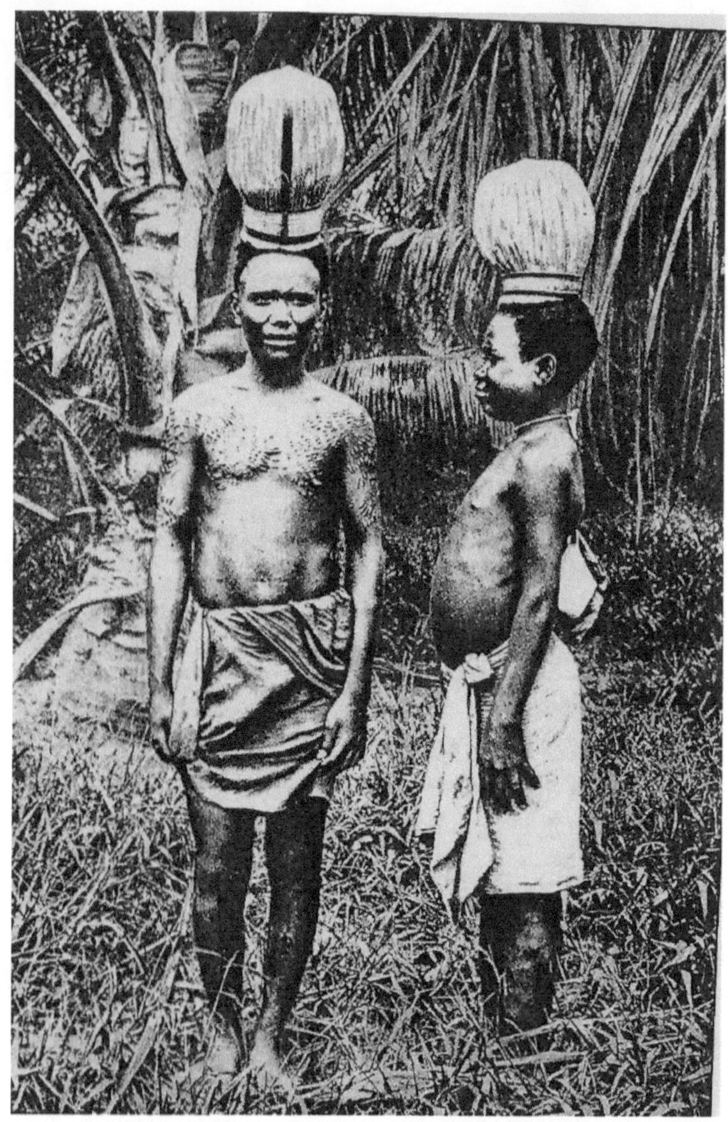

Fig. 4 Adolescent boys wearing 'bell-toppers',
Buka, Solomon Islands, 1918

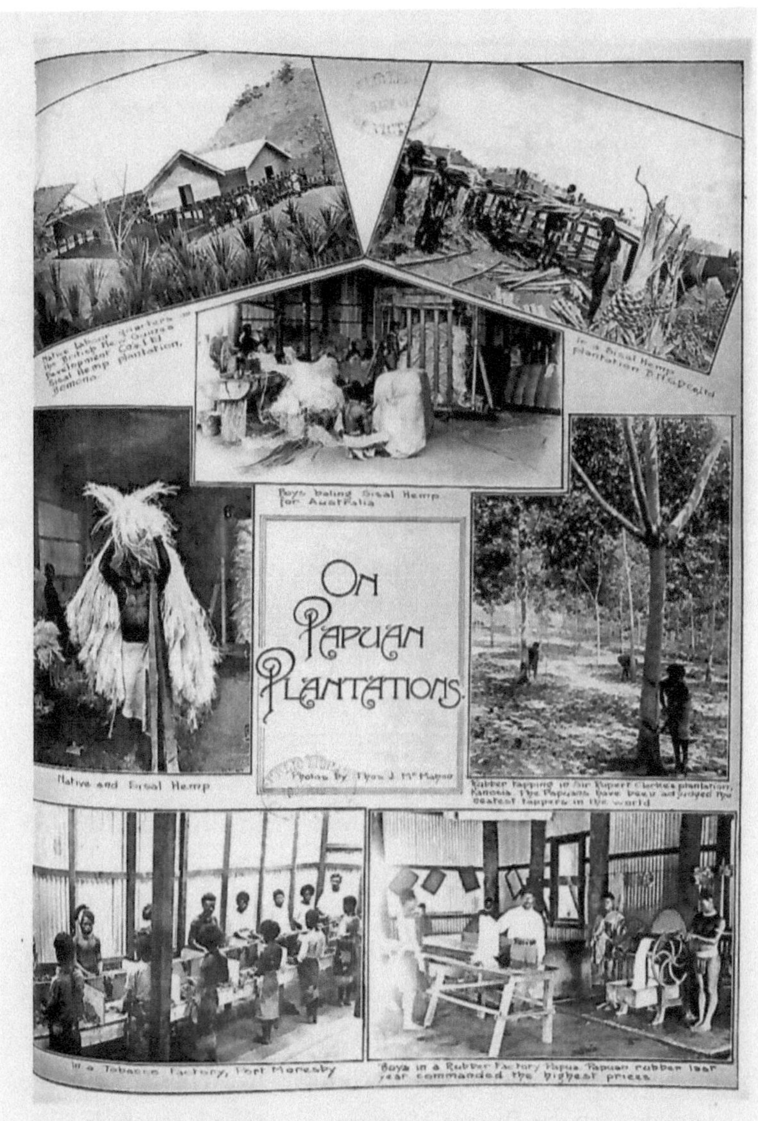

Fig. 5 Typical photomontage format used by McMahon, 1916

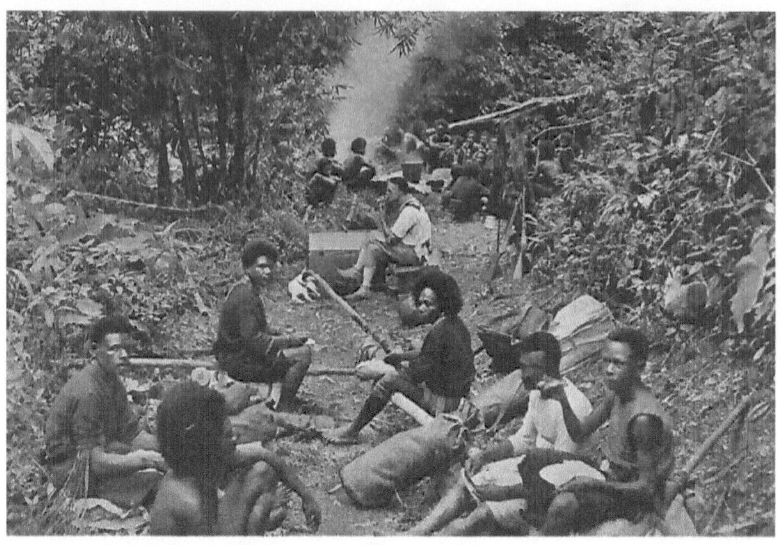

Fig. 6 On patrol inland to Mafula Mission
with the governor of Papua, 1915

two photographs), *The Queenslander* (forty-seven photographs),
Daily Telegraph (Brisbane, twelve photographs), *The Sydney Mail*
(seventy-three photographs) and *The Australasian* (Melbourne,
thirty-six photographs).[97] McMahon eventually published 763
photographs of Papua and German New Guinea in magazines,
newspapers and illustrated encyclopedia around the world.

Papua had been known as British New Guinea after annexation
in 1884. It was transferred to Australian control in 1901 and formally
enacted as an Australian Overseas Territory in 1906. The capital was
Port Moresby, a small port and township founded in 1873, jostling
alongside a sizeable Papuan Motu community at Hanuabada. The
only other European township was Samarai, a busy port in the China
Strait in eastern New Guinea. Papua was undergoing considerable

---

97   Weekend illustrated papers for rural areas were published, for example, by the
      Melbourne *Argus* (*The Australasian*), by *The Brisbane Courier* (*The Queenslander*) and
      the *Sydney Morning Herald* (*The Sydney Mail*).

change as tobacco, rubber and sisal plantations were being developed alongside the main export crop of copra, and there had already been a gold rush to Sudest and Misima in the eastern archipelago. Copper was rumoured to be potentially accessible, and McMahon photographed a railway being built to carry copper ore to Bootless Bay. There were missions all along the coast, but the interior was mostly unmapped by Europeans – no one guessed there were half a million people living in the Highlands.

As a visiting journalist, one of the first to visit for the purpose of recording Australia's effort as a colonial power, McMahon enjoyed privileges and access provided by the administration, missions and individual planters, including taking trips with the governor, Sir Hubert Murray. Papua was administered directly from Australia, and McMahon found planters and traders eager to complain about inappropriate policies, land and labour problems and inefficient administrators. Mostly, he had his camera ready to record economic potential that would attract attention back in Australia. The full archive of McMahon's published Papuan photographs includes general views of Samarai, Port Moresby and the coastal ranges (about ten per cent) and ethnographic subject matter (about eighteen per cent). The remaining seventy per cent were in the economic propaganda and commercial boosting category.

Papua was McMahon's first trip into the Pacific. After subsequent trips to Papua and German New Guinea in 1917 and 1921, and trips to other western and central Pacific islands, McMahon acquired an appreciation of the power and topicality of images. He never repeated the few blatantly stereotyped compositions such as partially clothed reclining belles, a native card party and sham fights.[98] In December 1915, after including three borrowed photographs

---

98   *Northern Herald*, 10.12.1915 (reclining belle composition); 10.12.1915 ('A friendly argument').

of semi-naked young girls in his first publication of his Papuan photographs, captioned 'a peal of belles', 'a mountain belle' and 'a lady and betel nut' (a classic reclining nude study),[99] McMahon never published voyeuristic imaging again. McMahon had purchased these three images at a photography outlet in Port Moresby or at Samarai. The inclusion of the three Papuan belle images may be explained by a reliance in Papua, during his first photography expedition, on stereotyped images and what he thought readers expected to find in photographs taken in so-called primitive, frontier colonies. These compositions and framing were abandoned as his photography skills increased, his understanding of Pacific Island peoples and cultures improved, and he took on the role of a traveller, author, photographer and promoter of the economic exploitation of island resources relying on carefully posed scenes, wide angle views and an *à la flaneur* approach to recording commercial developments as he came across them in the field.

The patrol to Mafula that McMahon took with Governor Murray was described in four of McMahon's illustrated articles[100] and individual photographs from this patrol appeared in newspapers and journals over the next seven years.[101] One

---

99   *Northern Herald*, 3.12.1915, p. 35; 10.12.1915, p. 26.

100   McMahon, TJ. (1916), 'The mists of Mafula', *The Lone Hand*, 1.7.1916, pp. 83–85; 'After outlaws in unknown New Guinea', *The Wide World*, Jan. 1917, pp. 372–82; 'Papua (British New Guinea): The wonderland of the great central mountains', paper read at the Royal Geographical Society (Qld), 1.3.1917, Box 4, Item 9053, Royal Geographical Society (Qld), Brisbane, published in the society's journal; see *Queensland Geographical Journal*, 1916–1918, Vol. 32, pp. 81–88; 'The wonderland of Papua', *Overland Monthly*, Aug. 1919, pp. 104–10.

101   *Northern Herald*, 3.12.1915, p. 25 and 10.12.1915, p. 26; *The Australasian*, 12.2.1916, p. iv; *The Queenslander*, 3.6.1916, p. 28 and 29.7.16, p. 23; *Travel*, Jan. 1917, p. 374; *Sydney Times*, 14.11.1920; *Trans-Pacific*, Mar. 1922, p. 81; Hammerton, J, ed, (1922), *Peoples of All Nations*, London, Amalgamated Press, p. 910; Moncrieff, ARH, ed. *The New World of Today*, London, Gresham (8 volumes), 1920–22, pp. 125, 133, 135, 137. McMahon also used the title, 'The wonderland of Papua' and several photographs from the Mafula trip for a general article on the Pacific Islands: see *Illustrated London News*, 15.11.1919, pp. 1776–80.

photograph from the Mafula patrol was often repeated. It depicted McMahon sitting with a large group of Papuan men, women and children, some in European-style clothing, and was variously captioned 'with types of a strange race', 'with the people of Mafula, central Papua' or more optimistically as 'civilization is starting'.[102] He described the seven-day, one-hundred-and-twenty-four-kilometre walk[103] as a trip to the remotest stations in the unknown 'wonderland of Papua' where 'cannibal savages roamed in great numbers'[104] and where waterfalls and ranges proved 'how magnificently grand nature can, under tropic skies, bloom forth'.[105] This was a slight exaggeration as by 1915, the Mafula track was a well-established and safe route for new arrivals, and going inland to Mafula had become a motif for many adventurers and storytellers.[106] Mafula was a mission and administration station and well within the boundary of the so-called settled or controlled area, but for McMahon, this was his first and only contact with Papuans away from Port Moresby and the coastal plantation districts. Beyond Mafula, there were indigenous tribal groups who were not integrated into the European-controlled economy or even located on administration maps, but McMahon was not interested. He was not in Papua to investigate ethnographic

102   *Northern Herald*, 3.12.1915, p. 35; *The Wide World*, Jan. 1917, p. 379; *Illustrated London News*, 15.11.1919, p. 776; *Mid-Pacific*, Vol. 24, 1922, p. 375.

103   Harry Downing walked the same track in 1920 and estimated the path, which he noted was worthy of being called a road, was 104 kilometres from the coast to the Mafula mission. Both McMahon and Downing noted it was a seven day walk up, but a four day walk down and out to the coast: see Downing, HL. 'A night in a cannibal village', *Sea Land Air*, 2.10.1922, p. 491; McMahon, TJ. 'The mists of Mafula', *The Lone Hand*, 1.7.1916, p. 83; McMahon, TJ. 'The wonderland of the Pacific', *Overland Monthly*, Aug. 1919, pp. 104–5.

104   McMahon, TJ. 'After outlaws in unknown New Guinea', *The Wide World*, Jan 1917, pp. 373–4.

105   McMahon, TJ. 'The wonderland of the Pacific', *Overland Monthly*, Aug. 1919, p. 104.

106   For example, see *Sydney Morning Herald* feature article, (anon.), 'A walk in Papua', 1921, subsequently reprinted in Allen, PS. *Stewart's Handbook of the Pacific Islands*, Sydney, Stewart and McCarron, pp. 325–34.

others but to report on 'the prospects for commercial men, both territories being very little exploited from a commercial point of view'.[107] The many hundreds of photographs he published after his visit were in response to this objective.

McMahon's photographs of tobacco crops at Katea and sisal hemp production at Bomana were displayed in Port Moresby and were judged 'descriptive of the work on these plantations'.[108] The agenda underlying this comment was a long-running debate about the level of support that the administration should offer for economic development by Europeans in the Territory. McMahon's photographs of fertile plantations, labour lines and Papuans performing a range of skilled and unskilled tasks were exactly the message that planters and traders wanted to send to Australia and the Commonwealth Parliament. They were pleased to see evidence published which might help over-turn Governor Murray's restrictive, pro-native policies. There was also criticism and frustration in Port Moresby over many writers in the Australian press who made a short visit (often lasting the turn-around time of the steamer service out of Cooktown) and who then wrote inaccurate and critical descriptions of development and the treatment of Papuans. Just two months before McMahon arrived, the *Papuan Times* had been critical of a journalist from Sydney who stayed for the thirty-six-hour turn-around in Port Moresby and then wrote a series of misleading articles about cannibalism, village conditions and treatment of Papuans.[109] This was the background when a Port Moresby resident was quoted in a Cairns newspaper referring to McMahon's visit. North Queensland readers should know, wrote the correspondent, that

---

107   McMahon, TJ. 'After outlaws in unknown New Guinea', *The Wide World,* Jan. 1917, p. 372.

108   *Papuan Times,* 13.10.1915.

109   *Papuan Times,* 28.7.1915.

when Mr McMahon returns, he will be able to speak with some authority and his articles must not be doubted or mis-allowed like some of the correspondents we have had amongst us previously, who after a stay of a couple of hours have gone back to Australia and written a lot of piffle. Mr McMahon when he returns will have seen more of this country than any previous paper representative and will be therefore in a position to speak with authority.[110]

McMahon certainly played the boosting role well, sending photographs with a short accompanying text to all the major eastern Australian city newspapers, and in December, after returning from Papua, he addressed the Brisbane Chamber of Commerce and the Royal Geographical Society (Queensland branch).

New Guinea: a land of revelation

McMahon's photographs of what he called a 'land of revelation' were immediately presented to readers in Cairns over an eight-month period in full-page formats with a lengthy text on adjoining pages. His first features were a miscellany of images, some borrowed, that served as a cultural and geographic introduction for readers to his following proclamations about plantations and boosting of the potential of Papua. Leaving no doubt as to his credentials as a booster of Papua's potential, he demanded that readers take note of 'Papua in its magnificent resources, commercial offerings, unparalleled and opportune prospects, existing wealth of coconut, rubber and hemp and in the immensity of its territory'.[111] To support these claims, he depicted economic activities such as 'boys' being paid off and groups of

---

110 *Northern Herald*, 19.11.1915.

111 *Northern Herald*, 10.12.1915, p. 20.

expatriate employees of the British New Guinea Company and Burns Philp. He depicted flourishing and successful examples of the European-controlled economy of Papua, including tobacco at Katea plantation, rubber at Kanosia plantation, sisal hemp at Bomana plantation and copra at Gili Gili plantation. At Kanosia plantation, the manager's residence and a group of married Papuan employees and their families were included. At Katea plantation, Papuans were shown lining up for work, rolling tobacco for packaging and a rare interior photograph recorded the 'inside of the native quarters with beds, bedding, mosquito nets, etc.'. McMahon also photographed attempts at rice cultivation. In a feature on Bomana plantation, a full-page spread of twelve photographs included the various stages of sisal hemp production and ended with a group of labourers and a view of the pristine, well-swept 'native boy quarters'. This format was repeated for Gili Gili plantation at Milne Bay with more photographs of the stages of production, a huge line-up of several hundred labourers, the labourers' quarters and three European overseers.[112] He published photographs of mining on Sudest Island, declared that 'considerable energy has been displayed' and listed an impressive array of minerals that allegedly were being mined: gold, silver, lead, copper, zinc, iron, obsidian, gypsum, manganese, sulphur, graphite and coal.[113] Investors in Australia would have been aroused by this list. McMahon's composition, focal length and content (mines, labour, quarters and plantation fields with flourishing crops) represented the economic success that could be achieved in Papua. On learning-by-looking through this series

---

112   McMahon, TJ. 'Unpublished prints' (uncatalogued), Box 4, Royal Geographical Society, Brisbane. McMahon published only one photograph of the Laloki copper mine railway (see *Trans-Pacific*, Mar. 1922, p. 80) and only one of rice planting (see *Importer and Exporter Journal of Australasia*, 24.6.1922, p. 56).

113   *The Sydney Mail*, 1.8.1917, p. 17. Two photographs of mining were included: ibid., p. 11.

of photographs, readers would have come to the same conclusion. There was no chance of misinterpretation. Others in this era such as the government anthropologist, FE Williams; the amateur photography enthusiasts, EWP Chinnery, FR Barton, OM Manning, RA Vivian and Archie Gibson; and the missionaries, WG Lawes, PJ Money and HM Dauncey amassed comparable sized photography collections, but for impact on the world stage in easily accessible formats for the reading public, McMahon stands alone as a photographer, essayist and image maker.

There were obviously no restrictions paced on McMahon by *The Cairns Post* and the *Northern Herald* because reworked material soon began to appear in *The Queenslander, The Sydney Mail, The Australasian* and *The Week. The Australasian* series in Melbourne began with a full-page feature titled 'In central Papua', including the administration yacht, *Elevala*, two scenes at Mafula mission, one photograph of a line of carriers on patrol, Resident Magistrate Hyndman-Jones with his wife and Armed Native Constabulary escort, and one of the Mafula children wearing cloaks against the rain. This format included the standard scene-setting and contextualising images, and following an established editorial format, the visual message in the rest of the series became more explicit. Photographs of sisal hemp, tobacco, rubber and coconut growing suggested that well-equipped production sheds, fertile crops, groves of trees and an ample supply of skilled labour were characteristic of the territory's economy.[114] In Brisbane, *The Queenslander* series opened with a full page on sisal production captioned 'Native labour in Papua' and was followed by full-page features respectively on 'Papuan plantations', 'Port Moresby; the capital of Papua', 'Mission work in Papua', 'Papuan byways' and

---

114   *The Australasian*, 12.2.1916, p. vi; 25.5.1916, p. i; 8.7.1916, p. viii.

'Scenes at Samarai'.[115] The accompanying text published under the 'Sketcher' by-line repeated McMahon's Cairns material. The full-page feature on Port Moresby began with a broad view of the Paga Hill wharves area but the remainder of the photographs were devoted to group portraits of European administrators surrounded by their Papuan staff. A feature page on Samarai Island included churches, wharves, the fire brigade and gaol. These were representing not Papua but European control, the imposition of colonial rule and the economic benefits derived from the bringing of commerce and industry to the colony. Only five of the forty-seven photographs in *The Queenslander* series were scenic views. Another five were of Papuan material culture, including the well-established iconic images – one of a tree house, two of suspension bridges and two of villages.[116]

An emphasis on export crops and commerce-backed colonial authority was clear from the start. A photograph captioned 'A Magistrate holding court on an unruly boy' depicted a very relaxed European magistrate, comfortably leaning back in his chair, legs crossed, with three uniformed police standing to the side. As many as 300 labourers were shown in other photographs. The underlying sign, or punctum, was that of authority being easily exerted over a large and pliable labour force. Three images in this opening feature relied on the uniformed martial figure as symbols of authority, in this instance, the ANC. One image relied on the symbol of the mounted figure (an overseer overlooking his shovel-laden labourers), and in another, Europeans were depicted surrounded by Papuans but sitting relaxed in the classic hierarchical framing of the colonial planter surrounded by his loyal 'boys'. The emphasis on labour continued throughout *The Queenslander* series.

---

115   *The Queenslander*, 1.4.1916, p. 24; 8.4.1916, p. 27; 27.5.1916, p. 24; 3.6.1916, p. 28; 15.7.1916, p. 22; 29.7.1916, pp. 23–24.

116   See previous footnote.

McMahon also toyed with innovative money-making uses for his images, particularly by photographing buildings, warehouses and staff portraits to be used in newspaper advertisements. *The Cairns Post, Northern Herald* and Port Moresby newspapers were soon using McMahon's photographs for advertisements for Patching's Cordial, Stewart's slipway and wharves, CR Baldwin's store, McCrann's Hotel Moresby, and Ryan's Papua Hotel. Photographs of buildings and warehouses that would be considered advertising in other contexts, but which to readers were symbolic of European progress in Papua, included Clunn's store, Burns Philp's Port Moresby store and British New Guinea Company's stores at Port Moresby and Samarai. Two of these were rare interior photographs. McMahon published group portraits of the staff at Whitten Brothers, Burns Philp (BP) and British New Guinea Company's stores and indulged in another advertising self-promotion technique in which Papuans were staged reading a copy of the journal or newspaper in which his article would later appear. He also used this gimmick during his later travels in the western Pacific.[117]

The emphasis on promoting Papua as a colonial possession and an economic opportunity continued as McMahon's solicited and unsolicited contributions spread around the world. For example, a single photograph of an extensive coconut plantation at Gili Gili and one of a mature rubber plantation at Kanosia appeared in Australia in the *Northern Herald*, *The Australasian*, *Sunday Times* (Sydney), *The Queenslander* and *The Lone Hand*, in England in *Our Quarterly Magazine* and in the United States in *Dun's Review*,

---

117 *Northern Herald*, 24.3.1916, pp. 18–22; 28.7.1916, pp. 22; 24.3.1916, p. 26; 28.7.1916, p. 27; 10.12.1915, p. 26; 30.11.1917, p. 34; *The Sydney Mail*, 9.3.1921, p. 20 (in New Ireland); *The Wide World*, Jan. 1921, p. 356; *The Queenslander*, 9.2.1918, p. 23 (in the Solomon Islands). These were clumsily touched up and the appropriate magazine name added.

Sunset: the Pacific Monthly and *Trans-Pacific*.[118] Two photographs of labour, one of a massed group portrait of labourers at Gili Gili and the other of labourers laden with their 'cargo' after being paid off, received a similar distribution.[119] Papua, as understood from the vicarious experience of learning-by-looking at these widely disseminated McMahon photographs, was indeed an economic revelation. McMahon wrote in 1918, that

> private enterprise is doing amazing things today in developing Papua's natural resources, and when capital in ample amounts finds its way to these shores ... it will surprise the world.[120]

Sisal hemp

In 1916, the headline for his first article on the sisal hemp industry, a full-page story accompanied by twelve photographs, clearly stated his enthusiasm for 'an industry that will show astonishing results in the future'.[121] Sisal hemp was looked at in Papua as a potential staple crop and was a topic McMahon apparently thought was of wider interest. When McMahon visited Papua, sisal production was expanding rapidly, doubling in

---

118   For 'natives' tapping rubber at Sir Rupert Clarke's Kanosia plantation, see *The Queenslander*, 8.4.1916, p. 27; *Northern Herald*, 21.7.1916, p. 30; *Our Quarterly Magazine*, Aug. 1918, p. 7; *Sunset: the Pacific Monthly*, Oct. 1918, p. 37; *Dun's Review*, Mar. 1918, p. 49; and *Sunday Times*, (Sydney), 14.11.1920. For Gili Gili plantation, see *Northern Herald*, 3.3.1916, p. 30; *The Lone Hand*, 1.7.1916, p. 85; *Australasian*, 8.7.1916, p. viii; and *Trans-Pacific*, Mar. 1922, p. 82.

119   For labourers at Gili Gili in Milne Bay, see *Northern Herald*, ibid; *The Australasian*, ibid; *Sunset: the Pacific Monthly*, Oct 1918, p. 37 and *World's Markets*, Aug. 1920, p. 31. For labourers being paid off, see *Northern Herald*, 10.12.1915, p. 26; *The Queenslander*, 1.4.1916, p. 24; *Sunset: the Pacific Monthly*, Oct. 1918, p. 37; *Trans-Pacific*, Mar. 1922, p. 83.

120   McMahon, TJ. 'Post Bellum Papua', *Sunset: Pacific Monthly*, Oct. 1918, p. 37.

121   By 1928, production had been abandoned. See McKillop, R., and Firth, SG. 'Foreign Intrusion; the first fifty years' in Denoon, D, and Snowden, C, eds. *A Time to Plant and a Time to Uproot; A history of agriculture in Papua New Guinea*, Port Moresby, Institute of Papua New Guinea Studies, 1981, pp. 97, 103.

hectares planted and tripling in export tonnage between 1913 and 1923. He reported that at Bomana Plantation, near the Laloki River, twenty kilometres from Port Moresby, the 'daily scene around the fibre mill is wonderful'. His images depicted large fields of sisal plants, the production sheds and labourer's sleeping quarters, and nine of the twelve photographs included labourers, supporting McMahon's assertion that skilled labour was available in Papua.[122] One image, repeated many times, showed labourers loading sisal onto trucks for transport along a temporary light rail track to the processing plant. Viewed in a full-page format, this was a persuasive statement of profitability and economic success, and readers would not have missed McMahon's emphasis on infrastructure – plant, railways, dormitories and bales of sisal hemp 'ready for export'.[123] He used these photographs in all his subsequent illustrated articles on the sisal industry.[124]

He did not publish on sisal again until 1918, a gap of three years. For the New York magazine, *Dun's Review*, he used seven of the photographs from his initial feature in 1916 and emphasised the many kilometres of 'two foot' tramway lines, rebutted accusations

---

122   For the sisal fields, see *Northern Herald*, 7.1.1916, p. 24; *The Australasian*, 20.5.1916, p. i; *Dun's Review*, Sept. 1918, p. 42; *World's Work*, Dec. 1919, p. 58; and *Sunday Times* (Sydney), 14.11.1920. For production sheds, see *Northern Herald*, 7.1.1916, p. 24; *The Queenslander*, 8.4.1916, p. 27; *The Australasian*, 20.5.1916, p. viii; *Dun's Review*, Sept. 1918, p. 44; *Town and Country Journal*, 23.4.1919, p. 20; *World's Work*, Dec. 1919, p. 60. For Papuans, see *Northern Herald*, 7.1.1916, p. 24; *The Queenslander*, 8.4.1916, p. 27; *Dun's Review*, Mar. 1918, p. 49; *Town and Country Journal*, 23.4.1919, p. 20; *World's Work*, Dec. 1919, p. 60.

123   The photographs of "bales of hemp from Papua ready for shipping" were used five years later, in 1922, in *Trans-Pacific, March 1922, p. 80; and Importer and Exporter Journal of Australia, June 24, 1922, p. 57*.

124   His illustrated articles on sisal appeared later in 1918 in *Dun's Review* and in 1919 in *The Times Trade Supplement* (London), *World's Work* and the *Town and Country Journal*. The *Town and Country Journal* was the weekend illustrated paper for rural areas published by the *Sydney Evening News*.

of mistreatment of labourers[125] and highlighted for his American readers that many of the experts in cultivation and production were American college graduates. He declared that opportunities abounded and that 'two Americans are already much interested and are taking up extensive areas of land'.[126] McMahon stressed in his captions and supporting text that labourers were cheap and efficient and could pass leaves through the shredding machine at the impressive rate of 120 leaves a minute. Other labourers had become mechanics and he reported 'one could not wish for more reliable and competent workers'.[127] Views of labourers cutting sisal in the field or preparing hemp in the production sheds were clearly documentary in their initial appearance as a roving report on the industry, but investors and intending settlers saw a different boosting or promotional message when these two photographs appeared thirty-five times in eleven magazines in three continents.

In 1919, he repeated the same boosting story in Sydney's *Town and Country Journal*, declaring that Papuan sisal was the 'best and most extensive in the world ... there is no reason why anyone thinking of going there should hesitate'. Four months later in *The Times* in London, he declared that Papua would be able to provide all the sisal the British Empire needed. These were grand claims not supported by import and export figures, costs or production projections. Four months later, in an eight-page article in *World's Work*, McMahon used eight of the original photographs published

---

125   For typical opinion being expressed in Australia in the 1920s and 1930s about Papuan labour, see anon. 'Savages and factory hands', *Sydney Morning Herald*, 6.7.1933, p. 10. For debate about the declining Papuan population, see anon. 'Depopulation of the Islands' (report on an address by Dr RW Cilento), *The Brisbane Courier*, 22.10.1932, p. 17; anon., 'Annihilation of native races' (report on Dr RA Bernatski's views), *The Brisbane Courier*, 21.4.1933, p. 12.

126   McMahon, TJ. 'Sisal hemp growing in the South Pacific', *Dun's Review*, September 1918, p. 43.

127   *Dun's Review*, Sept. 1918, pp. 42–43; McMahon, TJ. 'Sisal hemp growing in Papua', *The Times Trade Supplement* (London), 16.8.1919.

in 1916 and again noted that the Pacific provided the same strain of sisal as Florida and the Bahamas and there were opportunities in the south Pacific for men with small capital. He claimed, 'there is no reason why in Papua he should not be able to make 1000 acres of hemp pay in a few years and pay well'. In all these articles, he used Bomana plantation as an example of how, once the world was at peace again, hundreds of tons of sisal fibre would be produced for the 'benefit of the British Isles and the countries of the British Empire'.[128] This was a theme, as a reporter, photographer and patriot, that he pursued for the next decade as he sought fame by boosting Australia's role in the south-west Pacific.

Tobacco

In the absence of diaries and notebooks, the only evidence we have of McMahon's visit to a tobacco plantation at Katea are published and illustrated newspaper reports. He reported on his visit in a two-part feature in Cairns in August 1916 with a half-page column describing the operations at Katea, and a full-page gallery of five photographs, with two more on the following page.[129] McMahon used the line-up of tobacco workers being addressed at Katea by a European overseer in several publications. It had already appeared in the *Northern Herald* in late 1915, *The Queenslander* in April 1916 and *The Australasian* (Melbourne) in July 1916, and over subsequent years appeared along with other photographs of Papua.[130]

McMahon's photographs from Katea also focused on infrastructure such as a large building of European design probably used as a machinery shed, stable or workplace for drying, preparing

---

128   McMahon, TJ. 'Sisal hemp; its cultivation in the South Pacific Islands', *World's Work*, Dec. 1919, p. 61. *World's Work* was a New York publication with circulation of 100,000.

129   *Northern Herald*, 11.8.1916, pp. 30–33, 37.

130   McMahon, TJ. 'Native labour in Papua', *The Queenslander*, 1.4.1916, pp. 8, 24, 41; McMahon, TJ. 'On Papuan plantations', *The Queenslander*, 8.4.1916, p. 27.

and rolling the tobacco. McMahon was following a convention already in place in the photography of missions, company promotional material and official colonial reports. In the same way that a newly constructed church in a village could represent the work of a mission, a photograph of a processing shed staffed by local labour could represent an export industry and economic opportunity and success. When McMahon's readers saw Papuans from Katea plantation ploughing the ground in preparation for planting 'American' tobacco, Papuans driving a wagon laden with firewood for the driers, the plant nurseries, the processing sheds and scenes in the dormitory lines, it was both a human-interest story and a form of commercial propaganda.

McMahon's first Katea tobacco plantation photographs appeared in a newspaper only a few months after the photograph was taken. His visual reporting was of topical interest in Papua and in Australia in an atmosphere of planter acrimony over Governor Sir Hubert Murray's Papuan policies that prevented planters from gaining free and easy access to labour markets. McMahon was addressing a subject of interest, with the Australian military occupation of German New Guinea fresh in readers' minds, along with questions of how to make Papua pay its own way and how to apply appropriate government economic policy while protecting the 'native interest'. A line-up of willing, robust Papuan labourers on a tobacco plantation would have been interpreted as an innovative economic development in a colony otherwise dominated by plantation copra.

Labour

McMahon wrote about the contentious labour issue, a refrain he picked up from disgruntled planters. This was a theme he pursued later for Australian readers in relation to German New Guinea and the Solomon Islands. He demanded polemically that the Papuan administration in Port Moresby, which 'assiduously, faithfully and consistently administers its laws, especially these native labour laws', needed to change its misguided labour policies because they would cause 'a golden opportunity to be lost'.[131] He tackled Australian politicians, arguing that the responsibility to maximise Australia's economic growth in its new colonies required monitoring so that 'the new responsibilities are honoured in every way by Australian federal politicians'.[132] The impact of these photographs, accompanied by a text, that witnessed topical events and provided evidence, was an early example of photojournalism.[133]

In his feature on tobacco at Katea, McMahon contradicted his own view, expressed elsewhere, by declaring the 'Papuan is not in any sense a skilled labourer' and must be 'reclaimed from his savagery with all speed and learn to bend his back to the yoke'. In most other instances, he suggested there was ample labour, well-trained and skilled. His images suggested there was ready access to a large workforce and that some Papuans had already progressed from being simple field labourers to skilled industrial workers. The accompanying photographs depicted European overseers with a decidedly military appearance, emphasised by their elevated pose on horseback.[134] The line-up of tobacco workers at Katea highlighted for readers that surveillance and discipline controlled the workers' daily lives. This coercion was integral to the labour market, and rigid discipline was widely thought to be required. The faces, expressions, demeanour and posture of

---

131   *The Queenslander*, 1.4.1916, p. 24.

132   McMahon, TJ. 'Sisal hemp growing in Papua – a bright future', *Town and Country Journal*, Apr. 1919, p. 20.

133   The Golden Age of photojournalism is said to have started in the 1930s, even though photography had begun to infiltrate newspapers in the late 1890s.

134   The following section is based on an earlier publication: Quanchi, Max. 2015, 'Thomas McMahon's Pacific neighbours; an early Australian photojournalist' in Maxwell, Anne and Croci, Josephine, eds. *Shifting focus: colonial Australian photography 1860–1920*, Melbourne, Australian Scholarly Publishing, pp. 218–229.

the labourers in a carefully posed line-up suggest a compliant, subject labour force.

McMahon also took photographs of rubber, an equally innovative and speculative development that would hopefully provide Papua with an export staple. McMahon was acting here as a journalist, and as an imperialist, sending home evidence from the frontier of Australia's recently acquired tropical empire. McMahon did not have a personal background or experience in tropical plantation investments or economy, so he relied on opinions, grumbles and complaints gathered in bars, clubs and on a planter's verandah.

A new career

By 1922, he had used his Papuan set of photographs, with the addition of those collected on his second trip to German New Guinea between July and October 1917, in an ambitious range of publications including the *Sunday Times, Importers and Exporters Journal of Australasia, The Lone Hand, Town and Country Journal, Sydney Mail, The Australasian* in Melbourne, *Northern Herald* in Cairns, *Daily Telegraph, The Week, The Queenslander* and the *Journal of the Royal Geographical Society (Queensland)* in Brisbane, the *Illustrated London News, The Times (Trade Supplement), The Wide World* and *Our Quarterly Magazine* in London, and *Sunset: the Pacific Monthly, World's Work, Trans-Pacific, The World's Markets, Dun's Review, Overland Monthly, Pacific Ports* and *Travel* in the United States of America. The *Northern Herald* in Townsville continued to use single photographs by McMahon throughout 1917 and 1918, but by this time, McMahon had left for the Solomon Islands, a tour of the Northern Territory and Torres Strait and then to Nauru, Ocean Island (Banaba), the Gilbert Islands and the Marshall Islands.

The published photographs from his three visits to Papua in 1915, 1917 and (briefly) 1921, demonstrate McMahon's editorial awareness, responding to the demands of weekend illustrated newspapers and associated magazines for pictorial material supported by provocative polemics about government policies in Australia's Pacific backyard and sub-empire. McMahon was boosting Papua's appeal as a desirable place to invest, settle and keep under Australian colonial control, and his photography from Papua reinforced his message of European colonial authority, investment opportunities, success as settlers and the idea that plantations would be profitable due to the ready availability of a vigorous, semi-skilled and healthy workforce. He declared that accusations of slavery in Papua were misleading and used the headline, 'Non-existent and impossible' to stress his view.[135] His photographs reassured readers that colonial authority was well established, with loyal police, officialdom and portraits of magistrates and a Chief Inspector of Native Affairs.

The trip to Papua had allowed McMahon to establish a formula combining image and text, and his new career was about to bloom. He chose to change careers at the right time. He was now a photographer, an imperialist and a Pacific expert whose photographs were firsthand and topical. McMahon was reporting on emerging economic opportunities and the attempts being made in Papua to establish an export economy and reinforce Australia's possession parallel to the military occupation a year before of the neighbouring former German colony of New Guinea. McMahon's photographs of labour, plantations, copper mining, patrolling and Port Moresby and Samarai as port towns were educating Australian readers but also responding to a demand for events of interest to Australians. By late 1917, it was reported that 'photographs taken

---

135   *The Cairns Post*, 28.11.1916, p. 2.

by him on his previous trip (to Papua) have appeared in practically all the leading papers in Australia'.[136]

In the gaps between privately funded trips to the Islands, McMahon sought a regular income on commission as the back-country representative of the *Northern Herald* and *The Cairns Post*. McMahon was living in Malanda near Cairns and was said to be handy with his hands and a 'practical farmer' besides being an 'experienced pressman'.[137] This was the beginning of his parallel career as a self-funded Pacific Islands photographer and journalist and a paid photographer of rural Australian towns and districts. His first back-country job was to report on and photograph the Ravenshoe agricultural show. (His rural photography career is covered in chapter 14.)

In July 1917, he took off for his second tour of the Islands by returning to German New Guinea.

---

136 *Northern Herald*, 2.8.1917, p. 6.

137 *Northern Herald*, (Townsville), 13.2.1919, p. 4; 12.5.1917, p. 4; 2.8.1917, p. 6; 20.9.1917, p. 4.

Chapter 3

New Guinea: 'our new possession'

McMahon returned to eastern New Guinea in July 1917, visiting the Torres Strait, Port Moresby and Samarai en route to Rabaul, the capital of former German New Guinea. The large island of New Guinea had been divided into three territories by colonial powers, with the Dutch taking west of longitude 164° in 1824, the Germans creating a north-eastern colony under chartered company administration in 1884 and the British annexing Papua in the same year. In 1899, the German territory was restructured and became a formal colony under the Reich. It included the mainland, New Britain, New Ireland and the two most northern islands of the Solomons chain, Buka and Bougainville, and was successful economically with extensive copra plantations, shipping and trading.[138] Other than Rabaul, a major Pacific port and the capital of the colony, the German territory was not well known in Australia. McMahon

---

138   Firth, S. 'The Germans in New Guinea', in May, RJ. and Nelson, H, eds. *Melanesia beyond diversity*, Vol. 1, Canberra, 1982; Firth, S. 'The transformation of the labour trade in German New Guinea 1899–1914', *Journal of Pacific History*, 11, 1, 1976, pp. 51–65; Hempenstall, P. *Pacific Islanders under German rule: a study in the meaning of resistance*, Canberra, ANU Press, 1978; Latukefu, S. *Papua New Guinea; a century of colonial impact*, Port Moresby, UPNG Press, 1992; Waiko, JD. *A Short History of Papua New Guinea*, Melbourne, OUP, 1993; Moore, C. *New Guinea: crossing boundaries and history*, Honolulu, University of Hawaii Press, 2003; Quanchi, M. 'Melanesia: a region and a history' in *The Melanesian World*, edited by Hirsch, Eric and Rollason, Will, London, Routledge, 2019, pp. 63–76.

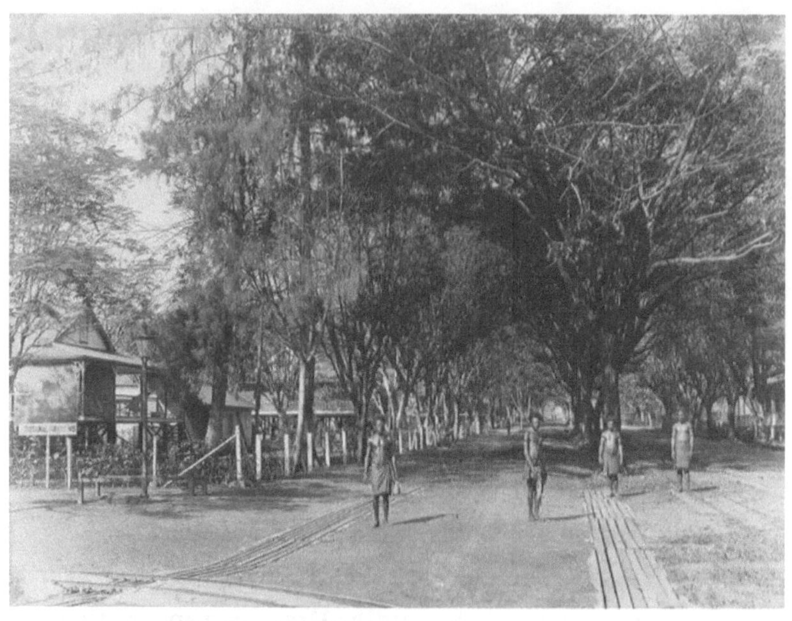

Fig. 7 'One of Rabaul's shady streets'

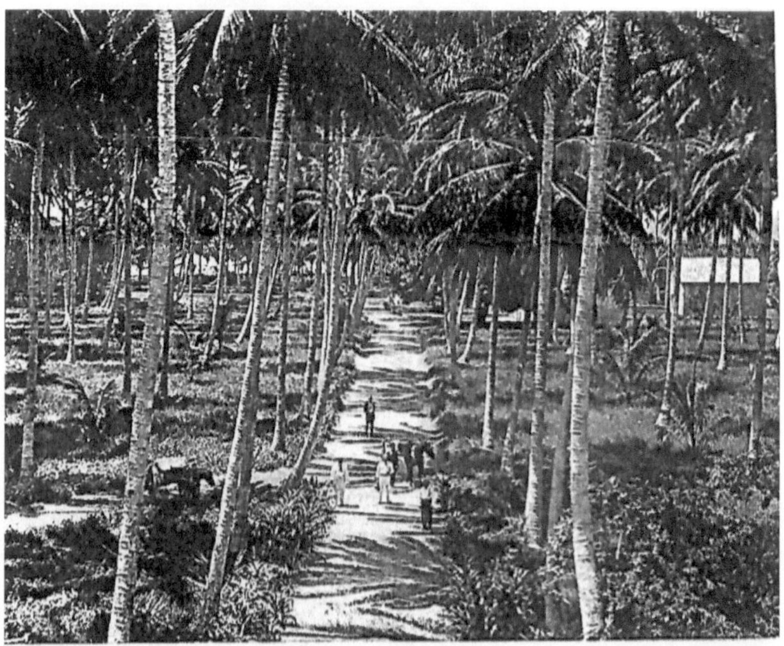

Fig. 8 A former German plantation on Mecklenburg, New Ireland, 1930

would have had difficulty finding English language background reading prior to his visit. There were several local identities such as the German Governor Wilhelm Solf, Queen Emma (whose trading and plantation empire was based at Ralum) and Baron Heinrich Rudolph von Wahlen (who had built a replica of a German 'burg' on his copra plantation in the Anchorite Islands)[139], but the extent of the German colonial presence would have surprised McMahon when he arrived in Rabaul.

At the outbreak of WWI, an Australian expeditionary force was quickly cobbled together and dispatched to capture the harbour at Rabaul and the Bitapaka wireless station. McMahon had visited Rabaul late in 1915 when the German presence was still strong, although the administration had been taken over by the Australian military, which took advantage of the infrastructure, local government and plantation system created by the Germans. In 1917 during his second visit, everyone in Rabaul was talking about Australia taking full control when the war ended. Ken Buckley and Kris Klugman's study of Burns Philp and Roger Thompson's study of Australian interest in the Pacific in the 1914–1920 period reveal a high level of newspaper editorial coverage of the debate over the fate of the former German New Guinea.[140] To symbolise the takeover, McMahon regularly published a photograph of the

---

139   Broomhead, Richard. *Living on the edge of paradise*, Buddina, Qld, Joshua Books, 2014. Broomhead went to the Hermit Islands as a young plantation manager in the 1960s and also tells the story of the pre-WWII, von Wahlen era.

140   Thompson, Roger. *Australian Imperialism in the Pacific: the expansionist era 1820–1920*, Melbourne, 1980, p. 216 and chs. 11–12; Buckley, Ken and Klugman, Ken. *The Australian Presence in the Pacific: Burns Philp 1914–16*, Sydney, 1983, chs. 1–6; Louis, William R. *Great Britain and Germany's Lost Colonies 1914–19*, Oxford, 1967. For documents on Australian links to the Pacific, see Evans, Moore, Saunders and Jamison, eds. *Our Future's Past: documenting Australia's federation*, Sydney, 1997, ch. 3; and Greenwood, Gordon and Grimshaw, Charles, eds. *Documents on Australia's International Affairs 1901–1918*, Sydney, 1977.

German naval yacht, *Komet*, now rearmed and commissioned as HMAS *Una*.[141]

1915: our new possession

His earlier short visit in 1915 had been limited to Rabaul, the cosmopolitan capital of the German colony. This had been a twenty-four-hour stopover, but it resulted in January 1916 in two articles with twelve photographs in *The Week* in Brisbane. Three photographs also appeared in *The Queenslander*, featuring the graves of Australian soldiers killed during the expeditionary force's capture of German New Guinea in 1914. The Battle of Bitapaka and the lives lost are now commemorated by an official Commonwealth War Graves Commission cemetery at the site of the German wireless station at the centre of the battle in August 1914.[142] The captions to two photographs in *The Queenslander* named six men who had died in the fighting at Herbertshöhe and Kabakaul. The third photograph was of eight graves in a broad vista of a graveyard at Rabaul. These were Australia's first casualties in World War I, but it was an incident overshadowed by the slaughter at Gallipoli and the Western Front. A series of commemorative postcards detailing the capture of German New Guinea by an Australian naval and military expeditionary force had been published by Reeves and Ellis of Hornsby, a Sydney suburb, and these postcards had a sense of journalistic immediacy with depictions of captured vessels, parade drills and flag raising. The celebratory reporting of a quick and glorious victory was

---

141   For example, *Life*, 1.3.1919, p. 175; and McKenzie, SS. *The Australians at Rabaul*, Melbourne, Angus and Robertson, 1927, p. 129. McKenzie used nine photographs by McMahon, all attributed.

142   The site also has the graves of Indians and Fijians killed in the war and a memorial to the lost submarine, AE1. For the story of Captain Pockley, killed in action, see McMullin, Ross. *Life So Full of Promise: Further Biographies of Australia's Lost Generation*, Melbourne, Scribe, 2023.

not undermined by other less laudable events including the flogging of a German doctor, the flogging of New Guineans and the embarrassment of looting and vandalism by the occupying Australian troops.[143] McMahon's photographs do not appear to have been used for postcards despite this interest in German New Guinea at the time.

He also published a three-page report with twelve photographs on German New Guinea in *The Sydney Mail* and another full-page collage of the graves in *The Australasian* in Melbourne. *The Sydney Mail* article in 1916, based on his earlier visit to Rabaul, was an impressive three-page report under three headings:

OUR NEW POSSESSION: GERMAN NEW GUINEA
GRAVES OF AUSTRALIAN HEROES IN NEW GUINEA
THE WHIPPING OF GERMANS AT RABAUL

He was wrong in claiming Australian possession of the former German Territory as this did not occur until the enacting of a League of Nations Mandate in 1921. McMahon devoted a full page of text to outlining the details of the whipping by Germans of a missionary, Rev. WH Cox, and then the retaliatory whipping by the military administration of the Germans involved. Strangely, McMahon did not mention the loss of *AE1*, an Australian submarine that disappeared with thirty-five crew near the Duke of York Islands in late 1914. (It was finally found on the seabed in 2017). Although visiting Rabual only briefly in 1915, McMahon

---

143   This flogging was punishment meted out after the Rev. Cox incident. By January 1915, postcards of the flogging were circulating in Sydney. The captions noted that 'natives' had not been allowed to witness the caning of Europeans. See Hiery, H. *The neglected war: the German South Pacific and the influence of World War I*, Honolulu, University of Hawaii Press, 1995, pp. 37–38; Rowley, CD. *The Australians in German New Guinea 1914–1921*, Melbourne, Melbourne University Press, 1958; and Mackenzie, SS. *The Australians at Rabaul*, 1927.

declared, 'there is a big future for our new territory when matters settle down'.[144]

1917: Australia's concern

Between his first visit in 1915 and return visit in 1917, McMahon stayed on his farm outside Cairns, and judging by the subsequent output in illustrated newspapers in 1916–1917, he must have spent a considerable amount of time and money developing and printing duplicate copies of his photographs, writing short captions and supplementary columns and then posting packages off to editors in Brisbane, Sydney and Melbourne. The subsequent level of acceptances and publication, notwithstanding rejections, suggests McMahon spent a great deal of money developing, printing and posting. He paid for this expense through his job as the back-country reporter for the *Northern Herald* and *The Cairns Post*.

In July 1917, McMahon carried a Letter of Introduction from the Australian Prime Minister, Billy Hughes, and was provided with a military escort as he travelled around the colony, meeting German traders, planters, missionaries, recently appointed Australian administrators, and soldiers in the military garrison. He also visited Buka and Bougainville Islands, the two most northern islands of the Solomon Islands archipelago which had been annexed by Germany in 1886, in agreement with Britain, so that Germany could access labour supplies from these two islands for their New Guinea plantations.

His first publications after the second trip appeared in *The Telegraph* in Brisbane in a series of eight illustrated articles from August to December 1917. It was headlined 'Australia's concern' and included sixteen photographs. At the same time as *The Telegraph* story, he published three articles on German New

---

144   *The Sydney Mail*, 19.4.1916, pp. 20–21, 24.

Guinea, each with two accompanying photographs in Brisbane's *The Week*. As he was sending back material to editors while in Rabaul, he must have been remarkably busy developing glass plate negatives and writing captions and short accompanying reports and then posting back to Brisbane. In a publication on a relatively unknown location such as German New Guinea, readers might have expected to see indigenous men, women and children, villages and picturesque scenes, but contextualising, geographic images are noticeably missing from McMahon's publications. He initially focused on government buildings, personnel serving in the administration and commercial opportunities. The emphasis on colonial infrastructure was a reflection of the imminent change of ownership awaiting the outcome of the war, and McMahon had begun to appreciate what he thought were popular views on colonial territories. He was also now able to compare the minimal and rather miserly colonial and administrative presence of the Australians in Papua, regarded as a backwater, against the extravagant, well-funded legacy that Germany had left in its territory, with grand government buildings, theatres, wharves, hospitals, roads, tunnels, tree-lined avenues and bridges.

McMahon's choice of photographs in *The Telegraph* was based on two themes: the Australians who lived in tropical territories, and the infrastructure that could support economic expansion. These themes continued through all his published photographs over the next five years. For example, he published a photograph of the fine building that housed the Commonwealth Bank of Australia in Rabaul and one of the Australian staff. He used the bank photograph for subsequent articles in *World's Work, The Lone Hand, The Sydney Mail* and his New Guinea album with McCarron's publishing in 1923. He also included a photograph of staff at the Native Affairs Department and a larger group portrait of 'the successful Administrative staff (Australian) at Rabaul'. Enjoying his status as a quasi-official representative of the Australian government, armed with his letter from the prime minister, he was also able to arrange a group portrait of the administrator, surveyor-general, judge, military commanders and the administrator's aide-de-camp, chauffeur and secretary. He later used these photographs in *Life, World's Work, The Sydney Mail* and *Munsey's Magazine*.[145] To provide supporting evidence of infrastructure, McMahon included portraits of the personnel he met and who were now running the territory. These were posed portraits at the Treasury, Customs Department, Postmaster General's Department and Native Affairs Department, and also the Administrator and his staff. He also captured lighter moments such as a large group enjoying a picnic on the Duke of York Islands, and another large group of senior officials during a road trip near Rabaul.[146] A panorama of a village said to be 'now under Australian administration' and a staged photograph of 'collecting tax from the natives' stressed to readers that control had passed from German to Australian hands.[147]

He photographed the road tunnel that linked Rabaul to New Mecklenburg, noting it had been blown up by the Germans but restored quickly by the Australian administration. On photographs of the harbour front and wharves, McMahon noted the harbourmaster, Captain Leach, was a Queenslander. He claimed the main wharf with dual railway lines and large sheds, built by Germans before the war, was capable of 'unloading vast quantities of coal'. A year later, for the same photograph, he

145   *Munsey's Magazine* was published in the US. It had had sales of 700,000 but by 1918 numbers had fallen below 100,000. It closed and merged with another magazine in 1929.

146   These photographs appeared in *The Sydney Mail* on 30.1.1918, 6.2.1918 and 20.2.1918. The borrowed German group portrait appeared on 23.1.1918, p. 8.

147   *The Sydney Mail*, 3.1.1918, p. 9; 6.2.1918, p. 9.

changed the caption in *The Sydney Mail* to state these sheds were 'capable of holding thousands of bags of copra'. Readers would not have noticed these changing details as they appeared in different publications, different cities and indeed in different countries.

He also emphasised that Rabaul was a fine city, without acknowledging it was the Germans who had developed it as a major Pacific trading port. McMahon depicted Rabaul as prosperous with tree-lined streets, a movie theatre, a hospital, Botanical Gardens, shipbuilding yards, wharves and a Chinatown. For example, a wide Rabaul street with a tramway and shaded by an avenue of *Poinciana regia* was said to demonstrate the 'possibilities of civic beautification in the islands'.[148] He captioned this road variously as a fine avenue in town, a road leading from the wharves to Namanula Hill Hospital or a road leading to Government House. It had been taken during his 1915 visit. McMahon used this image in *Life, The Sydney Mail, World's Work, Mid-Pacific Magazine* and *Munsey's Magazine*. He declared Rabaul was equal to the 'pretty residential suburb of some grand city'.[149] He also noted the looming presence of 'The Mother', the largest of the live volcanoes overlooking Rabaul.

Despite a large German presence still in the territory, McMahon only published one photograph of former German officials and planters, a borrowed photograph taken prior to the war. He photographed the former homes of the famed Queen Emma – Emma Forsythe or Mrs Kolbe. They never met as she had left the territory in 1914 before the war broke out.[150] McMahon reported

---

148   *World's Work*, November 1918, p. 483; *Life*, 1.6. 1918, p. 396. Another, more scenic vista of a jungle road built by the Germans appeared in a small Philippines and later China publication, *Far Eastern Review*, June 1921. p. 378.

149   McMahon, TJ. 'Rabaul; German New Guinea', *The Week*, 25.2.1916, p. 31.

150   For Queen Emma, see Robson, RW. *Queen Emma: The Samoan-American girl who founded an empire in 19th century New Guinea* (4th ed.), Sydney, Pacific Publications, 1971.

that she was energetic, of 'commanding personality' and strikingly handsome with charming manners and 'a remarkable business ability'. McMahon claimed from hearsay that her former company and plantations were worth 'hundreds of pounds sterling a year'.[151]

He ignored the missionary presence, as he did in his later photography around the region, despite enjoying their hospitality and their access and introduction to the local indigenous population. He published only a casual portrait of a missionary with two converts, a large 'native' congregation on a plantation and a church that he had photographed on his first visit in 1915. McMahon completely ignored the mainland component of the German colony and did not visit Madang, Berlinhafen or Konstantinhafen. The Germans had moved the capital from Herbertshöhe (today's Kokopo) to Simpsonhafen (today's Rabaul) just five years earlier in 1910, but this was not mentioned.

Although German New Guinea was under military administration from 1914 to 1919, McMahon may have thought there was little reader interest in Australia in nearby military matters, particularly with the war in Europe and the Middle East dominating the news. He did publish photographs of the AIF graves at Rabaul and Bitapaka,[152] the garrison headquarters, recreation house, officers mess and barracks at Rabaul and Kokopo and the daily quinine issues 'with a pannikin of rum to wash it down'. He photographed a footrace for soldiers, a group portrait of NCOs, one of the Army barbers at work and two group portraits of the Navy band and the Navy High Command. A military presence was not high on his agenda of key topics for Australian readers, investors and intending settlers.

His photographs of the 'native police' or Papuans and New

151   McMahon, TJ. 'Australia's new task', *Mid-Pacific*, Vol. 22, No 4, 1922, p. 378.

152   These appeared in *The Sydney Mail* on 16.1.1918, 23.1.1918, 24.6.1918 and 29.10.1919.

Guineans who had served with the Germans but who now were enlisted in the Australian Army, received a wide distribution, appearing in *Travel, World's Work, Munsey's Magazine, The Sydney Mail* and in SS McKenzie's account of the Rabaul campaign in 1927.

McMahon was rather loose with his terminology, variously labelling the same photograph as native soldiers, native constabulary or native police. He declared that under Australian officers, they were 'well drilled and useful ... very intelligent and eminently successful in maintaining order'. Mentioning order and loyal and diligent 'natives' was linked, of course, to McMahon's emphasis on economic potential and his appeal for the spread of Australian colonial control.[153]

McMahon stressed the Australian connection in captions, noting that a German planter on New Ireland, a Mr J Kirchner, was married to an 'Australian girl'. He included three photographs of planters' houses, noting for Australian readers that a planter's life was prosperous and that their homes were 'very cool and sometimes handsomely furnished'.[154] These houses also appeared in *Penny Pictorial, The Lone Hand, Munsey's Magazine, Sunday Times* and *The Sydney Mail,* in a period after the war when settling in the soon to be mandated territory might have been an option for some adventurous Australians. One panorama of a plantation at New Ireland (named Neu Mecklenburg in the German era) depicted a fine road leading through a grove of coconut trees with sheds in the background and labourers in the foreground and was said by McMahon in captions to be a 'typical plantation'. He claimed, probably based on second-hand information from discussions with ex-German planters unsupported by evidence

---

153   *World's Work*, 1918, p. 482; *The Sydney Mail*, 16.1.1918, p. 18.

154   *Sunday Times* (Sydney), 5.12.1920, p. 22.

or statistics, in a florid phrasing that McMahon often applied, that 'these islands abound in natural wealth' and that planters had experienced a reasonably high standard of wealth and living.[155] The copra industry had been moderately successful despite a slump in prices caused by the lack of shipping during the war, and the maritime strikes in Australia from 1919 to 1921. He added that 'New Guinea and Samoa before the war gave Germany large supplies of copra ... the Kaiser used to be deeply interested in their development'. [156] In an article in *Empire Review*, McMahon also argued that competition from America and Japan was detrimental to Australian and British trade in the Pacific.[157]

To support his boosting of the profitability of copra and a planter's life in the territory, McMahon published two photographs with large numbers of labourers and a line of females bringing in sweet potato for the worker's meals.[158] The female labourers had been photographed on a German plantation in 1915. He noted in 1918 that female labour was not permitted under the Australian administration. To demonstrate the extent of these enterprises, McMahon published a panorama of a shed swamped by unhusked nuts with thirty labourers in the foreground and the planter's substantial home on the ridge behind. This appeared in *PLA Monthly*, *Life*, in CAW Monkton's article in 1922 on New Guinea in the serial encyclopedia, *Countries of the World*, and in McMahon's album on New Guinea. He also documented the copra industry

---

155   *Penny Pictorial*, 6.12.1919, p. 77. For plantation development in Papua, see Lewis, David. *The plantation dream: developing British New Guinea and Papua, 1884–1942*, Canberra, JPH, 1996.

156   *The Queenslander*, 8.9.1917, p. 38.

157   McMahon, TJ. 'The South Pacific Islands Trade; Effect of the Australian strikes', *Empire Review*, Vol. 35, 1921, pp. 164-67. *Empire Review* was published in London, 1901–1944.

158   This photograph appeared in *The Sydney Mail* (1918), *Munsey's Magazine* (1918), *The Wide World* (1920), *World's Markets* (1920), *Travel* (1921), *Trans-Pacific* (1921), and in McMahon's *New Guinea* published by McCarron in 1923.

from field to wharf, starting with the coconut tree, a 'bull-a-ma-cow' cart bringing nuts in for processing, the husking of the nuts and sun-drying the kernels, to bagging the copra prior to shipping. McMahon later published photographs of the copra industry elsewhere in the Pacific, particularly after a visit to the Solomon Islands.[159]

Among the hundreds of photographs McMahon published on German New Guinea, there are only ten that might be catalogued as ethnography. This included three of *duk duk* dancers (mistakenly captioned 'Kap Kap' in the *Northern Herald*), two of the famed New Britain wicker fish traps and one of a widow in mourning. Another portrait was posed with a male standing and a female squatting, dressed in dance costume. McMahon alleged the 'natives of New Guinea, [are] still in a savage state. The Germans did very little to civilize the natives of the back country'.[160] His only other depictions of New Guineans were contrived settings of four people reading a copy of a Cairns newspaper and a group of men playing cards.[161]

Notable women of the Pacific

A photograph of an afternoon tea party in Rabaul, attended by three men in military uniforms and three in suits and ties attended by six New Guinean servants, had only one woman present. McMahon declared, 'Mrs Whiteman is a plucky and beautiful woman who has become one of the noted traders and planters of German New Guinea'.[162] He only published this

---

159   The *Journal of Pacific History* ran a special issue on copra and coconuts edited by Judith Bennett, Volume 53, no. 4, 2018.

160   McMahon TJ, 'German New Guinea', *Mid-Pacific*, Vol. 16, no. 4, 1918, p. 436.

161   *Northern Herald*, 3.12.1915 p. 27; 30.11.197, p. 34.

162   *The Telegraph*, 12.8.1917. He had published a photograph of Mr SA Whiteman, originally a merchant but who had now joined the administration, in his first German New Guinea article in *The Sydney Mail*, 19.4.1916, p. 22. The tea party photograph was taken during his second visit in 1917.

photograph once. Two years earlier, he had declared that in Papua, another woman, Mrs Mahoney, was 'a tall handsome lady' and the character on whom 'Mrs Carter' in Beatrice Grimshaw's novel, *Guinea Gold*, was based. According to McMahon, she was, 'undoubtably the most remarkable woman in Papua, and is known popularly as the "Queen of Sudest"'. When he chose eight 'notable women in the Pacific' to feature in an article in 1921, he did not include Mrs Whiteman, but did include Beatrice Grimshaw and Mrs Mahoney.

McMahon photographed relatively few expatriate women during his later travels around the islands. Females only appeared in association with something unusual, such as standing in the pinnacles in Nauru or riding the trolley railcars on Ocean Island. Some women appeared in large group portraits but with men in the central position. Then strangely in 1921, he published an article titled 'Notable women of the Pacific'. He chose eight women including Mrs Zahel (a Torres Strait Island administrator), Mrs Hyndman-Jones (the wife of a resident magistrate in Papua), Beatrice Grimshaw (the famed author who lived near Samarai Island), Mrs Mahoney (the 'Queen of Sudest'), Mother Elizabeth (the Superior of the Catholic Mission at Butaritari in the Gilbert Islands), Mrs Smith-Rewse (the wife of the Administrator of Nauru), Mrs Warren (the wife of Rev. Warren at Roper River Mission in the Northern Territory) and Mrs Warrington-Rogers (the manager of a cattle station at Paddy's Lagoon, also in the Northern Territory). This full-page story was accompanied by photographs of Mrs Smith-Rewse, Mother Elizabeth, Mrs Hyndman-Jones and Mrs Zahel. He did not include the 'plucky and beautiful Mrs Whiteman', whom he had praised in his reports on German New Guinea. He declared that all eight women, identified as 'truly distinguished', had demonstrated the 'sterling qualities of women who for good or bad fortune were compelled to live in what is truly isolation'.[163]

The only other occasion in which he featured expatriate women was in a column on the Solomon Islands in *The Queenslander* in 1918. The banner headline asked, 'Can white women live in the islands?' He then tackled a sensitive issue for some readers with a further headline which offered comment on 'The native wife and Mrs Grundy'. The reference to Mrs Grundy was to the well-known literary figure of a prudish, rigid overseer of feminine morals who censured men who lived with and married indigenous women in the colonies. The supporting full-page collage of six photographs did not include a 'native wife'. McMahon lauded the efforts of expatriate wives in the Islands who, despite loneliness and the absence of other European women, made amazing efforts to maintain diets, comforts, cleanliness and happy households. However, most of this article was about the failings of the British administration, taxation and a litany of settler complaints. Only one image included women – three expatriate women seated in a group of twenty men said to be 'pioneers'.[164] Photographing or writing about expatriate women was a diversion for McMahon. The trips to Papua and the former German New Guinea established his preference during visits later to other islands for mostly masculine portraits of male mining workers, male plantation labourers, male dancers, sturdy looking policemen and expatriate uniformed administrators.

A global audience

After his return to Cairns, McMahon embarked on a major effort to promote his German New Guinea photography and

---

163   McMahon, T.J. 'Notable women of the Pacific', *The Week*, 25.3.1921, pp. 16, 26.

164   'The British Solomons', *The Queenslander*, 5.1.1918, p. 49. A McMahon photograph was also used for the cover of the 'Pictorial' section on page 21.

recently won expertise to a wider market. This included illustrated articles and photographic collages, and some single photographs in *Life, Mid-Pacific Magazine, The Lone Hand, World's Work, Stead's Review* (Melbourne), *Munsey's Magazine, The Bulletin* and *The Age* (Melbourne).[165] A *Sydney Mail* series ran from January to February 1918 and included sixty-one photographs. This enthusiasm to publish as widely as possible and enhance his status as an 'expert' continued in 1919, with illustrated articles on German New Guinea in *The Wide World* (twice), *Chamber's Journal* (twice), *Penny Pictorial, The Morning Post* (London) and again in *Life* and *Munsey's Magazine*. He then moved away from publishing on German New Guinea until it became a topic of immediate interest regarding negotiations at the League of Nations and the imminent proclamation of an Australian mandate. In 1922, he returned to the topic with 'Australia's new task' in *Mid-Pacific Magazine*. His final publication was *New Guinea*, one of a series of eight small albums/booklets he published with McCarron in Sydney in 1923.

Surprisingly McMahon's photographs were not often used in the burgeoning postcard trade. This was probably due to McMahon's careful protection of his work. In the postcards produced globally on German New Guinea, there are few propaganda images of government patrols, oil, gold or artefact collecting expeditions, and there are relatively few images of mining, labourers, seedling plots, plantations or line-ups of workers. These were McMahon's stock in trade, so this gap is surprising as economic activities are otherwise well represented in the non-postcard photographic archive of this period and appeared

---

165   For example, a series of single photographs ran in *The Week* (Brisbane) for three weeks in January 1918.

in official publications, illustrated newspapers, magazines, and journals.[166]

The images published by McMahon after his return visit to Rabaul emphasised the enormous benefit Australia would gain by acquiring the former German colony. *The Sydney Mail* series therefore included the courthouse, the harbourmaster's office, the administrator's offices, the European Hospital, the Native Hospital, government stores, and the town water purification plant. This was the visual evidence for what McMahon was claiming to be, and indeed was, an important prize of the Great War. After the second visit, he engaged in a multi-pronged domestic publishing campaign in *The Telegraph*, *The Week*, *The Age*, *The Bulletin* and *The Sydney Mail*. In these illustrations, there was an equal emphasis on copra, administration and Rabaul, a city he extolled at length in the accompanying columns. Depictions of economic possibilities and infrastructure made up seventy per cent of the images, with single photographs of missions, 'natives', the military and picturesque scenery used sparingly. McMahon's main appeal to readers was to attract support for an Australian takeover in New Guinea. He declared, 'at all hazards Australians must strive to get the Germans out of these islands'.[167]

'Apostle of the Coconut'

In a flurry of articles McMahon published between 1917 and 1921 boosting the growth and profits of the copra industry, he regularly referred to Auguste Engelhardt, known as the 'Apostle of the

---

166   For the use of photography in promoting plantations, mining and tourism, see Quanchi, M. 'Thomas McMahon; photography as propaganda in the Pacific Islands', *History of Photography*, Vol. 21, no. 1, 1997, pp. 42–53; Quanchi, M. and Shekleton, M. 'Disorderly categories in postcards from Papua New Guinea', *History of Photography*, Vol. 25, no. 4, 2001, pp. 315–33; and Quanchi, M. 'Jewel of the Pacific and planter's paradise; the visual argument for Australian sub-imperialism in the Solomon Islands', *Journal of Pacific History*, Vol. 39, no. 1, 2004, pp. 43–58.

167   McMahon, T.J. 'German Possessions in the Pacific', *The Sydney Mail*, 16.1.1918, p. 6.

Coconut', a German originally from Württemberg, who lived at Kabakon plantation in the Duke of York Islands. McMahon first wrote about him in *The Sydney Mail* in 1918, declaring him to be a 'singularly handsome man of 35 years', sun-tanned from long exposure to the tropical sun and a 'polite man of the most perfect manners'. He maintained a library, said to be one of the finest in the southern hemisphere. It was Engelhardt's reputation as a naturepath [*sic.*][168] and sun worshipper, and his campaigning for dietary control, healthy eating and the life-giving qualities of the coconut, that attracted public attention. For eighteen years, he lived in the Islands promoting the coconut's curative powers and calling for restraint in food and drink. He had purchased his seventy-five-acre plantation on the Duke of York Islands from Emma Kolbe (Queen Emma) and claimed to his global audience of correspondents prior to WWI that included 400 in the US, and to visitors to Kabakon, that coconut meat and juice could promote clearness of the brain and renew the strength of the body.

McMahon published photographs of Engelhardt's library, sleeping quarters, home and dining table and self-portraits alongside Engelhardt. These fifteen photographs appeared globally in *Trans-Pacific, Sea Land Air, PLA Monthly, The Wide World, Chamber's Journal, World's Work, World's Markets, The Lone Hand,* and *Far Eastern Review* and in the Australian illustrated newspapers, *The Queenslander, The Sydney Mail* and *The Telegraph* (Brisbane). The captions always noted Engelhardt was the 'Apostle of the Coconut', sometimes spelt as cocoanut. McMahon's first essay on Engelhardt in *The Sydney Mail* was repeated nearly verbatim in subsequent articles the next year in *Chamber's Journal* and *The Wide World*. The next year, in a general article on copra in the Pacific, McMahon included a

---

168   In McMahon's articles after 1919, this spelling was changed to 'naturopath'.

portrait of Engelhardt, mistakenly naming him as an Austrian, and exaggerating the virtues of the coconut by repeating Engelhardt's claim that it could combat, 'the causes of all wickedness and strife in the world and the anger of man against man'.[169] In 1922, in a general article on copra, McMahon included a photograph of Engelhardt's home, with McMahon posing near Engelhardt, now described as the patron saint of the coconut. This article mentioned that Engelhardt had a recipe book with seventy different palatable dishes to be made from the cocoanut.[170] In McMahon's papers, there is a three-page printed pamphlet, *Man's original food: The truth about coconut*, on which Engelhardt had scribbled a request for McMahon to 'please publish in the most read newspaper in Los Angeles'. Engelhardt had scribbled in the margin that he was 'the pure coconut healer'. The pamphlet, printed in Newcastle in 1908, called for disciples to come to Kabakon, for a fee of £50 on arrival. He listed the fare from England via Sydney to Simpsonhafen on the German Lloyd steamer as £26.[171] Engelhardt died in 1919.[172]

New Guinea in twelve images

In 1923, McMahon published a small album or booklet with McCarron in Sydney, titled *New Guinea*, with twelve photographs, one to a page, taken during his brief visit to Rabaul in 1915, a second visit in 1917 and another short visit in 1921. A comparison, for example, between the twenty-four photographs he published in *The Week* in 1916 and the twelve chosen seven years later for his McCarron's album/booklet in 1923 reveals

---

169   McMahon, TJ. 'A dozen coconuts where one grew before: a vast South Pacific industry', *Trans-Pacific*, March 1921, pp. 76, 77.

170   McMahon, TJ. 'Cocoanut industry in the South Pacific', *Sea Land Air*, 1.2.1922, pp. 815–16.

171   In the McMahon papers, Royal Geographical Society (Qld), Brisbane.

172   In the long entry in Wikipedia on Engelhardt, McMahon's connection with Engelhardt is not listed. See https://en.wikipedia.org/wiki/August_Engelhardt.

that McMahon had sharpened his focus, moving away from an emphasis on infrastructure and the impressive city of Rabaul, and was now boosting the potential of copra plantation life and economic benefits of imperial control, administered by Australia. The earlier choices may have been partially determined by the periodical in which he was publishing, as *The Week* was according to its banner, 'a journal of commerce, farming, mining and general information'.[173] By 1923, in a stand-alone publication, he was offering audiences a much more nuanced and balanced view of the mandated territory, now securely under Australian control. In 1923, McMahon had to carefully select twelve images from the several hundred he had taken. He chose to emphasise the copra industry with photographs of plantations, a planter's home, the copra-making process, labour and a substantial bank to suggest security and stability in the industry. To cater for a wider readership perhaps unfamiliar with the territory, he added one photograph each of missions, a picturesque scene, the 'native' police and a *duk duk* dancer. Photographs of Rabaul and the administrative apparatus and military were excluded.

By 1923, he had travelled around the wider Pacific region and seen the diversity of the Australian, British, French, Japanese and German colonial presence and various developments in agriculture, mining, shipping and the growth of port towns, and had witnessed the former German New Guinea become an Australian territory. His choice of images in 1923 was based on a much wider and intimate view of the region. These choices also reflected McMahon's changing focus over the period as he self-promoted his status as an Islands expert based on a campaign

---

173 *The Week*, based in Brisbane, ran from 1876 to 1934. Each Friday issue, in which McMahon published, included two pages of illustrations, usually linked to a story elsewhere in the issue.

of clamorous and polemical declarations about Australian engagement in the economy and governance of the Pacific Islands and their importance to Australia.

His next trip was to the Solomon Islands.

Chapter 4

Solomon Islands: jewel of the Pacific

A series of pictorial features by Thomas McMahon, titled 'In the British Solomons', appeared in Brisbane's illustrated weekend newspaper, *The Queenslander*, between December 1917 and July 1918. This was at a time when the British Empire was rallying to survive key battles on the Western Front in World War I. Surprisingly, the series mounted an argument critical of the British administration of the British Solomon Islands Protectorate and argued that Australia would not be welcomed should the status of the Solomon Islands change in the post-war rearranging of colonies to be negotiated as Germany lost her Pacific possessions and New Zealand, Australia and Japan jostled for vacated territories. As non-Australian subjects had been seriously curtailed when illustrated newspapers concentrated their visual and text content on the war, a ten-part series with two thousand-word columns, each with eight to ten photographs, was historically quite remarkable.[174] McMahon's photographs of the Solomon Islands were drawn from a hundred or more photographs taken during a month-long visit, October–November 1917.[175] The

---

174   An earlier version of this chapter was presented at the Pacific History Association conference in 1998 and later published as 'Jewel of the Pacific and Planter's Paradise: The Visual Argument for Australian Sub-imperialism in the Solomon Islands', *JPH*, Vol. 39, no. 1, 2004, pp. 43–58.

175   *The Queenslander*, 22.12.1917; 29.12.1917; 19.1.1918, 9.2.1918, 2.3.1918; 23.3.1918; 11.5.1918; 5.7.1918.

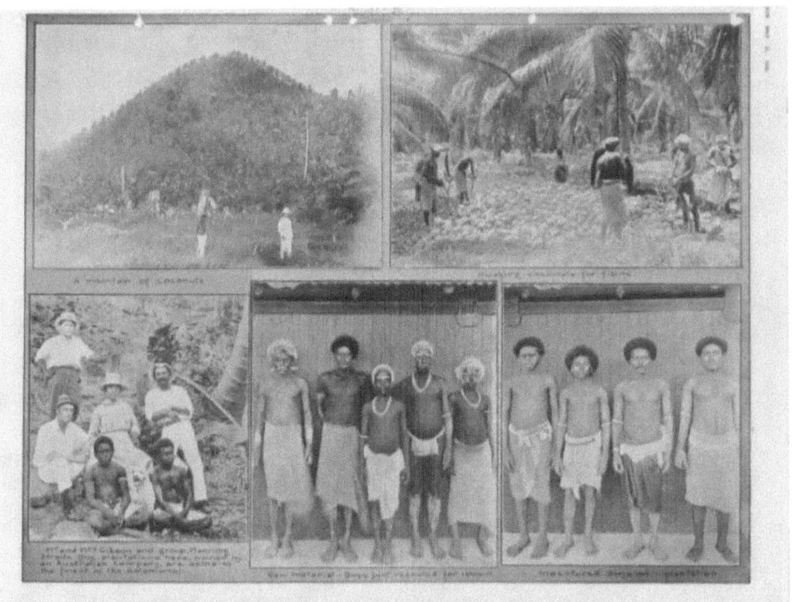

Fig. 9 Solomon Islands, 1918; typical format in the
'Pictorial' supplement of *The Queenslander*

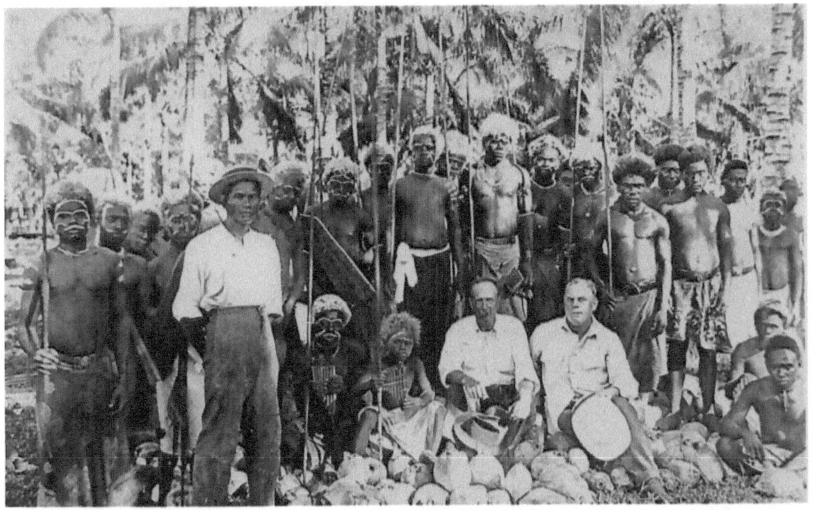

Fig. 10 'The writer [sitting centre right] with an overseer and a group of
natives on a Solomon Islands plantation', 1918

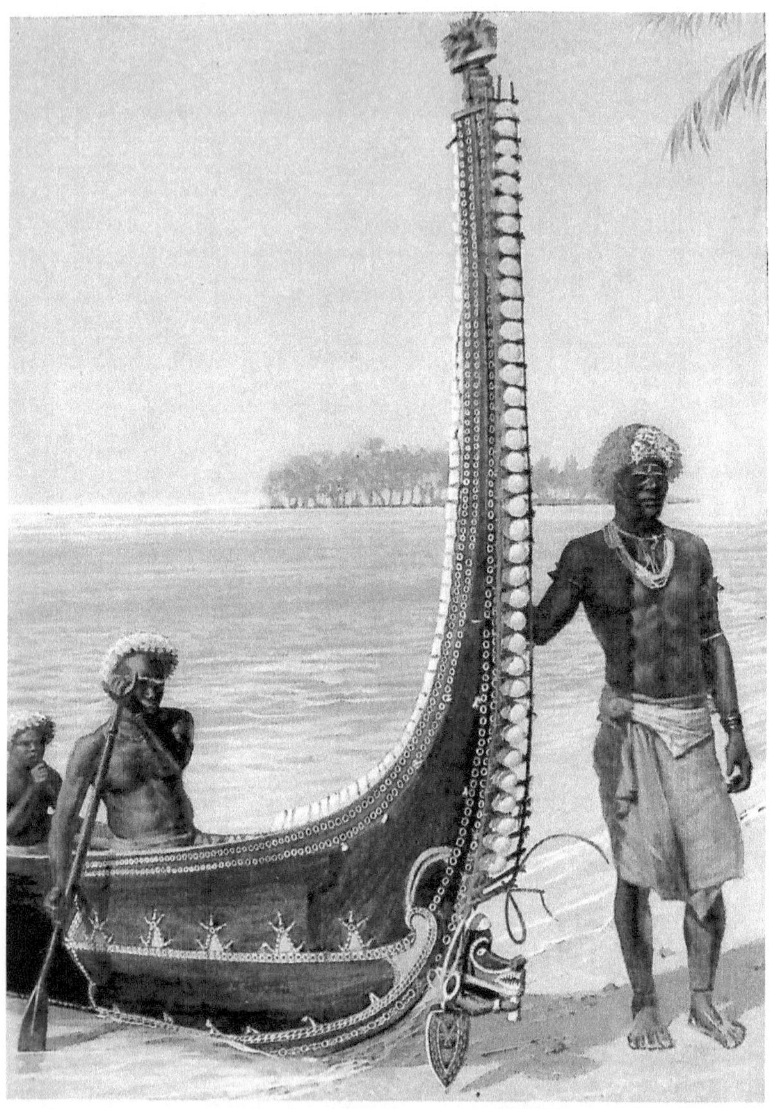

Fig. 11 Solomon Islands canoe, 1918

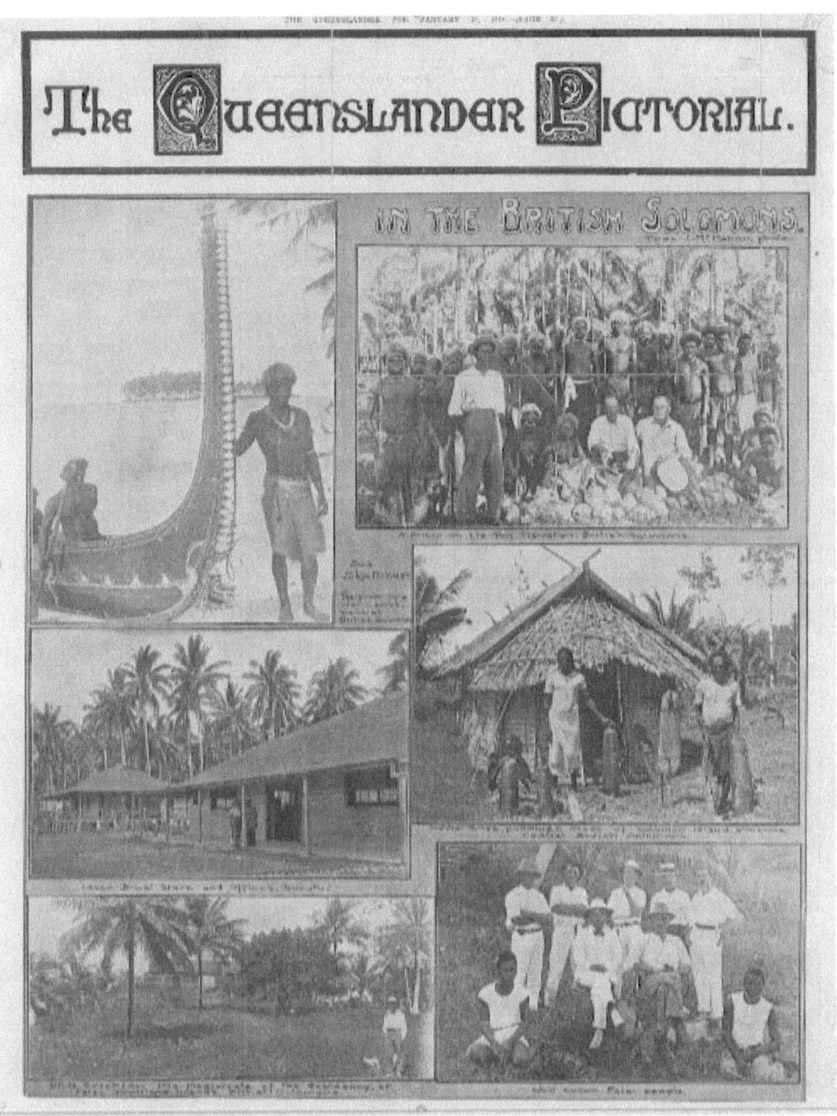

Fig. 12 'In the British Solomons', 1918

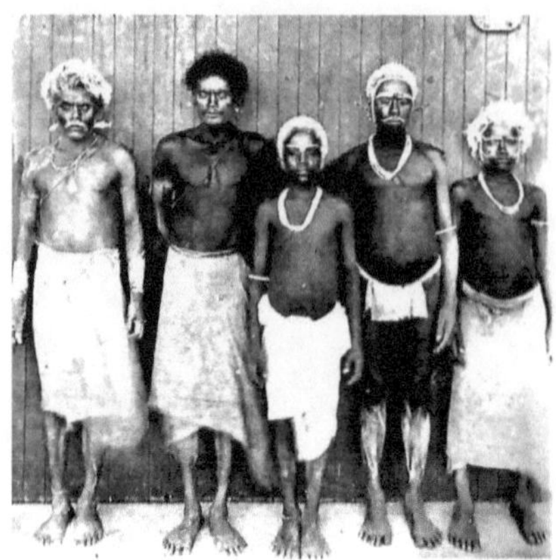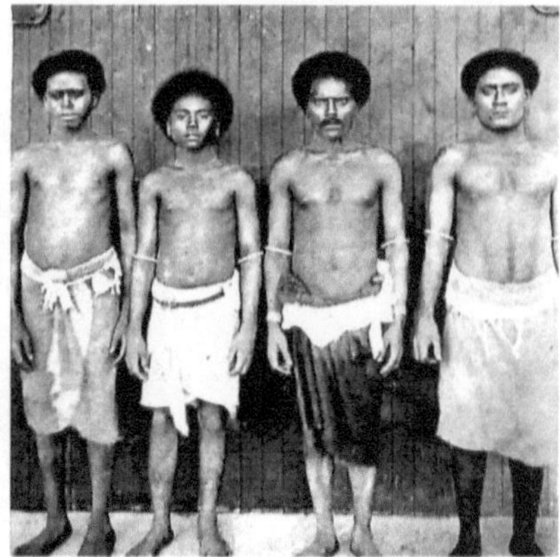

Fig. 13 Comparison of wild men and recruited labour, Solomon Islands

Solomon Islands had been a British protectorate since 1892, but while plantation development had occurred, there was minimal colonial presence. 'In the British Solomons' also raised in readers' minds the possibility that international recognition and status might well be won through a renamed 'Australian Solomon Islands'.

The Queenslander's decision to publish the series maintained a pattern of photographic imaging of sub-empire going back to the 1890s, but historians generally have ignored this significant body of visual evidence.[176] Acknowledgement of the role of photography is therefore overdue, because in shaping public opinion, the mass-dissemination of visual material in the early twentieth century offers convincing evidence of Australia's diverse links with the region and of Australia's thwarted claims for a closer relationship

176   Benito Vargas has shown the importance of photography in the American colonial imaging of the Philippines, but this approach has not been applied to the south Pacific. See Vargas, Benito. *Displaying Filipinos: photography and colonialism in early 20th century Philippines*, Manila, 1995. For example, a general history of the region by Donald Denoon, Philippa Mein-Smith and Marivic Wyndham, *A History of Australia, New Zealand and the Pacific*, London, 2000, and *The Cambridge History of the Pacific Islands*, edited by Paul D'Arcy (with eighty-five chapters), 2022, ignored the role of photography and visual propaganda in creating colonial identities and global knowledge of the region.

with the Solomon Islands. Public awareness of the region was being shaped by new media and photographs. McMahon's series in *The Queenslander* demonstrated the importance of illustrated newspapers and magazines in the history of Australian, and particularly Queensland's, engagement with the south-west Pacific.[177] The decision to publish such an extensive series indicates an editorial commitment to monitoring the economy, administration and future of nearby colonial possessions and suggests that editors were responding to readers' associations with the Islands through work, investment, friends, travel, novels or missions.

This level of coverage also suggests significant public interest in the fate of colonial possessions and the economic opportunities believed to exist in the neighbouring Pacific Islands. McMahon's widely published images of the Solomon Islands lauded the economic potential and targeted reader interest in the shape of the world that would evolve in the post-war period. Having already visited Australian Papua and German New Guinea, McMahon was developing considerable firsthand experience and was making comparisons between colonial administrations. Rabaul, for example, was presented as impressive in all respects in comparison to Port Moresby. Then, during his visit to the Solomons he visited Tulagi, the capital of the protectorate, a small ramshackle collection of huts and sheds overwhelmed by the adjacent Levers and Burns Philp wharves, storage and indentured labour quarters on Macombo and Guvatu Islands respectively. [178]

The views of McMahon were paralleled in journal and

---

177   For a pioneering essay on links through the Coral Sea, see Moore, Clive. 'Queensland and its Coral Sea: implications of historical links between Australia and Melanesia', in Gillies, Malcolm, ed. *Northern Exposures*, Canberra, 1997, pp. 79–102.

178   For Tulagi, see Moore, C. *Tulagi: Pacific outpost of British Empire*, Canberra, ANU Press, 2019.

magazine articles by a small but vocal cohort of commentators.[179] The Solomon Islands, a British protectorate, was not on the negotiating table but there were optimists in Australia who thought the two northern islands of the archipelago, formerly in German hands, might be rejoined to the south in a wider re-distribution by the Allies and pass fully to British or perhaps Australian control. The New Hebrides (now Vanuatu) was equally not open for negotiation, but Australian expansionists thought post-war deals might lead to the New Hebrides passing by annexation or mandate from condominium control by Britain and France to France and Australia as the joint administering authority or to possibly Australia alone. Commentators at this time also noted the fate of Nauru, New Zealand's aspirations in Samoa and Japan's move for a mandate over the northern Pacific Islands vacated by Germany.[180]

McMahon's series, 'In the British Solomons' was therefore both topical and visually arresting to Australian readers in a world being reshaped by the Great War. When he flooded illustrated newspapers with stories and images of the potential

179   McGregor, William. 'The Pacific Islands and their political settlement', *United Empire*, March 1918, pp. 107–10; McGregor, William. 'The settlement of the Pacific', *Scottish Geographical Magazine*, May 1918, pp. 161–77; Im Thurn Edward, 'The present state of the Pacific Islands', *Journal of the Royal Society of Arts*, Nov. 1918, pp. 38–45; Scholefield, GH. 'Problems of reconstruction in the Pacific', *United Empire*, July 1919, pp. 326–9; McLaren, AD. 'A Monroe doctrine for Australasia', *Contemporary Review*, Aug. 1918, pp. 158–63; Hughes, William. 'Australia and the Pacific', *United Empire*, Sept. 1918, pp. 293–5; Eggleston, FW. 'Australia's view of Pacific problems', *Pacific Affairs*, 3, 1930; Eggleston, FW., ed, *The Australian Mandate in New Guinea*, Melbourne, 1928; Eggleston, FW, 'The British Empire, Australia and the Pacific', *Australian Quarterly*, 4, 1936.

180   Fitzhardinge, LF. 'Australia, Japan and Great Britain 1914–18', *Historical Studies*, 14:54, 1970, pp. 250–9; Louis, WR. 'Australia and the German colonies in the Pacific 1914–19', *Journal of Modern History*, Vol. 38, 1966, pp. 407–21; Snelling, RC. 'Peacemaking 1919: Australia, New Zealand and the British empire delegation at Versailles', *Journal of Imperial and Commonwealth History*, Vol. 40, 1975, pp. 15–28; Thompson, R. 'The Labor Party and Australian imperialism in the Pacific 1901–1919', *Labour History*, Vol. 23, 1972, pp. 27–37.

waiting for Australia and Australians to develop in Papua and the Islands, readers were being primed for expansion. When McMahon asked whether the maps of the future would 'show these attractive islands of the Pacific coloured red for British or black for Germany', and when he suggested 'there is a moral force of national pride demanding that Australia strike for the future now ... and inquire more diligently into the progress and prospect of these Pacific Islands',[181] readers probably agreed that Australia's relationship with the region should expand or be strengthened. McMahon's photography of the Solomon Islands appeared immediately in illustrated newspapers and magazines in Australia after he returned to Australia in December 1917 and continued throughout 1918.[182] They reappeared in features in journals, magazines, postcards, albums, illustrated books by other authors and serial encyclopedias twenty-six times over the next decade.[183] By 1923, his Solomon Island photographs had appeared on more than a hundred separate occasions.

McMahon was not an ethnographer, a student of the emerging

---

181   McMahon, TJ. 'The Pacific Islands. What of their future? Australia's relationship', *The Queenslander*, 29.12.1917, p. 14.

182   As well as Brisbane's *The Queenslander*, *The Daily Telegraph*, *The Week*, *Daily Mail* and *The Queensland News Budget*, McMahon's material appeared in Sydney in *The Bulletin* (31.1.1918), *The Sydney Mail* (27.2.1918, 15.1.1919) and in Melbourne in *The Age* (27.4.1918). In 1920, McMahon wrote on the Solomon Islands again for *The Queenslander* (28.8.1920), *The Leader* (Melbourne) (21.8.1920) and for Brisbane's *Daily Mail* (30.8.1921).

183   'Coconut growing as a career', *World's Work*, 31 (1918), pp. 338–47; 'The octopus: Germany in the Pacific', *Evening News* (London), 6.12.1918; 'The islands of the South Pacific', *Dun's Review*, Mar. 1918, pp. 48–9, 51; 'The Gordon of the Pacific; my visit to Germany's South Sea possessions', *The Wide World*, 42 (1918), pp. 349–57; 'Coconut cultivation' *The World's Markets*, Aug. 1920, pp. 27–31; 'British Solomon Islands and their administration' *Bulletin* (Sydney), 31.1.1918, pp. 6–7, 31; 'Among the natives', *The Sydney Mail*, 15.1.1919; 'German Solomon Islands: an asset of the Commonwealth', *The Leader* (Melbourne), 21 .8.1920, p. 51; 'A Commonwealth dominion: the German Solomon Islands', *The Queenslander*, 28.8.1920, p. 15; 'The jewels of the Pacific', *The Wide World*, Vol. 46 (1921), pp. 350–6; 'The jewels of the Pacific', *Daily Mail* (Brisbane), 30.1.1921, p. 15; 'The Solomon Islands', *The Blue Peter* (London) 1921, pp. 163–7.

social sciences or a trained fieldworker, but he was by now an astute photographer. The photographs in his 'In the British Solomons' series were usually six to a page, graphically laid out with handwritten captions in *The Queenslander*'s regular 'Pictorial' photography segment. This section was printed on art paper, with individual images measuring 18 cm by 14 cm. The final in the British Solomons series in May 1918 was magnificently laid out across two full pages with nine 24 cm by 16 cm images. The text appeared separately in the newsprint sections under the by-line, 'The Sketcher'.

After his first visit to the Pacific in 1915, McMahon adopted a strategy of submitting to editors a portfolio of photographs accompanied by short, anecdotal and pithy articles. His expertise, or local knowledge, typically came from short visits of a day or two on a scheduled mail boat or cargo run through the archipelago. He also collected stories from casual discussions with traders, planters and labour recruiters, mostly anecdotal details on trade, economy and administration. He then reported through his images, accompanied by a text of borrowed opinions and personal observations. Reference was made to early European explorers in the Solomon Islands along with lyrical descriptions of fauna, flora and topography. His writing was closer in style to the popular travelogue and illustrated format developed at the turn of the century in response to reader demand for colonial adventures, imperial expansion and exotic settings.

McMahon targeted public interest in eastern Australia in the potential to invest in or migrate to the neighbouring western Pacific Islands and make a profit from planting, trading or mining.[184] At a personal level, McMahon's images offered readers

---

184   Halter, Nic and Quanchi, Max. 'Boosting the Frontier: Australian Settler
        Colonialism in the Pacific 1860s-1900s', *Australian Historical Studies*, Vol. 53, no. 3,
        2022, pp. 415–32.

a tantalising glimpse of successful private enterprise and a secure future for those willing to take a risk. In an era when Solomon Island copra had nearly doubled in price per ton between 1908 and 1913,[185] and both Australian investors and Island administrations were favouring capital investment in plantations, the coconut was so promising it was known as the 'Consol of the East'. The coconut, McMahon announced, was the reason that islands were 'bursting out in grand fruitfulness and profitableness'.[186] It was an offer that attracted attention in the eastern Australian states weary of war news and with the problem ahead of what to do with several hundred thousand military personnel wanting to rejoin the workforce or start a new life. McMahon's determination to seek out editors on three continents and make a career in photojournalism was based on this double-edged visual appeal to readers – the promotion of Australian sub-imperialism and the depiction of a planter's life as a pathway to personal, material and financial success.

The first feature in *The Queenslander* series mixed contextual and propaganda material with two portraits of Solomon Islanders, one of the crew of the Choiseul Plantation Company inter-island trader, *Rogeia* (the vessel in which McMahon toured the Islands), a coconut plantation, an impressive Lever Brothers plantation residence and labourers bringing in a canoe-load of nuts for husking. The two portraits fixed the location of the story – exotic

---

185   Bennett, Judith. *Wealth of the Solomons: a history of a Pacific archipelago 1800–1978*, Honolulu, University of Hawaii Press, 1987, p. 138. In Papua, the exported value of copra increased threefold over the same period; see Lewis, David. *The Plantation Dream: developing British New Guinea and Papua 1884–1942*, Canberra, JPH Press, 1996, 4, p. 311; Buckley, K and Klugman, K. *The Australian Presence*, pp. 49–52.

186   In *The Queenslander*, McMahon claimed this could be reworded as 'Consol of the Islands': *The Queenslander*, 2.3.1918, p. 19; McMahon, TJ. 'Coconut growing as a career', *World's Work*, 1918, p. 339; Bennett, ibid, p. 139. A consol was a valued government-issued bond that offered secure profits, a metaphor for the promise of the copra industry.

and western Pacific – and the views of plantations, residences and labourers suggested a planter's prospects were assured by substantial infrastructure, plentiful labour and accessible, fertile land. The rest of the series repeated the promise of a stable colonial environment for both investors and immigrants seeking to try their luck as planters. Wharves, trade stores, government buildings and group portraits of the local planter community were shown, with images of canoes and village housing to maintain the geographic location.

Pointedly for his Brisbane readers, one caption read, 'Marmora plantation, a Queensland owned property'. A fifth of the captions stressed a connection to Australia. McMahon reminded readers that either ownership or management of a plantation was Australian, and in one instance noted the manager's residence at Lavero plantation, another Queensland-owned property, had previously been an office building in Brisbane. McMahon was alert to contemporary concerns in Australia when he noted in captions that artisans and overseers pictured were returned WWI soldiers from Sydney. He claimed a man with capital would succeed within ten years and a young man without capital might, over a fifteen- to twenty-year period, move from a salaried position to one of slowly acquiring two or three hundred acres and setting himself and his family up as small planters, earning the comfortable income of £1000 a year.

Photographs of sowing, harvesting, processing, horticulture, labour and shipping scenes were included. Readers were offered a panoramic glimpse of the process by which plantation seedlings matured and were harvested as nuts and turned to copra by husking and drying before finally being carried in bags on the shoulders of sturdy labourers to the waiting ships. The importance of shipping during the war years, despite commercial cargo space on British flagships being curtailed, was highlighted by images of vessels unloading at wharves at Faisi and Guvatu, and off the beach at unnamed locations. A whaleboat filled to the gunnels was pictured unloading coconuts for husking at a plantation in the Manning Straits. These images gave the impression that Solomon Islands copra could be harvested from remote plantations, processed, bagged and shipped within the archipelago to a depot, then to Sydney or direct to the west coast of the United States of America. Visually readers could see the link between plantations, harvesting and processing and copra delivered quickly to the world market.

The Queenslander's readers saw well-built, substantial homes, cheap labour, a crop in world demand, and land with 'superabundance' fertility, and read that a moderate capital outlay and patience would pay back with interest the initial investment of labour, capital and time. A caption noted a vista of one-year-old seedling palms was the result of a commitment by Lever Brothers, 'the giant British soap makers (who) have invested millions in this group of islands and have many fine plantations'. McMahon photographed innovations such as running cattle to keep the grass down in a plantation and then later selling them as meat on the Australian market. The photographs hardly needed captions: the message was clear – copra planting was a success just waiting for Australian capital and men.[187]

The early twentieth-century practice of using photographs as propaganda for investment and a prospectus for intending planters could be seen in McMahon's photograph of five Europeans, presumably planters, managers or overseers depicted lounging on a whaleboat, one of three drawn up in a coconut grove by a

---

187   Although expatriate women appeared in several group portraits, presumably the wives of managers, overall, McMahon's imaging was masculine, following the gendered perspective that the colonial frontier, tropical adventures and plantation life were man's work. In 1917, there were few European women, perhaps forty, in the expatriate population in the Solomon Islands.

beach. Several buildings are scattered in the grove of palms. The nonchalant posture of the men suggests affluence and a pleasant way of life, a relaxed moment amid their prosperous and busy economic activity. McMahon used this image in illustrated articles in *The Sydney Mail* (1919), *World's Markets* (1920) and *The Wide World* (1921) as well as his McCarron pamphlet in 1923. In another photograph, the same group of men is shown wandering in 'a fine coconut plantation owned by a Queensland company'. In an Australia still imbued with the spirit and reliability of Empire, this imaging was a persuasive argument for investors.

Visually, the impact of McMahon's full-page features on the Solomon Islands was in stark contrast to *The Queenslander*'s main weekend pictorial section, dominated by battlefield scenes, studio portraits of embarking soldiers and an increasing number of portraits captioned 'killed in action'. Pages of relaxed, tropical planters and prospering plantations stood out among the carnage of war. The opening article in *The Queenslander* series carried the triple headline:

WONDERFUL DEVELOPMENT

AUSTRALIAN TRADE PROSPECTS

QUEENSLAND'S CONCERN

The authority came from the 'I was there' visit. The willingness of the Brisbane editors of *The Queenslander* to publish opinion on the Solomon Islands was matched in the United Kingdom and the United States of America. After some rephrasing and re-captioning by McMahon, this gallery and text appeared in magazines worldwide.[188]

188　Several copies of *The Queenslander*'s 'Sketcher' columns, in Royal Geographical Society (Queensland), McMahon Papers, Files 9038 and 9053, Box 4, have scribbled new captions and subheadings, deletions and reordering as they were prepared for other publications such as *World's Work*, the *Evening Post*, *Blue Peter* and *The Wide World*.

Five years later in 1923, McMahon selected thirteen images for his Solomon Islands booklet in the 'Pacific Islands Illustrated' series published in Sydney by McCarron and Stewart.[189] With 15 cm by 10 cm photographs, one to a page, these booklets sold for one shilling and ninepence to the tourist, mission, ex-colonial official and ex-residents market. There were seven booklets in the series. The opening image in the Solomons album was the nonchalant planters mentioned above, lounging on a whaleboat pulled up on the shore. The following photographs were explicit: an attractive European residence, a steamer loading copra, an old growth plantation doubling as a cattle property and a team of labourers husking a pile of coconuts in a seedling nursery. He used this image of an 'experimental coconut seedling nursery' several times. Taken in Bougainville in 1917, the composition and framing stressed the important role of the expatriate supervisor, with a European standing to the rear overseeing the two labourers with the seedlings. This photograph appeared in magazines worldwide, illustrated newspapers and pictorial encyclopedias and was a classic example of promotional framing and hammering home a message of opportunity and expansion.[190]

The few mandatory ethnographic images included fishing, bamboo flutes, drums, paddlers in a fleet of so-called war canoes, grass 'top hats' of adolescent north Solomon males and Vella Lavella dwellings with unique banana-leaf food storage containers. Two views of substantial rivers hinted at a well-watered, arable archipelago. The economic and political agenda of the

---

189   A copy is held by the Royal Geographical Society, London, PR/056713. The image on the cover was mistakenly a Nauruan male. On McMahon's *New Guinea* booklet, a Fijian man appeared on the cover. In thousands of McMahon's published images, there are relatively few mis-captioned or misplaced images, usually the fault of subeditors.

190   It appeared first in *The Queenslander*, 2.3.1918, p. 22. It was used mostly for articles on the Solomon Islands, even though it had been taken on Bougainville in the former German territory.

1923 album was obvious in his choice of images – five from the formerly German northern islands of Buka and Bougainville and the remainder from the southern British protectorate. However, McMahon's proposal for a reunion of the two sectors under Australian rule had been overrun by the declaration of mandates and resumptions of control in the post-war period. By 1923, the northern Solomon Islands were already under Australian control through the mandate granted over the former German mainland and islands of north-east New Guinea, and the British had made no change to their protectorate status in the south.

Australia and the Solomons

McMahon argued that Australia was perceived in the Islands as a victim of trade union tyranny on its wharves. Planters, reported McMahon, thought Australia was obsessive about maintaining monopoly mail routes and cargo rates and was unsuitable as a governing authority. Readers were told British rule in the Islands was also unpopular, unsympathetic and inimical to economic development, and that expatriates were contemptuous of the final authority held by the Western Pacific High Commission (WPHC), ruling from Fiji. A leaked copy of a report on labour by the Lieutenant Governor of Papua, Sir Hubert Murray, was cited as evidence of the fear held by the expatriate community should Australian policy in Papua be applied in the Solomon Islands.[191] McMahon called for 'an end forever of the species of government called British, but distinctly un-British in methods ... a constant complaint of planters, of missionaries, traders and settlers of all other classes'.[192] Readers were told Solomon Islanders were given a bank holiday in an archipelago that did not have any banks, that

---

191   *The Queenslander*, 11.5.1918, p. 29; Buckley and Klugman, *The Australian Presence*, pp. 28–31.

192   *The Queenslander*, 19.1.1918, p. 19; 9.2.1918, p. 15.

£10,000 was spent on a rarely used jetty at Tulagi and in 1916 a costly government steamer had lain idle for 290 days. He called for a renewed effort by Australia to improve its reputation among the planter community, to grasp the opportunity provided by post-war realignments, to establish a sub-empire in the western Pacific and, should it assume control, to adopt a governing practice based primarily in the interests of expatriate European investors, settlers and traders.

Privately, the British administration in the Solomons was concerned that McMahon's articles would give the wrong impression to Australian readers. As noted earlier, the District Officer on Malaita, William Bell, wrote in response to a request from the Assistant Resident Commissioner, Charles Workman, that McMahon's articles were 'libelous epistles' typically voiced in colonial circles by disgruntled planters wishing to exploit both the indigenous landowners and the resources. Bell noted that McMahon merely repeated these complaints and neither fully explained the nature of the complaints nor offered any solutions.[193] This exchange remained private, and no censure appeared in the Letters to the Editor columns of the Brisbane press. McMahon's journalistic practice was later attacked on similar grounds in 1921 after he criticised the Papuan administration for inactivity and not fostering economic development. This became a public debate when both the Minister and Acting Minister for Home and Territories published rebuttals in Melbourne's *The Argus* attacking McMahon's practice of listening to gossip and collecting anecdotal evidence from the expatriate but not the official community.[194]

---

193   Workman to Bell, 28.5.1918, 14/46, Bell to Workman, 10.6.1918, 14/12, Honiara, National Archives, BSIP, 33/1918. I am grateful to Clive Moore for alerting me to this correspondence.

194   This exchange occurred as the Minister and Acting Minister returned from separate tours of Papua and New Guinea; *The Argus* (Melbourne), 13.5.1921, 14.5.1921, 22.7.1921.

This did not detract from McMahon's popularity with editors, although it may have influenced his later decision to travel to Asia in 1922 and abandon photography in the Islands.

McMahon's text in the 'Sketcher' pages usually pursued a separate theme from the pictorial segment, which meant readers could absorb opinions expressed in the text or draw conclusions based on their own interpretation of events depicted in the photographs. The text was didactic but claimed authority by reference to individual planters, ship's captains and the names of local ships, plantations and ports. The focus on Australia's national interest, promises of individual prosperity and calls for increased imperial responsibility resonated with readers. In Melbourne, *The Age* voiced the opinion at the start of the war that 'we have long realized that we have a Pacific destiny' and the post-war path could open an Australian empire in the Pacific.[195] James Burns, the head of Burns Philp, argued in 1915, 'the natural destiny of the Pacific Islands is that they come under the control of Australia'.[196] In two memoranda on Australia's post-war role in the Pacific, Burns suggested the transfer to Australia of power over all British colonies and territories in the Pacific, or at least their administration from a base in Australia, closer to merchants, traders and others interested in the Islands. This transfer would involve a lesser role in the Solomon Islands by the Fiji-based Western Pacific High Commission. In 1915, Burns went to London, arguing the case for a post-war realignment including the possible transfer of the Gilbert (now Kiribati), Ellice (now Tuvalu), Tonga and Solomon Islands to Australian control. These arguments, with specific references to the administration

---

195   *The Age* (Melbourne), 12.8.1914, cited in Thompson, *Australian Imperialism*, p. 203; Buckley and Klugman, *The Australian Presence*, pp. 4–7.

196   Cited in McIntyre, Stuart. *The Oxford History of Australia: the succeeding age 1901–1942*, Melbourne, MUP, 1986, p. 178.

of the Solomon Islands, were laid out in an anonymous series of articles in the *Sydney Morning Herald* in 1915 and in a pamphlet titled *British Mismanagement in the Pacific No. 2*.[197] McMahon's private papers include annotated copies of this pamphlet, and sentiments he expressed in his *Queenslander* series reworked many of these ideas.[198]

Prime Minister Hughes announced in London that Australia favoured using the equator as a demarcation line, with Japan conceding control of the north and Australia the south. Hughes called it an 'Australasian Monroe doctrine in the South Pacific'.[199] Roger Thompson's evaluation of Hughes's campaigns in London and at the Versailles Treaty negotiations regarding the New Hebrides and former German colonies in Nauru, New Guinea and the Marshall and Caroline Islands was that Hughes's achievements were considerable for a small, semi-independent power. Hughes was reported to have said in London, 'the voice of the colonies will be dead against the return of colonies to the Huns ... it is safety not aggrandizement we are playing for'.[200] The personal reputation of Hughes, his demand for separate dominion representation in the negotiations and his alleged confrontation with the great powers over control of the Pacific were exaggerated in Australia,

---

197   Buckley and Klugman, *The Australian Presence*, pp. 7, 19–20, 26–8.

198   The Western Pacific High Commission had been criticised in London in 1902 by Alfred Deakin. He claimed the Commissioner 'had never yet justified his title' (*Morning Post*, London, 11.3.1902, cited in Evans et al., eds. *1901 Our future's past*, pp. 216–17).

199   An Australian 'Monroe doctrine' in the Pacific Islands was noted in 1898 (*Adelaide Advertiser*, 7.6.1898, cited in Evans, ibid., pp. 215–16). In 1902, the visiting British colonial official, journalist and author, Archibald Colquhoun, claimed, 'the Australian Monroe Doctrine has not yet been officially promulgated or incorporated in the national policy, but its spirit is breathed by all Australians', in Colquhoun, AR. *The Mastery of the Pacific*, New York, 1902, pp. 204. See also McLaren, AD. 'A Monroe doctrine', pp. 158–63; Tate, M. 'The Australasian Munroe doctrine', *Political Science Quarterly*, 1961, p. 76.

200   Extract from the *London Evening News*, 14.6.1918; *The Week* (Brisbane), 21.6.1918. See also editorials in *The Week*, 28.6.1918; 19.7.1918.

where newspapers were forced to rely on 'scrappy and sensational cabled news' and Hughes's self-aggrandising reports. On his return, Hughes claimed he had secured for Australia the islands that were 'the ramparts of Australia's security' as well as a valuable monopoly over the economic trade and resources of Nauru and German New Guinea.[201] By the time Prime Minister Billy Hughes arrived in London in June 1918 to argue for Australia in the post-war realignment of colonial territories, other illustrated newspapers in Brisbane such as *The Week* and *The Queensland News Budget* had run news items on the fate of ex-German colonies. There is nothing in Hughes' speeches to suggest McMahon's call for greater Australian involvement had influenced Hughes.

Apart from mandates over Nauru (jointly with New Zealand and Great Britain) and German New Guinea, Australia's relationship with the rest of the western Pacific remained as it had been before the war.[202] McMahon's views on empire and descriptions of the Solomon Islands had become rapidly out of step with post-war planning and imperial developments.[203] As Roger Thompson pointed out, by 1920 the expansionist period was over. The governor-general claimed Imperial issues was a

---

201   Anon., 'The return of Mr Hughes', *Round Table*, 10.12.1919, pp. 179–85; *Commonwealth Parliamentary Debates*, House of Representatives, 10.9.1919, pp. 1266–79; 14.9.1920, pp. 4454–7; and Hudson, WJ. *Billy Hughes in Paris*, Melbourne, MUP, 1978.

202   Hughes's initial request was for control over the south Pacific (excluding New Zealand's link with Samoa). Sole control of Nauru's valuable phosphate resources was adjusted to a lesser demand for a joint administration: Williams, Maslyn and Macdonald, Barrie. *The Phosphateers: a history of the British Phosphate Commission and the Christmas Island Phosphate Commission*, Melbourne, MUP, 1985, pp. 126–31.

203   Extracts from McMahon's writing on mandates were reprinted in *The Lone Hand*, on German New Guinea in the *Bulletin* (Sydney) and the *Sydney Sun*, and his descriptions of the New Hebrides, Torres Strait Islands and Norfolk Island were reprinted in *Stewart's Handbook of the Pacific Islands* in 1921, and for Fiji in the 1923 edition.

topic not much mentioned at public meetings in Australia[204] and neither McMahon's predictions, nor those of Hughes and other expansionists, came true. The Solomon Islands remained a British protectorate until gaining independence in 1978.[205]

Planters and plantations

As well as photographs on specific colonies and territories, McMahon also published more generally on the copra industry across the Pacific (often misspelt as 'cocoanut'), even as late as 1928, well after he had changed careers. Fifteen photographs of the copra industry accompanied his article in *World's Markets* in 1920. He focused on US trade as it was an American journal. Two years later, in *Sea Land Air*, an Australian wireless communication magazine, he claimed the copra industry in the Pacific could reach an annual value of £50 million, a figure he often cited without evidence. He asked, 'Why should not Australia make a bid for much of this trade?' A year later in a new magazine published in Japan, *Trans-Pacific*, he increased his estimate to £100 million. Nine photographs accompanied this article. In 1928, in the Port of London's magazine, *The PLA Monthly*, McMahon used three photographs from his earlier copra articles but adjusted the annual value of the copra trade to only £12 million. These publications on copra demonstrate McMahon's awareness of the demand for illustrated material on the Pacific in the US, UK, Japan, New Zealand and Australia.

Photographs of plantation crops, exports, shipping, and

---

204   Cited in Thompson, *Australian Imperialism*, pp. 213, 218. The anonymous writer of 'Australia and the empire' (*Round Table*, 1.8.1911, p. 500) claimed, 'The average citizen of the Commonwealth (of Australia) troubles himself very little about imperial affairs at all'. The outbreak of the Great War in 1914 and the rise of Japan in the north Pacific challenged public indifference, but sub-imperialism in the Pacific was not a regular subject of debate in federal and state parliaments.

205   Thompson, *Australian Imperialism*, p. 221.

labour in *The Queenslander* series in 1918 were similarly out of step regarding post-war plantation development and the general level of planter prosperity. The pre-war potential for prospective Australian planters in the tropics was first affected by the outbreak of war and then by a levelling off and subsequent decline as trade passed into a recession in the 1920s. The plantation boom in the Solomon Islands, German New Guinea and Papua ended respectively before McMahon's visits. In neighbouring Papua, settler-occupiers dominated agriculture and there were few holdings by foreign-owned companies. Half the owner-occupiers and managers of company estates in Papua had arrived without previous tropical experience, and in the Solomon Islands, as Judith Bennett points out, many planters had moved across from a start as traders. Despite familiarity with local customs, tenure and practice, they struggled for success.[206]

In the Solomon Islands, the large foreign-owned companies were more significant. In 1914, Levers Pacific plantations held 230,000 of the 250,000 acres granted by the administration to Europeans. Another 170,000 acres had been purchased direct from Solomon Islanders, although later only 145,000 acres were acknowledged as appropriated and occupied. Valuable coastal plantation lands totalling 463,425 acres were claimed to have been alienated in the Solomon Islands.[207]

David Lewis noted that in Papua before the war, a planter's prosperity had seemed assured by substantial influences 'at work in the larger world of investment in tropical commodities', with the world price of copra doubling between 1903 and 1914 and rubber

---

206 Bennett. *Wealth of the Solomons*, pp. 138, 142; Lewis, *The Plantation Dream*, pp. 89, 104–5.

207 Lewis, *The Plantation Dream*, pp. 72–4 (ch. 7 is titled 'The country of chances'). Bennett notes an Australian newspaper article in 1910 was titled 'The wealth of the Solomons'; Bennett, Wealth of the Solomons, pp. 138, 148; Scarr, Deryck. *Kingdoms of the Reefs: the history of the Pacific Islands*, Sydney, Macmillan, 1990, p. 256.

undergoing an even more spectacular boom. But in the Solomon Islands, copra's value per ton exported fell during and after the war, with only the good years of 1920 and 1921 to break the slump. Solomon Islands copra was regarded as the world's lowest quality. Access to and retaining labour, which was calculated to about sixty to seventy-five per cent of the cost of developing a plantation, was a problem in the Solomon Islands, with demand exceeding supply.[208] Images of seedling lots, mature plantations, lines of workers, wharves, shipping and group portraits of the planter community misled Australian readers into believing the Solomon Islands was a planter's paradise. The planters lounging about the beach in the beachfront plantation scene referred to earlier would have been discussing, in late 1917, not whether more would be enticed to the Islands by the pose they adopted for the camera but whether their own futures were secure in the copra slump of the late war and immediate post-war period.

In 1919, McMahon left on a speaking tour to London. In a series of journal and magazine articles, he reminded British audiences there was 'no greater obstacle to the British advancement of trade and enterprise ... than the strange and unpardonable ignorance of English people in not knowing how commercially wonderful these lands of the South Pacific are'.[209] His call for economic expansion attracted a good response at the Royal Colonial Society and the Chamber of Commerce in London and in journals like *Empire Review*. On tour, he was speaking to sympathetic audiences who lamented the fading of the empire and who saw renewed hope in McMahon's vision of post-war prosperity on the colonial periphery,

---

208   Although world prices were high, the war limited shipping available for commercial freight. Copra was the major export but was smoke-dried rather than hot-air- or sun-dried and produced only 0.7% to 0.8% of the world supply; see Bennett, *Wealth of the Solomons*, pp. 199, 219; Buckley and Klugman, *The Australian Presence*, pp. 28–31, 33.

209   McMahon, TJ. 'The South Pacific Islands; their resources and prospects', *Empire Review*, 1919, p. 250.

but investors and planters did not rush to the Solomon Islands to exploit the island's resources. In 1925, *Round Table*, a new journal on imperial affairs, reviewed the first twenty-year period of Australian administration in neighbouring Papua and asked why plantations had not been profitable.[210] The problems that were listed – inappropriate administration policies, falling commodity prices, the world war, unavailability of labour and the 'crowning horror' of the Navigation Act (Australia, 1912) – were problems that applied equally to the Solomons.[211]

Editorial policy and reader interest

The photographs published in 1918 in McMahon's series, 'In the British Solomons', and the widespread publication afterwards of his Solomon Islands photographs, indicate a lingering fascination with sub-empire and tropical potential. There was enough continuing public interest in exotic locations, indigenous cultures and Europeans living on the colonial frontier in the Pacific for Merl La Voy, an American contemporary of McMahon in photographing the Pacific, to publish fifty-five photographs in *The Sydney Mail* in 1921, in a four-part series titled 'With a camera in the Solomon Islands'.[212] La Voy emphasised the ethnographic over the economic, preferring portraits and village scenes, canoes and musical instruments to plantations and colonial infrastructure. There were some images of planters, residences, husking nuts, loading copra and labourers returning

---

210   Anon., 'Australian administration in Papua', *Round Table*, June 1925, pp. 15, 573–82.

211   The Navigation Act was passed in 1912 but not proclaimed until 1921. Its purpose was to protect Australian shipping, ensure shipping used Australian crews and develop Australia's maritime capabilities. It was attacked for raising import and export costs, preventing trade and having done little to develop Australia's maritime industries.

212   La Voy, Merl. 'With a camera in the Solomon Islands', *The Sydney Mail*, 7.12.1921; 28.12.1921; 4.1.1922; 1.2.1922.

to Santa Cruz after a two-year indenture on a copra plantation, but La Voy's imaging contrasts with the political and economic agenda of McMahon's *Queenslander* series just a few years earlier.

Prior to running McMahon's series, *The Queenslander* had published several pictorial features on the Solomon Islands. In 1910, the anonymously attributed 'The mysterious Solomons' had forty-eight photographs of plantations, crops and infrastructure, and 'Development in the Solomon Islands' included photographs depicting economic opportunities and potential prosperity. In 1915, *The Queenslander* ran more anonymously attributed pictorial features on 'The future of the Solomons', and in January 1916, another titled, 'In the Solomon Islands'.[213] McMahon's series in late 1917 and early 1918, therefore, continued an established commitment by editorial staff, and we can assume a consistently high level of reader interest. What *The Queenslander* series also demonstrates is the popularity of early twentieth-century photographically illustrated publications, particularly illustrated weekend newspapers and magazines, and the ease with which Australian audiences could access evidence about events in the neighbouring south-west Pacific region.

The links to the Solomon Islands reported on in McMahon's photographs and text now need recognition and inclusion in a wider revision of the early twentieth-century history of Australia and Australian-Pacific relations. This gap includes overdue acknowledgement of the post-WWI takeover of German New Guinea and Nauru, attempts to exert greater influence in other archipelagos and Australia's considerable early twentieth-century human, political and economic links with the region. Because

---

213   Anon., 'The mysterious Solomons', *The Queenslander*, 13.8.1910; 27.8.1910; 3.9.1910; 17.9.1910; Anon., 'Development in the Solomon Islands', ibid., 15.10.1910, 29.10.1910; 'Future of the Solomons', ibid., 16.1.1915; anon., 'In the Solomon Islands', ibid., 1.1.1916.

the widely disseminated illustrated material on the region by McMahon and others has been undervalued, it is necessary that more attention now be paid to the photographic evidence and its complex, contrary meanings.

In 1918, McMahon left on Burns Philp's 'islands run' to continue his investigations and gather photographs of Ocean Island (Banaba), Nauru, the Gilberts (Kiribati) and the Marshall Islands.

Chapter 5

The phosphate islands (i):
a mighty British enterprise

In 1918, in his first publication on the phosphate of lime extraction industries on Nauru and Ocean Island (now Banaba), McMahon could not restrain himself and claimed that British effort and determination had created 'splendid and most complete industries for the mining and distribution of the magic fertilizer.'[214] A month later in a two-part illustrated feature in *The Telegraph* (Brisbane) and in a double-page illustrated feature in *The Sydney Mail*, he mentioned that the Pacific Phosphate Company ran the mining operations, declaring 'there is no exaggeration in the opinion that in the history of British enterprise there is to be found no more progressive demonstration of British pluck and endeavour'.[215] This pro-British boosting continued into 1919, when in an article without illustration in *The Daily Telegraph* in London, he declared, 'British enterprise has turned these islands from wastes of unproductiveness, from the haunts of aggressive savages, to prosperous lands and Christianised people'. McMahon stressed that the king and people of Nauru, aware of diplomatic negotiations on post-war German colonies, had petitioned the

---

214 McMahon, TJ. 'A mighty British enterprise', *The Scientific Australian*, Dec. 1918, Vol. 24, no. 2, p. 27.

215 McMahon, TJ. 'Central Pacific Islands', *The Telegraph* (Brisbane), part 1, 1.2.1919, p. 13; part 2, 8.2.1919, p. 13; McMahon, TJ. 'The amazing story of Ocean and Nauru Islands', *The Sydney Mail*, 22.1.1919, pp. 16–17.

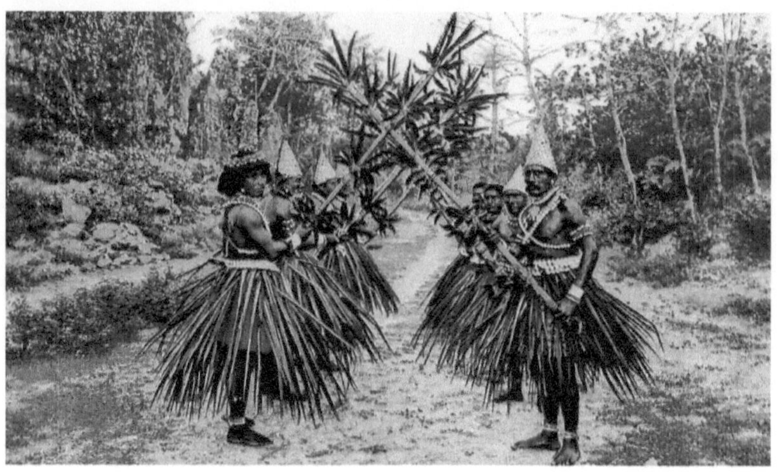

Fig. 14 'The Karanga (native dance), Ocean Island', 1923

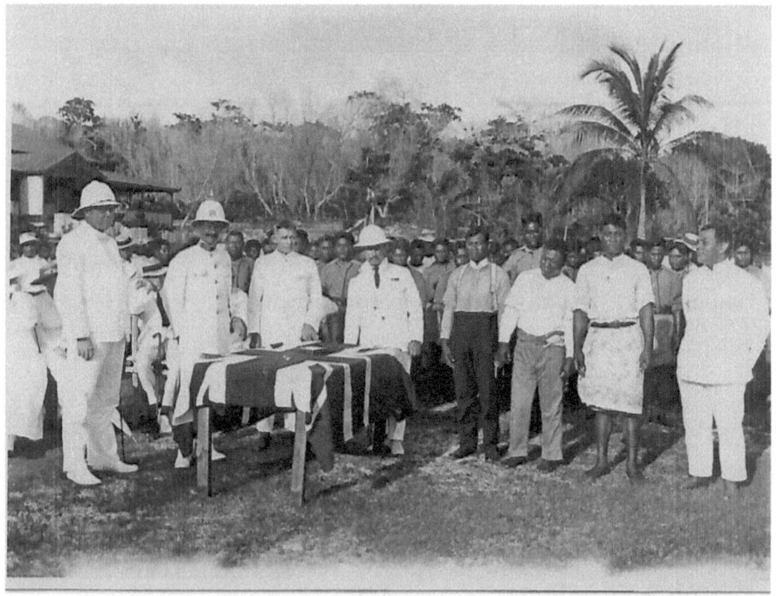

Fig. 15 The Tambo heroes at the awards ceremony, Ocean Island, 1918

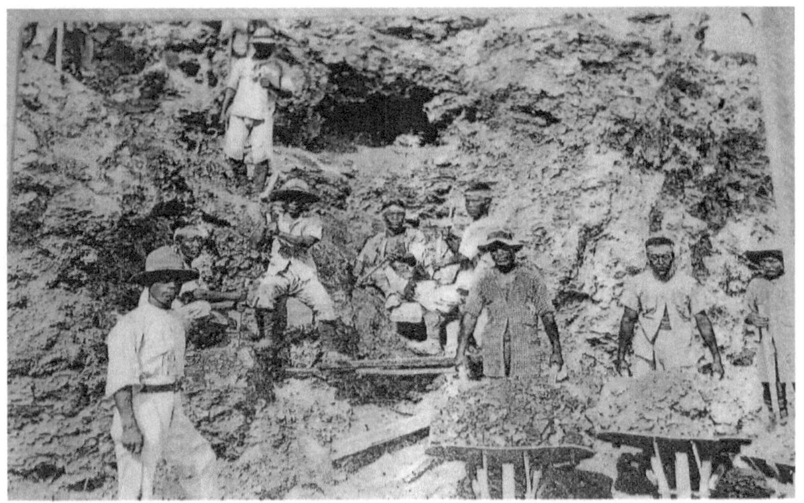

Fig. 16 Japanese work gang in the phosphate fields, 1919

British monarch, King George V, for the island to remain under British protection and administration. This boosting language continued in features he published in *World's Work* and *Dun's Review* in 1919. McMahon published 146 photographs of the two phosphate islands.[216] Before turning to each island (chs. 6 and 7), this chapter looks at McMahon's boosting of British colonial rule and prospective Australian involvement.

McMahon took Burns Philp's 'islands run', intending to report on the British economic and colonial presence in Nauru, Ocean Island (Banaba), the Gilbert Islands (Kiribati) and specifically on the relatively new phosphate mining industry on Nauru and Ocean Island. McMahon took passage on the *Tambo*, passing through the Solomon Islands, then north and east along the equator to

---

216   This figure is based on known publications found after thirty years of library sleuthing. There may be more McMahon photographs in as yet unsighted publications and repositories.

what he called the 'atoll-lands'.[217] This was the famous Burns Philp's 'islands run' that wound its way 4000 kilometres from Sydney to Tarawa in the Gilbert Islands and then veered north into the Marshall Islands on the other side of the equator. Japan had occupied the Marshalls, with Allied approval, at the outbreak of the war in 1914. Three Burns Philp ships were allocated to the two-month-long return trip eight times a year. As well as carrying phosphate, this was an Australian government subsidised mail run that also carried freight and passengers, and later tourists, and served also to maintain Australian interests in the region, where commercial competition from Japan and the US was increasing.

The trip exposed McMahon to several colonial administrations as Nauru, a former German colony, was under Australian military administration after being occupied at the start of the war, while Ocean Island was the capital for the recently merged British Crown Colony – the Gilberts and Ellice Island Colony (known as the GEIC).[218] Finally, he encountered a Japanese colonial administration in the Marshall Islands just as it was about to be awarded to Japan as a mandate under the League of Nations.[219] At the war's end, these small Pacific Island entities were of global interest. McMahon had highlighted this geopolitical transformation after his trips to Papua and the former German New Guinea in 1915 and 1917 and had already published an impressive array of photographically illustrated articles on the

---

217 This was inaccurate as Nauru and Ocean Island were not atolls but raised coral islands, elevated well above sea level by tectonic uplift. Atolls in the classic doughnut shape were flat, just above sea level, narrow and usually encircling a lagoon open to the sea.

218 The following chapters on Nauru and Ocean Island are based on earlier publications: 'A trip in the islands in 1918; the photography of TJ McMahon', *Meanjin*, Vol. 53, no. 4, 1994, pp. 715–22; 'TJ McMahon; photographer, essayist and patriot in colonial Australia, the Pacific and empire' in Quanchi, Max and Talu, Alaima, eds. *Messy Entanglements*, Brisbane, Pacific History Association, 1995, pp. 49–62.

219 In 1918, Japan, with Allied approval, controlled Palau and the Marshall, Caroline and Marianas archipelagos, excepting Guam.

south-west Pacific, in over 150 different magazines, illustrated with his own photographs.

The phosphate industry

The phosphate from Nauru and Ocean Island was being shipped to the US, Australia, Japan, New Zealand and Europe for use as fertiliser to enhance pasture and farm productivity. The relative exports from Nauru and Ocean Island for 1920–1924 were 950,000 tons to Australia, 300,000 tons to Japan, 160,000 tons to New Zealand and 30,000 tons to Britain. The Nauru and Ocean Island operations were large-scale industrial enterprises overseen by the British Phosphate Commissioners, a joint British, Australian and New Zealand body that had replaced a former pre-war German–British consortium.

The extent of the industrial infrastructure was made obvious to readers by McMahon's choice of photographs of machinery, shipping, plants and rail networks bringing the phosphate rock from the diggings. McMahon did not publish many photographs of the pinnacles or broken landscape from which the phosphate was extracted by hand – only a few images highlighted that this was a manual labour-intensive industry relying on shovels and wheelbarrows and hand-pushed light rail trolleys. Viewers would have noticed the reliance on imported labourers from China and Japan. In Nauru, there had been a short-lived experiment to use indentured labour from New Guinea, but it was abandoned after two years due to health problems caused by an inappropriate diet.[220] On Nauru, the former German colony, Nauruans were employed along with imported Chinese labour.

---

220   Barrar, W. *op. cit.*, pp. 89–90. Barrar includes a photograph of a New Guinea labour gang c.1921, probably taken by CN Hayward. Despite initially asking for five hundred workers, the first New Guinea group in Nauru only consisted of forty-one men. See also Williams, M. and Macdonald, B. *The phosphateers*, 1985, pp. 162, 166–67.

According to McMahon, the secret behind these two successful mid-Pacific operations was the railway network. He published numerous photographs of lines, trains and wagons including several posed group portraits of expatriate staff and family, and of himself seated rather majestically on trolley cars poled along by labourers.[221] The phosphate industry in the Pacific, known earlier as the guano industry, is well documented historically. Guano or phosphate mining occurred on several islands where phosphate of lime from bird droppings had accumulated over millennia. Guano mining started on Caroline, Howland and Baker Islands in 1874,[222] and early in the twentieth century on Malden, Nauru, Ocean Island, Angaur in the north Pacific (1909–1955) and Maketea in French Polynesia (1917–1964).[223]

During phosphate mining on Angaur Island in the north Pacific, the historian David Hanlon noted that 'the construction of a railroad, drying plant, sawmill, loading dock, warehouses, thirty-two European residences and eleven workers' dormitories further blighted a landscape already ravaged by the open-pit technique used to extract phosphate'.[224] Three million tons of phosphate were mined on Angaur. Hanlon's description, mirrored in McMahon's imaging, could be applied equally to Angaur, Maketea, Nauru and Ocean Islands.

---

221 These were propelled by imported Asian labourers, or Nauruans and Banabans using poles.

222 The US claimed many islands as potential mining sites in the infamous Guano Acts of 1856. See Cushman, GT. *Guano and the Opening of the Pacific World: A Global Ecological History*, Cambridge, Cambridge University Press, 2013. Few of these islands and atolls were able to sustain long-term intensive mining.

223 For phosphate, see Binder, P. *Treasure Islands: The Trials of the Ocean Islanders*, London, Blond & Briggs, 1977; Quanchi, M. 'Life on Malden', *Pacific Islands Monthly*, May 1978, pp. 59–62; Teaiwa, K. *Consuming Ocean Island: Stories of People and Phosphate from Banaba*, Urbana, Indiana University Press, 2005; Cushman, GT. *Guano and the Opening of the Pacific World: A Global Ecological History*, Cambridge, Cambridge University Press, 2013.

224 Hanlon, D. *Remaking Micronesia: Discourses Over Development in a Pacific Territory, 1944–1982*, Honolulu, University of Hawaii Press, 1998.

The photographs

On the outward leg of the 'islands run', he visited Ocean Island first, and then Nauru on the return leg after visiting the Gilberts and Marshalls. The *Tambo* took on a full cargo of phosphate on Nauru on the return leg to Sydney. McMahon's photographs of the two phosphate islands depicted an extraordinarily complex extraction, processing and exporting infrastructure that had been developed to mine the phosphate of lime and potassium deposits.[225] Photographically, the trip was very profitable for McMahon and soon after he returned, *The Queenslander* ran a series of his photomontage feature pages and associated short commentaries. This series began in April 1919 with two features about Nauru with eleven photographs. This was followed by illustrated articles on Ocean Island, the Gilbert Islands and the Marshall Islands. The series ended in 1921 with two more features on the Gilberts and Ocean Island. *The Queenslander* series presented thirty-nine photographs to readers. McMahon also sold five illustrated features with thirty-six photographs to the *Auckland Weekly News*.

The investment in making the 'islands run' to the central Pacific had produced a sizeable financial return, and McMahon, no doubt with an element of conceit, felt confident in his path towards being acknowledged as a Pacific expert and patriot.[226] This firsthand experience also enabled him to deliver a lecture on

---

225   Buckley, K. and Klugman, K. *South Pacific Focus: Burns Philip's trading viewed through photographs early this century*, Sydney, Allen and Unwin, 1986; Buckley, K. and Klugman, K. *The history of Burns Philp; The Australian company in the South Pacific*, Sydney, Burns Philp, 1981; Williams, M. and Macdonald, B. *The Phosphateers*, Melbourne, Melbourne University Press, 1985.

226   Because of the absence of personal papers, we do not know how much McMahon was paid for publications, or his overall personal wealth and financial rewards from publishing. Editorial advertisements asking for contributions rarely indicated the fee. In his will, he declared he wanted all his papers destroyed except for some donated to a WWI Veteran's Museum in Melbourne and the RGS (Qld) in Brisbane.

post-war realignment in the Pacific, including the former German colonies, at the Lyceum Hall in Sydney, to a large and applauding audience. He argued that Britain should take over the former German colonies, including Nauru, declaring they would benefit if awarded to British enterprise.[227]

McMahon dramatically depicted the industrial infrastructure, environmental impact and reshaping of the landscape. Only a few photographs were repeated, such as a scene in the diggings with labourers filling wheelbarrows with rock, and a photograph of a cantilever jetty with a freighter offshore in deeper water. A third of his published photographs were industrial, depicting the fields, the railways, the crushing and drying plant and the loading and unloading jetty. Another third depicted the expatriate overseers, managers and officials of the phosphate company and the fine amenities they enjoyed – a billiard room, theatre, tennis courts, substantial houses and tree-lined streets. The remaining third were devoted to the customs and appearance of the indigenous Nauruan and Banaban inhabitants.

McMahon's boosting of the British presence in the Pacific and his photographs from the central Pacific trip are a valuable archive because they were taken over a short, defined period in a sequence, in a region that had mostly escaped outside notice, a region in a state of flux, unsure of changes to come in the post-war period. Historically, they also offer access to the variety and unevenness of Australian, British, German and Japanese colonial rule, and the arrival of movies, new clothing fashions, bicycles, steamships and trips to Japan. McMahon thought he might stand out by being one of the few to photographically record British enterprise in the phosphate industry, which he noted in articles in 1918 and 1919

227   Cited in Williams, M. and Macdonald, B. *The Phosphateers*, Melbourne, Melbourne University Press, 1985, p. 194. McMahon's portrait of King Oweida appears on p. 246. One McMahon publication from 1919 is listed in their bibliography.

was known in Australia only through the Cockle Creek works near Newcastle. His photographs are also important as an archive of the wider history of mining in the Pacific.[228]

After the 'islands run', he returned to Cairns in late 1918 and embarked on a busy schedule of sending photographs and accompanying text to newspapers and literary, scientific, commercial and other magazines domestically and abroad. McMahon's amazement at finding this industrial landscape on two tiny specks along the equator took precedence, although he did publish photographs of Islanders riding bicycles, frigate bird racing and wearing top hats. He also supplemented the focus on phosphate by including several excellent ethnographic studies of dance and costume, important today for Nauruans and Banabans searching for aspects of their early twentieth-century material culture and heritage. But the constant theme through his central Pacific publications was British pluck and enterprise, terms he repeated in nearly all articles. The phosphate industries of Nauru and Ocean Island were, he declared, 'a mighty British enterprise'.

The next two chapters separately present McMahon's photography of the phosphate industry on Ocean Island and Nauru.

---

228   As well as Angaur and Maketea, this field includes the history of West Papua's Freeport mine, Southern Highlands gas, New Caledonian nickel, Bougainville copper, magnesium mining in Vanuatu, Ok Tedi, the Misima, Sudest and Bulolo gold fields, Emperor gold mines in Fiji, ocean floor mining off New Guinea and others. See Denoon, D. 'Mining colonies', *The Cambridge History of the Pacific Islanders*, Cambridge, CUP, 1997, pp. 236–43; Sugihara, K. 'The economy since 1800', *Pacific Histories: Ocean, Land, People*, edited by David Armitage and Alison Bashford, London, Palgrave, 2014, pp. 166–190; Banks, G. 'Extractive industries in Melanesia' in *The Melanesian World*, edited by Eric Hirsch and Will Rollason, London, Routledge, 2019, pp. 501–16.

The phosphate islands (ii): Ocean Island (Banaba)

The first known sighting of Ocean Island (Banaba) by Europeans occurred in January 1804, but it was not until 1900 that high-grade phosphate was discovered in the coral-based rock of Ocean Island. A British company, the Pacific Phosphate Company, built railways, processing and shipping facilities between 1900 and 1919, when it was taken over by the governments of the United Kingdom, Australia and New Zealand. McMahon's visit occurred as this transfer was happening. Because of its export income-generating potential, Ocean Island had just been made the capital of the British Crown Colony of the Gilbert and Ellice Islands formed a few years earlier in 1916.[229] McMahon's political and economic agenda on Ocean Island was revealed by the photographs he took while the *Tambo* was loading and unloading passengers, mail and supplies. Despite some Islanders being heroes and deserving of Royal Life Saving Society medals, he concentrated not on Islanders and their lives, but on the presence of healthy, well-built workers. His camera did wander on Banaba

229   For Banaba, see Sigrah, Raobeia Ken and King, Stacey M. *Te Rii ni Banaba; Backbone of Banaba*, Runaway Bay, Qld, Banaban Vision Publications (2nd ed.), 2019; Binder, P. *Treasure Islands: The Trials of the Ocean Islanders*, London, Blond & Briggs, 1977; Teaiwa, K. *Consuming Ocean Island: Stories of People and Phosphate from Banaba*, Urbana, Indiana University Press, 2005. For photography, see Barrar, W, *Fields of vision; Photography, phosphate, and landscape from a Pacific History*, unpublished, Master of Design, Massey University 1995, pp. 25–34.

to costumed dance groups and chiefs, but his main interest as a freelance photographer and journalist was to depict European-led economic progress and examples of successful colonial and capitalist development.[230]

McMahon's visit to Ocean Island was the first of his two-part visit to the phosphate islands, and there is a noticeable difference between the images collected on Ocean Island on the outward leg and in Nauru on the return leg of the 'islands run'. Demonstrating his awareness of audience on Ocean Island, he stressed the Australian connection to a British Colonial possession and an industrial operation staffed mostly by Australians, with direct shipping to Australia.

McMahon's first article on Ocean Island appeared in the *Scientific Australian* in December 1918, not long after returning from the trip. In January 1919, a reworked story and twenty-five photographs in different combinations appeared in *The Sun* and *The Sydney Mail* in Sydney, *The Leader* in Melbourne, the *Daily Telegraph* in Brisbane and the *Illustrated London News* in London. The series of three articles in the *Daily Telegraph* was a typical McMahon foray, using the format of a full page or double spread of photographs with the text located elsewhere in the paper. Even without captions, those learning-by-looking would have been impressed with the enterprise, achievement and authority of European-led resource exploitation on this remote island. *The Sydney Mail* features linked the histories of Nauru and Ocean Island as an 'amazing story', and readers were informed visually that Ocean Island was a revelation.[231] In 1918, the two phosphate-

---

230   Parts of this chapter are based on an earlier publication: Quanchi, M. 'A trip through the islands in 1918; the photography of TJ McMahon', *Meanjin*, Vol. 53, No 4, 1994, pp. 714–22.

231   McMahon, TJ. 1919, 'The amazing story of Ocean and Nauru Islands', *The Sydney Mail*, 22.1.1919, p. 16.

rich islands were indeed booming in terms of industrial output, and the colonial administration was tailored to maximise, in McMahon's phrasing, 'a mighty British enterprise'.[232]

McMahon's photographs of Ocean Island also appeared regularly in the *Auckland Weekly News* and the *Otago Witness*, the respective weekend illustrated news review and magazines of Auckland and Dunedin. A full-page collage in the *Auckland Weekly News* was headlined, 'The phosphate of lime industry in the central Pacific'. The images highlighted the tramways and rail lines, Japanese workers, the diggings and cattle being kept for food. This was an acknowledgement of rural interest in the source of the fertiliser on which Australia and New Zealand relied.[233] The sub-title, 'Picturesque phases of life on Ocean Island', suggests that McMahon was aware New Zealanders were less interested in imperial and industrial accomplishments. Four more photographs were published in May 1922 in the *Auckland Weekly News*, including the Residency and tennis court, Uma village (misspelt as 'Ooma'), the wharves and the crushing plant.[234] The *Auckland Weekly News* had already published photomontages with forty-four photographs by McMahon on Ocean Island, Nauru, the Gilbert Islands and the Marshall Islands. Emphasising the level of interest in New Zealand, the *Otago Witness* also ran a full-page feature in July 1922 titled 'Ocean Island and our phosphate supplies'.[235]

---

232 McMahon, TJ. 1918, 'A mighty British enterprise: the phosphate and lime industries of Ocean Island and Nauru', *Scientific Australian*, December 1918, pp. 27–31.

233 CN Hayward, whose photographs were used by Albert Ellis in 1935, published photographs of phosphate mining in the *Auckland Weekly News* in the same period as McMahon: see Hayward, CN. 'Views of Nauru Island: the source of New Zealand's supplies of phosphate', *Auckland Weekly News*, 9.1.1919 with eight photographs.

234 *Auckland Weekly News*, 18.5.1922, p. 41.

235 Anon., 'Ocean Island and our phosphate supplies', *Otago Witness*, 18.7.1922 (with five photographs).

Industrial history

A much repeated photograph depicted a scene in the diggings with a group of Japanese indentured labourers with picks and shovels and using wheelbarrows to take alluvial rock to the rail network. A Japanese supervisor looks over the operations.[236] McMahon noted that Japan was a purchaser of Ocean Island phosphate and supplied a large portion of the labour force on Ocean Island. At the time of McMahon's visit, the labour force on Ocean Island was roughly four hundred Japanese and a thousand indentured Pacific Islanders from the Marshalls, Gilbert and Ellice Islands. There was a small police detachment of Fijians and about eighty European expatriates.

The emphasis on neat streets, railway lines, machinery, the crusher, huge mooring buoys and a line-up of labourers at the paymaster's office suggests that McMahon was aware of symbols and their impact on readers. Shipping magnates, Sydney investors, colonial officials, League of Nations Mandate Commissioners and Australian and New Zealand farmers would have probably felt secure with the evidence before them of a prosperous, well-governed, industrialised, colonial landscape. Anthropologists and museum curators might have longed for more details of the Banaban people and their allegedly disappearing maritime culture, but people in dentists' or doctors' waiting rooms or relaxing at home would have been nodding in agreement that Ocean Island was indeed a revelation.

McMahon published several photographs of Ocean Island's railways, said admiringly and surprisingly to extend to 160 kilometres. It was mostly light rail on which trolleys were hand-pushed to the main network where steam locomotives hauled the

---

236   *Dun's International Review*, June 1919, p. 1333; *Trans-Pacific Magazine*, Nov. 1920, p. 56; *Geografisk Tidskrift*, 1920, p. 224.

rock from the diggings to the crushing, drying and sorting plant. McMahon also published photography of himself on passenger trolleys being pushed along to visit the Deputy Commissioner's residence or to the transfer site where trolleys from the diggings were unloaded and the prepared rock sent by aerial cantilever to the jetty for exporting. One often-published photograph had four small children being pushed along by two Islanders. In this photograph, an extensive rail network with three rail lines can be seen running towards the large plant behind.

McMahon's published industrial photographs are historically important. More than half of the photographs he published depicted railway lines, diggings, processing plants, shipping and infrastructure related to phosphate mining. McMahon published very few depictions of the guano fields where phosphate was extracted as alluvial deposit or hard rock dug out from between the coral pinnacles, often six or more metres tall. Readers would not have been able to tell which were the worked-out fields, but the jagged, unworldly aspect of pinnacles and diggings would have been impressive. In two photographs, McMahon used a man standing in a worked-out field with two coconut palms on the horizon to offer perspective, adding in a caption that a dug-out field had a 'weird but very picturesque appearance'.[237]

A carefully framed empire

Images of the hospital, police band, billiard room and a social outing at the recreation ground on Ocean Island carried a message of normality, control and European-ness. Labourers are depicted everywhere – lining up for pay, working the railway skips, digging among the pinnacles, posing in front of huge machinery or in the streets outside their living quarters. These were not the generic

---

237   *The Sydney Mail,* 22.1.1919, p. 19.

'native' found widely in Pacific photography but workers. Women and Asian workers on Banaba were not included in his selective visual record of progress. McMahon's depiction of an industrial paradise, with modern plant, technology and amenities, a willing labour force and silent, quaint 'natives' was very explicit. Wayne Barrar's study of central Pacific phosphate photography noted that McMahon's 'self-generated ventures would have been seen favourably by the colonial community in Nauru and the Pacific generally ... enhancing trade awareness and support for further industrial development'. Barrar concluded that McMahon's imaging was 'not unlike today's corporate photography used to establish and confirm a company identity'.[238] McMahon would have rejected this description, seeing himself as not in advertising or marketing but as a geographer, a journalist and an expert commentator. His Ocean Island photographs of the phosphate industry certainly promoted the 'company' aspect of the operations, but McMahon also framed this in terms of colonial initiative and spirit and British- and Australian-led enterprise.

A portrait of an expatriate woman with a parasol travelling on a railcar propelled by a shirtless Banaban reveals how McMahon carefully framed his subject matter. In one composition using the same location, the woman sits on the railcar with a male companion, with a Banaban poling the car along the rails, with a second Banaban, dressed in *laplap* and shirt, sitting alongside. In the second image, the woman sits alone while the male companion stands aside leaning on a tree in the cutting through which the railcar is passing and the Banaban in *laplap* and shirt is now sitting five metres away to the side. The latter image was captioned 'How a lady travels on Ocean Island' and emphasised the privileged

---

238   Barrar, W. *Fields of vision; Photography, phosphate, and landscape from a Pacific History*, unpublished, Master of Design, Massey University, 1995, pp. 28, 34.

treatment of European women. The caption, 'Muscular boys ... give their passengers a thrilling ride', highlighted the servitude of indigenous workers and the racial superiority enjoyed by expatriates.[239]

A view of a neat streetscape lined on both sides by dwellings with corrugated iron roofing and water tanks was said to be 'the married men's quarters'. For a street said to be the 'single men's quarters', he noted that electric light was supplied.[240] Another repeated photograph was a scenic view from the ridge above the company manager's house showing his tennis court and overlooking Home Bay, the township, plant and wharves.[241] By 1920, this was a stock-in-trade image – the pocket of civilisation on a distant colonial frontier. Similar views could be found in albums, magazines and postcards from the French Cameroons, Portuguese Goa, German Samoa and Dutch West New Guinea. This stereotypical composition was not picturesque but served a practical and functional purpose by visualising a message of colonial order, stability, security for investment and comfortable expatriate surroundings.

McMahon also published three photographs in the curiosity category: one of a signboard in four languages and two of European children dwarfed by the residual coral pinnacles left behind after mining. His most used photograph from Ocean Island was of a costumed male Banaban dancer. This appeared from 1919 to 1922 in Sweden, America, Australia and London,

---

239   *The Sydney Mail*, 22.1.1919, p. 17; *Sunset: the Pacific Monthly*, Sept. 1919, p. 39. Nic Halter used this photograph by McMahon to emphasise the 'Victorian values' in depictions of women in the colonial Pacific: Halter, N. *Australian travellers in the South Seas*, Canberra: ANU Press, 2021, p. 142.

240   Both first appeared in *The Sydney Mail*, 22.1.1919, p. 18, then in *World's Work, The Quiver, Trans-Pacific* and *Geografisk Tidskrift*.

241   *The Sydney Mail*, 20.4.1921, p. 18, then in *Dun's Review, Trans-Pacific* and *Geografisk Tidskrift*.

in black-and-white and colourised versions, suggesting McMahon also knew his earning power as a photojournalist relied on the continuing fascination of international audiences with the 'other' or the 'native' in a south Pacific setting.

In McMahon's depiction of how colonialism brought order and authority to Island peoples, the 'native' police are shown carrying rifles with bayonets fixed, dressed in an attractive combination of *laplap* and tailored uniform shirt and, although bare-footed, wearing a leather belt with polished buckle. (Some images of the police squads on Nauru and Ocean Island, first published in April 1919 in *The Sydney Mail*, were later miscaptioned. The police on Nauru and Ocean Island and the medical orderlies in the Gilbert Islands in 1918 were wearing the same uniform, so a mistake by editors in Sydney or London is perhaps excusable.)[242] McMahon took no chance that learners-by-looking would mistake his message of colonial authority and hegemony, so he added a caption that informed readers that these were 'men of intelligence qualified to assume responsibility' and that they gained promotion and emoluments by attending night school and learning to read, write and speak English. A caption in *Peoples of All Nations* declared they were staunch supporters of British discipline and 'fine strapping men, possessing remarkable ability for acquiring the principles of European civilization'.[243] McMahon did not mention their policing roles, their varied geographic homelands, marital status or what their age or their absence from home meant to their ethnic ancestry, clan or village. Although we may look today for Islander agency and achievement within these images

---

242   For police detachments on parade, see *The Sydney Mail*, 9.4.1919, p. 8; *The Wide World*, June 1919, p. 54; *Pacific Ports*, Aug. 1919, p. 87; *Sunset: the Pacific Monthly*, Sept. 1919, p. 38; *Bulletin of the Pan-American Union*, Jun 1922, p. 604; *Australian Museum Magazine*, Jul 1922, p. 157; and the pictorial serial encyclopedia, *Peoples of All Nations*, 1923, p. 964.

243   *Peoples of All Nations*, op. cit., p. 964.

of the police detachments, for these staged scenes, McMahon was looking through the lens and saw only Empire. About half of his Ocean Island photographs were used only once, such as one of the huge buoys used for offshore anchorage, the police band playing in a rotunda, scenes of men wrestling and doing gymnastics and labourers lining up to be paid.

The Banabans

Banabans had arrived in several waves of migration and had occupied Banaba for perhaps 3000 years. By 1979, eighty per cent of the island's surface had been strip-mined and Banabans successfully took the British to court over royalties and the cost of rehabilitating the island. This story was told in the famous BBC television documentary, 'Go tell it to the judge' (1977).

A highlight of McMahon's imaging of the Banaban people was a line-up of male dancers performing the *te karanga Are E Uarereke*, or war club dance, shortened by McMahon to just *karanga*. This appeared in his first published article on Ocean Island in *The Sydney Mail*, and subsequently in *Sunset: the Pacific Monthly, Australian Museum Magazine, Illustrated London News* and *Geografisk Tidskrift* (the Danish Journal of Geography) and in the pictorial encyclopedias *Countries of the World, Lands and Peoples*, and *The New World of Today*. A colourised print appeared as a full-page plate in both *Countries of the World* and *Lands and Peoples* (see Fig. 14).[244] On Ocean Island, he also posed a portrait of a single male *karanga* dancer, two group portraits of men lined up to attention in full dance costume, and one of himself with the same group of dancers standing behind a group of expatriate officials.[245]

The most fascinating of McMahon's Ocean Island photographs

---

244 *Countries of the World*, Vol. 6, p. 3756; *Lands and Peoples*, Vol. 5, p. 306.
245 *World's Work*, June 1919, p. 56.

involved a technique that he used several times in other islands and territories. This involved lining up men or women, some wearing so-called traditional costume and some wearing modern Western or European clothes. On Ocean Island, he depicted a Banaban woman in a neck-to-ankle 'Mother Hubbard' cotton dress, standing beside a younger female in traditional (pre-European) dress with a grass skirt, shell necklaces and bare-breasted. The 'belles' of Banaba, captioned McMahon, 'crave modern styles ... elaborately adorn themselves'.[246] It was, according to McMahon, a depiction of how the islands of the Pacific had been 'civilised', a comment repeated in many of his feature articles. To emphasise this transition, in a second, more dramatic example, McMahon created a sequence of four men: the first in traditional indigenous style, the second in worker attire, the third in fancy shoes and garters and the fourth in high-fashion 'dude' style. McMahon suggested that these four, like the other Banabans, Gilbert Islanders and Ellice Islanders he met on Banaba, were great 'swells' and dressed ostentatiously for church or their day off. He noted that on Ocean Island, 'the men earn good wages and spend their money freely on clothes'. This sequence on the 'evolution of dress' appeared first in *The Sydney Mail* in 1919, and then three years later in the serial encyclopedia, *Peoples of All Nations*, in 1922.[247] He also noted that a full body covering, and the tendency for it to be worn either wet, dry or unclean, meant 'diseases and lung troubles have become prevalent', an opinion probably gathered from mining managers or administration officials.

The *Tambo* heroes

On the outward leg of the 'islands run' in 1918, the *SS Tambo*

---

246 This was the opening illustration (of seven) for 'A real Treasure Island', *Sunset: the Pacific Monthly*, Sept. 1919, p. 37.

247 *The Sydney Mail*, 8.1.1919, p. 15; *Peoples of All Nations*, 1922, p. 963.

was fully laden with passengers and cargo when the rudder malfunctioned halfway along its regular supply and mail run to the first port of call at Ocean Island. Three Tuvaluan and Marshallese men leapt overboard and, working day and night, re-rigged the rudder while the vessel drifted for several days in rough seas. The crew shot sharks with rifles from the deck while the men worked in blood-stained waters. The *Tambo* limped back to Brisbane, and after three weeks, the voyage resumed. Upon arrival at Ocean Island, the Resident Commissioner for the Gilbert and Ellice Islands Colony, EC Elliot, presented the three heroes with silver watches and promised to approach the Royal Life Saving Society for medals to be awarded. Thomas McMahon recorded this presentation ceremony by taking six photographs and publishing a short note, 'Recognition of bravery', with two supporting photographs in the Melbourne illustrated weekly newspaper, *The Leader*.[248] There is no record in Australia or London of any medals being requested or awarded.

At the presentation, he took several staged photographs of the police detachment; however, when publishing a photograph of the detachment, he cropped the image to remove the European officers at each end of the squad, leaving only the Islanders.[249] The photographs taken of the presentation include one of the three men standing awkwardly on the sports ground surrounded by several hundred Banabans and imported phosphate mine workers, a small group of European managers and their families and an armed detachment of eighteen police. In an unusual composition, McMahon positioned himself behind and overlooking the official desk and crowd, meaning the three heroes are lost in the mass

---

248   *Leader* (Melbourne), 11.1.1919, p. 30.

249   Compare *Sea Land and Air*, Feb. 1919, p. 658, and *Penny Pictorial Magazine*, 6.12.1919, p. 79. The *Penny Pictorial Magazine*, an English publication, ran from 1899 to 1922.

of bodies, officials and spectators.[250] The three men were not named by McMahon, merely referred to as 'three natives, two Ellice Island boys and one from the Marshall Islands'. Two other photographs, not staged, captured the scene around the Resident Commissioner's flag-draped presentation table with the three heroes dressed in a combination of *laplap*, collared shirts and trousers, braces, cufflinks and armbands. Other than the two photographs in his *The Leader* article, McMahon did not write about this incident again or use the presentation day photographs in any of the fourteen articles and fifty photographs he published about Ocean Island.

From real life

McMahon's photographs of Ocean Island had the same veracity and legitimacy as the text in a colonial handbook, a governor's annual report or the statistics in a company balance sheet. They were accepted by readers as pictures from so-called real life. To readers, they were re-presenting Banaba, not representations. For distant readers unlikely to have heard of Ocean Island, McMahon's photographs were a record of a new place and people and unexpected events. There is a temptation today to reinterpret these images of wharves, dredges, police parades and European outings as symbolic of a destructive civilising mission and oppressive hegemony, to interrogate images for ideologically driven discourses and to draw out subliminal messages (which neither McMahon nor his readers would have acknowledged). Simply put, McMahon's Ocean Island photographs are an artefact of three galleries: of McMahon's life journey, of

---

250   This photograph was only published once as a 'filler' in a page full of unrelated photographs in *The Telegraph*, (Brisbane), 23.10.1918, p. 16.

learning-by-looking about others by distant audiences, and of the history of European-controlled industrial resource exploitation.

As the *Tambo* headed further eastwards on its run along the equator, McMahon had to change focus, as ahead lay the Gilbert and Ellice Island Colony (GEIC) and the Marshall Islands archipelago, a long string of coral atolls inhabited by people living mostly unaffected by modern industrial developments (there was no phosphate mining) and administered as colonial territories by two quite different colonial rulers – one British and one Japanese.

On the return leg, the *Tambo* called at Nauru, the major phosphate island on the 'Islands' run.

The phosphate islands (iii): Nauru

The indigenous people of Nauru had settled on the island 3000 years previously. The population of the small raised coral island was of Micronesian ancestry and numbered fewer than a thousand. In 1798, the first European to visit Nauru had named it 'Pleasant Island'. It had been annexed by Germany in 1888 and included in a larger German protectorate governed from Jaliut in the Marshall Islands. Phosphate mining had commenced in 1906 with the establishment of the Pacific Phosphate Company, a German–British consortium, with the first exports in 1907. At the start of World War I, after capturing the German colony of Western Samoa, *HMAS Melbourne* had sailed to Nauru on 9 August 1914 and captured Nauru just ahead of the Japanese navy intending to land and claim it. Acknowledging this takeover, in October 1918, The *Sydney Mail* published photographs of Nauru by F Danvers Power, a metallurgist and geologist who had visited Nauru before the war. His feature included photographs of the central lagoon on 'topside', Nauruans with 'noddy' birds and lighting a fire, German officials bathing and the German official residence.[251] McMahon arrived later in Nauru in 1918,

---

251   Power, FD. 'Naru: Another of Germany's lost Pacific colonies', *The Sydney Mail*, 7.10.1914, pp. 27, 37. (Nauru was misspelt in the title). Power was a lecturer at Sydney University and a keen photographer. His feature did not include photographs of the phosphate industry.

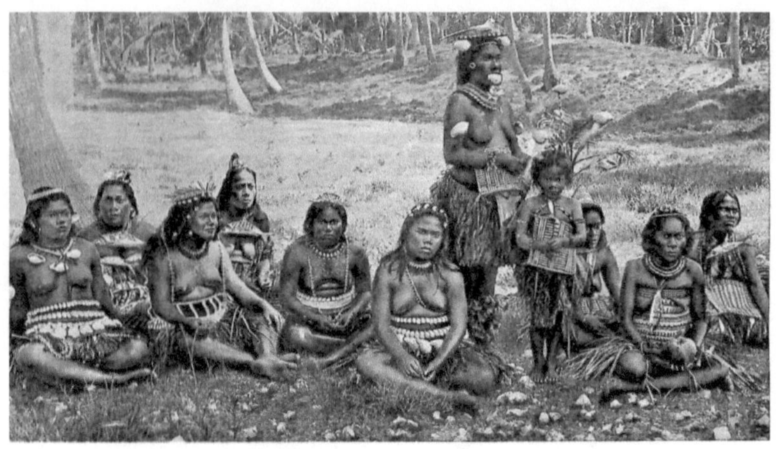

Fig. 17 'Remarkable flower, fish and shell paraphernalia
of the ballerina of Nauru Island', 1922

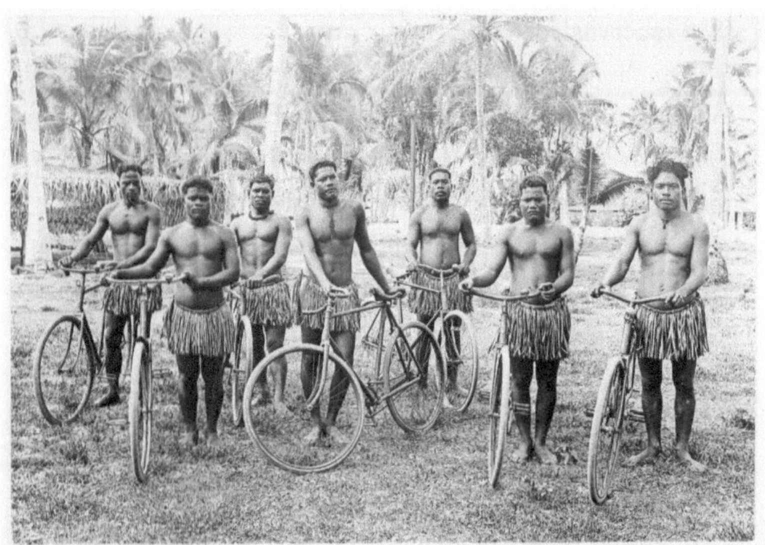

Fig. 18 'No Nauru man or boy will walk
if he can get an American bicycle', 1919

on the return leg of the 'islands run' along the equator on Burns Philp's ship, Tambo. At the time of McMahon's visit, the former German colony was under an Australian military occupation and was about to become a jointly administered League of Nations mandate under Britain, Australia and New Zealand, with mining operations under a new consortium of Britain, Australia and New Zealand interests – the British Phosphate Commission.[252]

McMahon's first publication on Nauru, in the *Scientific Australian* in December 1918, was wholly devoted to the phosphate industry with photographs of the cantilever jetty, the guano fields, the railway, European staff housing and an expatriate family posing at the base of six-metre pinnacles in a worked-out area of the diggings. In January to April of 1919, his series on Nauru in *The Sydney Mail* and *The Telegraph* in Brisbane retained the overall emphasis on phosphate operations but added portraits of King Oweida of Nauru, twice, along with frigate birds and group portraits of female dancers. McMahon's photographs of Nauru then appeared widely in *Sea Land Air, Pacific Ports, Illustrated London News, The Wide World, Scientific Australian, Dun's Review, Stead's Review, Penny Pictorial, Sunset: the Pacific Monthly, The Mid-Pacific* and the *Bulletin of the Pan-American Union*, and in New Zealand in the *Auckland Weekly News* and *Otago Witness*. From 1923 to 1929, they appeared in the serialised pictorial encyclopedias *Peoples of All Nations, The New World of Today, Countries of the World* and *Lands and People*. In this impressive output, fifty-seven of McMahon's photographs of Nauru were used on ninety occasions, some being repeated in four to five different publications. In a noticeable change of focus, McMahon placed more emphasis on indigenous people and customs compared

---

252   This story is told in Albert Ellis, *Ocean Island and Nauru; Their Story*, Sydney, Angus and Robertson, 1935; Williams, Maslyn and Macdonald, Barrie. *The Phosphateers*, Melbourne, Melbourne University Press, 1985. Ellis used three photographs attributed to McMahon and listed four of McMahon's publications in his bibliography.

to his earlier published photography of Papua, German New Guinea and the Solomon Islands. McMahon noted that in Nauru, the workers were either Chinese or local Nauruans, compared to Ocean Island where the workforce was imported Japanese, Gilbertese and Ellice Islanders.

His *The Sydney Mail* series contained eight full-page and double-page photomontages with accompanying text and covered Nauru and Ocean Island as well as the fate of post-war German colonies, the Marshall Islands, and broader issues such as the rise of Japan as a trading nation and competitor. The banner headlines alerted readers to the accompanying photographs of the phosphate industry and post-war changes.

Date	Number of photos	Article title
1.1.1919	10	The Marshall Islands: Wonderful work by the Japanese
8.1.1919	6	Among the natives of the Pacific (i)
15.1.1919	6	Among the natives of the Pacific (ii)
22.1.1919	16	The great phosphate industry of the Central Pacific
5.2.1919	6	Among the natives of the Pacific (iii)
12.3.1919	4	How Japan is winning the trade of the islands
26.3.1919	2	Treasure Island of Nauru: Who is to control it?
9.4.1919	7	A new chapter in Nauru

Table 1: *The Sydney Mail* series on McMahon's central Pacific trip

This was an impressive display of McMahon's photography, and in the case of Nauru, very topical, as the fate of Nauru after the war was then being discussed in Europe, and Australian farmers and pastoralists were reaping the benefits from the use of Nauru's phosphate fertiliser.

The Naurans

The aspect of Nauruan life most photographed by McMahon was a female custom, captioned a 'fish dance', one he sometimes humorously labelled the 'Royal Ballet'. The photographs were not of the dancing but posed and static, with a focus primarily on the costumes and decoration. Each woman was adorned with numerous, 20-cm-long fish attached to their costume or body. McMahon published photographs of these elaborately costumed females, starting in *The Sydney Mail* in early 1919, then in *Sunset: the Pacific Monthly*, *Pacific Ports* and the *Illustrated London News*. Two also were used by Basil Thompson in the serial encyclopedia, *Peoples of All Nations*. The taking of the photographs appears to have been arranged especially for McMahon as the background is not near a village and not as part of a ceremony but in a secluded forest grove. The group portraits have three, four or five women in costume and adorned with fish, and some are in larger groups of up to nineteen women. Several present the women sitting down, and some are posed with either King Oweida or McMahon in the centre of the group, while in other framings, they stand frozen looking at the photographer. McMahon assumed that Australian readers would be fascinated by the unusual practice of dancers being adorned with small fish. McMahon noted in captions that Nauruan women danced beautifully and afterwards all feasted on the fish.

This genre of exotic imaging of indigenous peoples, known

today as 'othering', was common in early twentieth-century publications on the Pacific. For example, in 1908, mostly bare-breasted women of Polynesia, Melanesia and Micronesia featured in the pictorial encyclopedia *Women of All Nations*, despite its academic pretensions of being authored by scholars and edited by two fellows of the Royal Anthropological Institute in London. *Women of All Nations* came out in a single volume, and later in a two-volume edition, with three hundred and fifty photographs and thirteen colour paintings by Norman H Hardy.[253] Some of McMahon's photography of clothing and costume for dance followed this style of female portraiture, but he never noted having seen or read *Women of All Nations*.

McMahon's photographs were mostly *in situ*, carefully arranged but giving the impression of being *à la flaneur*. He published nine scenes of women's dancing, three on the keeping of frigate birds, five of King Oweida with his servants and numerous portraits of Nauruan footballers, cyclists, gymnasts, policemen and watermelon sellers. Over half the photographs he took on Nauru were of Nauruan culture and Nauruan adaptation or adoption of non-indigenous ideas and habits. For example, seven Nauruans were photographed in coconut or fibre *ridis* (loincloths), then regrouped and photographed as cyclists. Dancers were rearranged for small or large group portraits, with and without King Oweida. Emphasising McMahon's attention to readers' interest in the so-called kings, queens and chiefs of other lands and peoples, King Oweida is shown in portraits wearing or holding his top hat and being waited upon by a policeman or a manservant. Oweida's clothing varied from a top hat and dress suit with a white cane to a planter's suit and felt hat.

---

253   Joyce, T. and Thomas, N W, eds, *Women of All Nations: A record of their characteristics, habits, manners, custom and influence*, London, Cassell and Company, 1908. In the second, two-volume edition, two photographs of Nauruan women were included. There were numerous editions published in England and the US up to 1923.

The Nauruans in the police are shown in full regimental dress on parade with rifles and then re-posed in sports clothing. In a typical full-page photomontage with seven photographs in *Pacific Ports*, McMahon offered readers four views of Nauruan life and customs (including a costumed female dance group and frigate bird catching), two of bicycle riding, Chinese labourers and a police detachment but only three of the diggings.[254] The roughly 4:3 ratio between ethnographic and industrial photography continued throughout his published Nauru photographs.

In a double-page montage with eight large photographs in the *Auckland Weekly News* in March 1919, McMahon noted the 'Peace conference has decided to place Nauru under the control of Britain, New Zealand and Australia'. This feature included standard shots of King Oweida, a railway crossing signpost in four languages, football players, dancing girls ('the handsomest of the South Pacific Islanders') and sewing machines and bicycles, both easily recognised symbols of modernisation in 1920. He claimed that 'every woman wants a sewing machine'.[255] As New Zealand had a direct interest in Nauru as it was its major source of fertiliser, illustrated weekend newspapers in New Zealand often included coverage of Nauru. For example, a month after McMahon's article appeared, a photomontage of ten photographs was published in the *Auckland Weekly News* noting the images were of 'Nauru in the central Pacific from whence New Zealand receives its chief supplies of phosphate'.[256] In the *Otago Witness*

---

254   McMahon, TJ. 'A bit of Pacific romance unfolded on Nauru (Pleasant Island)', *Pacific Ports*, Aug. 1919, p. 85.

255   McMahon, TJ. 'Formerly under German Rule', *Auckland Weekly News*, 10.4.1919, pp. 32–33.

256   Hayward, CN. 'Scenes from Nauru', *Auckland Weekly News*, 23.5.1922, p. 41. Hayward had previously published 'Views of Nauru Island' with eight photographs, ibid., 17.2.1921, p. 37. Later, four more photographs of Nauru were published by AA Hintz, ibid., 28.5.1925, p. 44.

in July 1920, fourteen photographs of Nauru were published primarily of mining.[257]

Photographs: single-use and repetition

McMahon repeatedly published several of his Nauru photographs, such as two photographs of labourers loading rock on railway trucks in the phosphate diggings and one of a line-up of smartly dressed and uniformed indigenous police, a favourite composition of McMahon's in Papua and New Guinea. As the line-up in a colonial context was a commonly published composition, readers could sense the authority and discipline that Europeans had brought to these colonial enclaves and outposts. Another much republished image was of Nauru's King Oweida, ambivalently presented as a 'native' but in a dress suit with a cane and top hat and bicycle. McMahon clearly wanted to show readers that civilisation involved the adoption of Western dress codes, but there is also an acknowledgement of the indigenous leader's power, status and prestige and the hierarchical social order affecting Nauruans. It is also likely that readers ridiculed Oweida and laughed at 'natives' who foolishly copied European ways. Like all photographs, the meaning here was not singular, and audiences could take away their own conclusions.

The popularity of bicycles, at the time a craze in Australia, was noticed by McMahon on Nauru, and he took photographs of King Oweida, a group of men with bicycles and a Nauruan wheeling home a bicycle laden with palm leaf to be used for roof thatching. Australian viewers would have been fascinated that, far away on the equator, cycling was a keen interest. McMahon noted in a caption that 'No Nauruan man or boy will walk if he can get an

---

257   Rowley, H. 'Views of Nauru', *Otago Witness*, 20.7.1920, pp. 33–4.

American bicycle ... practically every islander owns a bicycle'.[258] Frigate bird catching, an ancient Nauruan craft, also captured McMahon's attention, and he photographed the birds and their elaborate roosts, calling the birds 'man-of-war hawks'. After being caught, they were trained to fly out to sea to attract other birds or to help in identifying shoals of passing fish.[259] He declared it was the national sport.

The photographs that McMahon repeated reveal how his priorities changed when he returned to Australia and began selecting images for publication. Without his notes or diaries, it is now mostly guesswork as to why McMahon repeatedly chose to publish the same three or four photographs or how he decided on the balance between publishing ethnographic and industrial images. The repeated use of a particular image suggests McMahon was aware of the multifaceted powers of photographic imaging (representation), recording details (documentary, re-presentation) and propaganda (the boosting of commerce and Australian capital and investment). On Ocean Island, the first port of call on Burns Philps' 'islands run', he concentrated on industrial activity and the European staff and seems to have had little interest in Banaban culture. The choice to focus more on people and customs and less on the expatriate community during his visit to Nauru on the way home a month later may have been because he had just been immersed among indigenous peoples in the Gilberts and Marshall Islands and had enjoyed the time spent photographing people and customs. It was also a longer stay on Nauru while the phosphate for Sydney was loaded. In Nauru, his photographs suggest he had

---

258   *Sea Land Air*, Feb. 1919, p. 658; *The Wide World*, 1921, p. 244; *Pacific Ports*, Aug. 1919, p. 85; and the serial encyclopedia, *The New World of Today*, Vol. 8, 1922, p. 212.

259   *The Sydney Mail*, 9.4.1919, p. 8, then in *Pacific Ports*, *The Wide World*, *Sunset: the Pacific Monthly*, *The Telegraph* (Brisbane) and two photographs reproduced in Albert Ellis in *Ocean Island and Nauru* (pp. 32, 85.)

begun to appreciate more the people and cultures of the Islands, and he retained this emphasis and restricted his boosting of British enterprise to expatriate managers, industrial activity, billiard rooms, tennis courts, railways and streets illuminated by electricity.

Two sites, changing emphasis

Although Nauru and Ocean Island had similar railway lines, wharves, worker's quarters, offices and clubs, on Nauru McMahon took fewer European portraits and scenes involving expatriate officials and families and fewer of the industrial landscape. The motivation for McMahon's decision to publish more industrial photography of Ocean Island and more ethnographic photography of Nauru is partially explained by Ocean Island being the first of the phosphate islands he visited and by the shorter time available there to wander about among the Banaban people due to a day taken by an award ceremony. The access provided by the different administrations – Australian military in Nauru, British colonial officials on Ocean Island – may also have affected McMahon's choice of subject. Nauru was under military occupation replacing the former German rule, whereas Ocean Island was a British Crown Colony possession and capital of the recently formed GEIC. For example, in Nauru, McMahon took only six formal and casual portraits of officials, while on Ocean Island he took many more, including one of the Administrator, an Australian, in a classic, colonial composition sitting relaxed in a chair surrounded by twenty 'loyal' Islander servants and staff. The greeting by European residents, mostly Australian, on Ocean Island was probably warm and friendly, due to the day given over to welcome the *Tambo* heroes who had dived overboard to repair the ship's rudder.

The *Tambo*'s visit to Nauru was slightly longer, and this

allowed McMahon to take twice as many photographs compared to Ocean Island, and to take opportune non-industrial shots of dances, Nauruans playing sport, costumes, bicycle riding and police parades. It was also significant that resource exploitation on Ocean Island had been a totally British enterprise. As the number of photographs that could be published in one feature was limited, the answer on image selection lies somewhere in McMahon's perception that photographs, in the reductionist and stereotypical fashion (discussed in ch. 2), had to capture for readers, in one or two images, the spirit, environment and atmosphere of a place.

The next chapter returns to the latter part of his 'islands run' on the *Tambo* through the atolls of the Gilbert and Marshall Islands.

Chapter 8

The atoll lands: Gilbert and Marshall Islands

After the excitement of observing and photographing an industrial complex on Ocean Island, McMahon must have felt transported back in time when he landed in the Gilberts in late 1918. He found a colonial backwater with narrow strips of flat land extending to the horizon, with ocean on one side and a lagoon on the other but no industries to extol or claim Australian dominance. This was a new experience for McMahon as he had so far only visited the heavily populated, densely forested, mountainous islands of the western Pacific or Melanesia. Now in the atolls, he found himself in a territory where there were no port towns with wharves and colonnaded buildings, no mountain villages and no sweeping vistas of copra, rubber, sisal or cotton plantations. Micronesians were also culturally distinct from the Melanesians whom McMahon had been photographing for the previous four years. Micronesians had adapted, adopted, borrowed and rejected Western influences during a century of European contact, and in the case of the Marshall Islands, were under a form of colonial administration – by Japan – that McMahon had not previously encountered.

The natives always salute as they pass

The Gilbertese (now known as I-Kiribati) came from Asia to

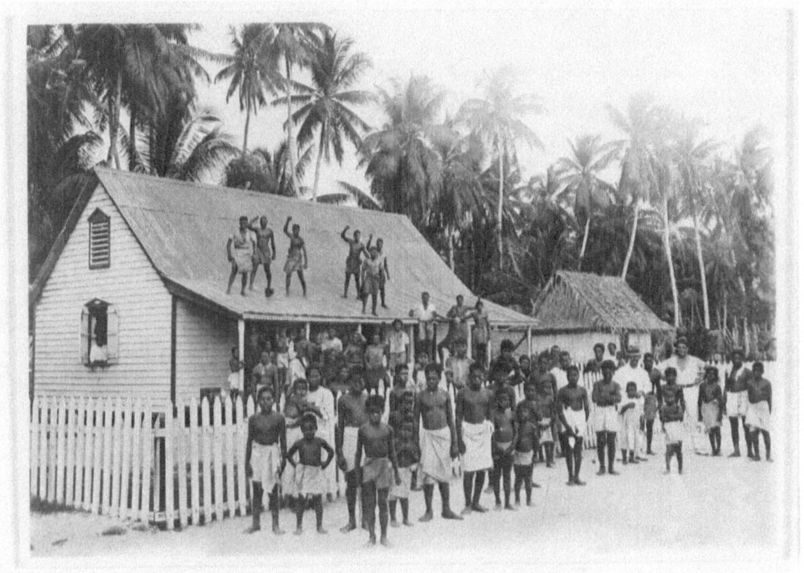

Fig. 19 'A British trader's store;
In Little Makin, one of the Gilbert Islands', 1920

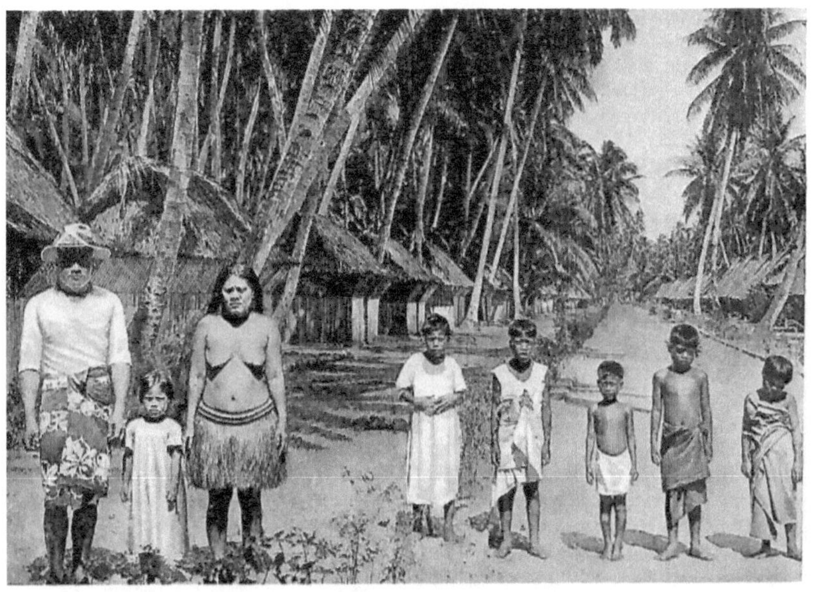

Fig. 20 'At home with the children on tropical Tarawa', 1923

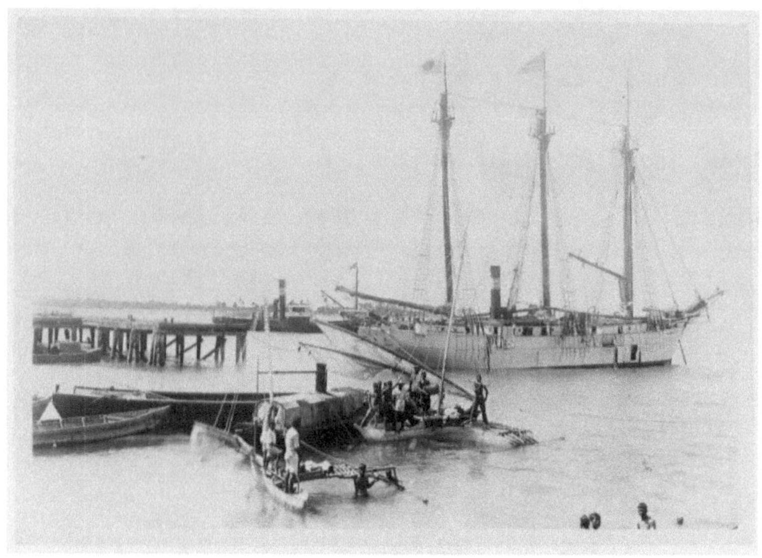

Fig. 21 'Japanese trading vessels, Jaluit harbor', 1919

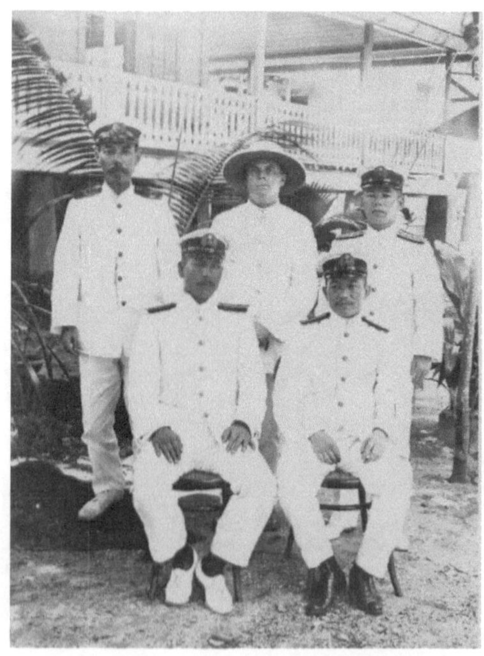

Fig. 22 McMahon, back row, middle, with Japanese naval officers, Marshall Islands

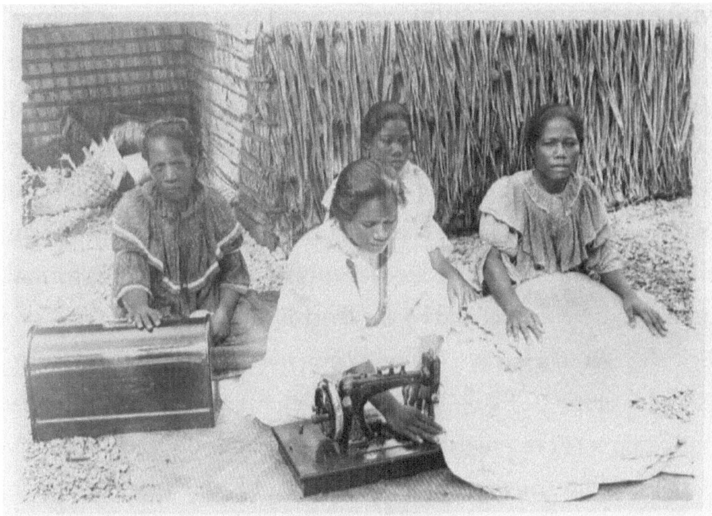

Fig. 23 Marshall Islands women with sewing machines from Japan

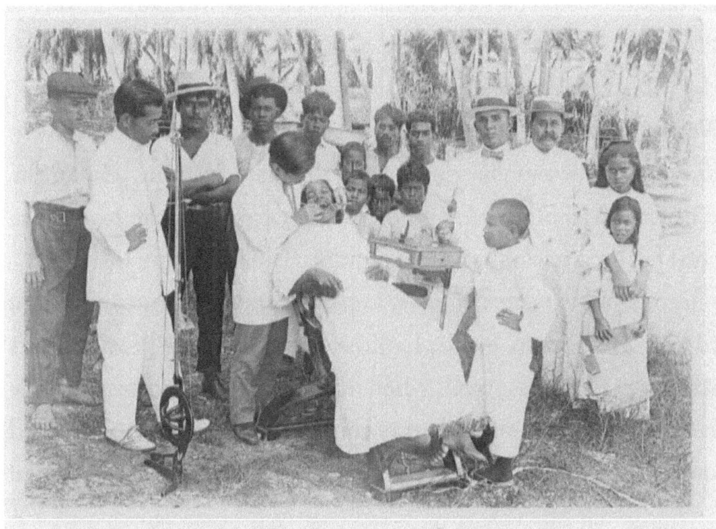

Fig. 24 Japanese travelling dentists at work in the Marshalls

Micronesia 4000 to 5000 years ago. The atolls were sighted first by Europeans in 1606 during a Spanish expedition and then surveyed 250 years later in 1841 during the famed USXX expedition (the United States Exploring Expedition). In 1886, an Anglo–German agreement partitioned the central Pacific, with Nauru and the Marshall Islands going to Germany, and Ocean Island, the Gilberts and Ellice Islands to the British.[260] A formal protectorate was declared by the British in 1892, and in 1916 the British created a Crown Colony known as the Gilbert and Ellice Island Colony (GEIC). The Gilbert chain of sixteen atolls was one component of a myriad of atolls and islands merged into a new British colony, including the Gilbert and Ellice Islands, Ocean Island, the Line Islands, Phoenix Islands and the Tokelau Islands. McMahon visited three years after this merger.

Many well-known trading companies were based in Makin and Butaritari atolls such as On Chong, Randall and Durant, Burns Philp, the German WPHG (*Handels-und Plantagen-Gesellschaft der Südsee-Inseln zu Hamburg*), the Japanese trading company *Nanyo Boeki Kabushiki Kaisha* and WR Carpenters. Makin and then later Butaritari had been the major trading port in the Gilberts. Although McMahon did not focus on the stores, the staff or the interiors as he had done on Samarai Island in 1915, his photographs of the environs, streetscapes and people are important historically. Burns Philps had recently moved its headquarters south to Tarawa Atoll when it became the administrative headquarters and major port of the protectorate, until the capital moved a second time to Ocean Island in 1908. McMahon noted

---

260   The German presence in the Pacific was substantial with colonies or protectorates in German New Guinea, Western Samoa and Nauru in the south Pacific and the Marshall, Caroline and Marianas Islands in the north Pacific. During McMahon's visit in 1918, their reassignment to other colonial powers was being considered and they were subsequently given as mandates by the League of Nations to Britain, New Zealand, Australia and Japan.

that trade was shifting to Japan and suggested that although considered commercially unimportant by Australia, the Gilberts would soon come 'into general prominence'.[261]

His photographs of the Gilberts first appeared during 1919–1920 in *The Telegraph* (Brisbane), *Sunday Times* (Sydney), *The Sydney Mail* and *The Australian Photo-Review*. A few photographs appeared later in serial encyclopedias and in *The Quiver*, in his article on the 'South Seas myth'. In 1923, he used eight photographs for his booklet/album on the Gilbert and Ellice Islands in the McCarron series.[262] After the excitement of boosting Australian economic and Imperial opportunities in the bustling phosphate industry, the Gilbert Islands must have seemed lacking in photo opportunities, and this lack of patriotic composition explains the attention McMahon now gave to indigenous life, people and customs, and picturesque and panorama views of villages.

In short visits to Tarawa, Little Makin and Butaritari, McMahon had less time and less official assistance in arranging posed groups, performances and police parades, and there was a much smaller European population of government officials and missionaries. McMahon found it a difficult landscape to photograph. The flat, narrow atolls were a new experience for McMahon and for readers back in Australia. The Gilbert Islands' coral atolls were barely above the high-water mark, stretching as an archipelago roughly in a north–south line. The origins of coral atolls, as the tops of submerged mountains visible only because of the coral reefs that encircled the former peaks, had only just been investigated by an Australian, Professor Edgeworth David

---

261 McMahon, TJ. 'The Gilberts Islands', *Chamber's Journal*, 14.2.1920, pp. 161–63. There were no photographs.

262 The cover of *Pacific Islands Illustrated; Gilbert and Ellice* (Sydney, McCarron, 1923) was mistakenly of a Papuan warrior.

in 1897, following the early theorising of Charles Darwin.[263] The six southern atolls had been occupied by Polynesians and the ten northern atolls by Micronesians. The population was 30,000. There was a copra industry, and while some Gilbertese had previously signed on as indentured labour to Peruvian guano mines and Fiji's plantations, most people lived a traditional lifestyle, moderated to some extent by Christian missions. McMahon had to comply with the route taken by the *Tambo*. Although he was only able to visit Tarawa Atoll in the central Gilberts and the two northern atolls of Butaritari and Little Makin, McMahon's thirty-one published photographs of the Gilberts are a significant historical record.

The visual impact in his article in *World's Work* in 1920 was dramatic, and many readers may have skipped the text and perused only the thirteen images, laid out in a double-page opening devoted fully to photographs.[264] He had adopted a new compositional approach, positioning his tripod in the middle of a roadway, with Islanders spread randomly across the foreground stiffly posing but not specifically positioned. This composition had the dual effect of being a group portrait and a panorama of a village. This gave readers a visual sense of looking down at a street and seeing life played out in Little Makin, Butaritari or Tarawa. Five of the illustrations in his article, 'The gateway of the Pacific', in *World's Work* offered readers this type of streetscape. His pro-British rhetoric was most prominent in *World's Work*. Without the compelling industrial motivation found on Nauru and Banaba

---

263 Edgeworth David's exploratory drilling took place on Funafuti Atoll in the Ellice islands. As well as scientific papers, his wife published an account of the expedition: David, Mrs Edgeworth, *Funafuti, or Three Months on a Coral Island; an Unscientific Account of a Scientific Expedition*, London, John Murray, 1899.

264 McMahon, TJ. 'The gateway of the Pacific: The wonders of British administration in the Gilbert Islands,' *The World's Work*, 1920, Vol. 39, pp. 144–151. *The World's Work* (1900–1932) was a monthly American business and national affairs magazine.

and finding little of interest in his role as a watchdog of unsecured colonies and potential British advancement, McMahon's photographs of the Gilberts presented to viewers a quiet and secure British enclave with an emphasis on indigenous colonial subjects benefiting from a sympathetic colonial administration.

As he had already published at length about copra's potential in illustrated articles on Papua, New Guinea and the Solomon Islands, perhaps this explains why copra never attracted his attention in the Gilberts. His photographs of the Gilberts have a distinct *à la flaneur* feel, and readers would have felt they were being taken on a tour. The Gilbertese stand rigidly at attention for the camera, but readers might have concluded that McMahon just looked for opportunist scenes and said, 'Oh, I'd better get a shot here!' He took five photographs of government buildings and officials, four village scenes, a trader's store on Little Makin and three photographs of Butaritari. An obscure building on Butaritari, for example, only took on meaning for the audience when a caption informed readers it was formerly the house where famed author Robert Louis Stevenson had lived for five days in 1889. He noted in captions that there was a street named after Stevenson and that Stevenson's horse had survived.[265] He declared Butaritari to be one of the 'prettiest villages of the Gilberts', but readers were not told he had seen only three villages from among a hundred or more scattered across sixteen atolls.

McMahon informed readers that the British were undertaking a remarkable colonial experiment in administration and self-government that promoted indigenous involvement by appointing Gilbertese as magistrates, in the civil service and the police.[266] McMahon's depiction of the Gilberts is therefore a documentary

---

265 As horses have a longevity of thirty years and Stevenson's house had been pulled down long before McMahon's visit, both stories were misleading.

266 McMahon, TJ. 'The central Pacific', *Australasian Photo-Review*, 15.3.1919, p. 212.

record of 'native' doctors, councillors, magistrates, police and clerks. A portrait of three magistrates sitting formally on chairs with their hands resting on their knees, surrounded by twenty policemen was proof, McMahon suggested, of the 'successful native self-government in the Gilbert Islands'.[267] In an important photograph in terms of archival evidence, he also photographed a *maneaba*, a huge open-sided building used as a government forum or meeting place on Tarawa. As *maneaba* are still constructed in Kiribati today, photographs like these are historically valuable as a guide to earlier practices and architecture. McMahon noted that the *maneaba* contained a picture of King George of England and that people always saluted as they passed by.

This travelogue-type narrative was repeated in *Chamber's Journal* in 1920 with McMahon adding that neatness and well-looked-after roads, houses and stores were features of the head station or administrative centre. He declared the GEIC was a 'triumph of British administration'. Readers probably did not notice that McMahon's opinion was being expressed only three years after the Crown Colony had been proclaimed.[268]

Two photographs best illustrate McMahon's reporting on the Gilberts. In one composition, he arranged for a family of eight to stand stiffly in a line across a road in Tarawa, but his captions do not refer to their individual names (see Fig. 20). Instead, it became a propaganda image for a text that praised British colonial rule for imposing cleanliness and order on villages, using fines and punishments and only partially acknowledging that Gilbertese had in place customs for keeping homes and surrounds swept and tidy well before the British arrived. The version of this photograph

---

267 This photograph sat beside a portrait of the Resident Commissioner and his wife and a classic-style composition of a Gilbertese man and woman in traditional attire, *The World's Work*, Vol. 39, 1920, p. 145.

268 McMahon, TJ. 'The Gilbert Islands', *Chamber's Journal*, 14.2.1920, pp. 161–63.

published in the pictorial encyclopedia, *Countries of the World*, in 1922, was not cropped as it had been in *The Telegraph* in 1919, and the later readers were able to see a small crowd gathered on the side of the road watching McMahon's staging of the family portrait.[269] The straight lines of the roadway lined by houses and a kerbside stretching into the distance with overarching palms framed a vista that demonstrated McMahon's appreciation of aesthetics, art and photography. In a second photograph in the same location, McMahon relied on a conventional portrait format, with two figures standing to attention, dressed especially to demonstrate their indigenous customs, or 'native' way of life. The setting was like that of studio poses, only taken outdoors, divorced from the dance, performance or ceremony for which the dressing up usually occurred. Staged and posed portraits had been used widely by photographers across Africa and Asia and became known as depicting 'types' with a caption stating they were, for example, Zulu types, Borneo types or Papuan types;[270] McMahon did not use this terminology. The man is wearing a unique Gilbertese woven suit of armour, made of coconut fibre, and the woman is wearing a woven pandanus mat worn as a dress and adorned with shell and fibre necklaces. McMahon declared the upper body armour was 'bulletproof' and that the pandanus leaf mats were 'remarkable for their scant simplicity' and were worn for everyday use. This phrasing was McMahon's but may have been edited when it appeared as a full gravure plate in an entry by Basil Thompson in the pictorial encyclopedia, *Peoples of All Nations*.[271]

His New Zealand publications also comprise a small but

---

269   This appeared twice, in *The Telegraph* (Brisbane), 3.2.1919, p. 13 and *Countries of the World*, 1922, Vol. 6, p. 3787.

270   For example, see Quanchi, M. 2013, 'Kanaka portraits; the photographic record of indentured labour in colonial Australia', *Pacific Arts*, Vol. 13, no. 2, 2014, pp. 33–44.

271   This image was published twice, in *The World's Work*, Vol. 39, 1920, p. 145 and *Peoples of All Nations*, 1922, Vol. 2, p. 965.

historically valuable record on the GEIC in 1918 and allow us today to see how New Zealand audiences at the time were learning-by-looking at distant places through the agency of photography. For example, a double-page collage in 1919 in the *Auckland Weekly News* included the same twelve photographs that appeared fifteen months later in the *Otago Witness* under the headline, 'Quaint life and scenes in the Gilbert Islands'.[272] These photographs have an ethnographic feel, not in the sense of capturing types, material culture or artefacts in a zone of cross-cultural entanglement, but in the Edwardian sense of capturing what a twentieth-century 'native' would look like under sound, British colonial administration.[273]

In 'The central Pacific', an article in the *Australasian Photo-Review* in February 1920, McMahon wrote briefly about photographers and equipment and included a product endorsement for Kodak's Anti-Therm plates and acid-fixing salts. He noted seeing the albums of several Chinese traders in the Gilberts, 'all keen photographers', and declared that all Japanese and Chinese traders in the Gilberts and Marshalls had a camera.

After a short mail and freight stopover in the Gilberts, the *Tambo* then steamed north into the Marshall Islands where Jaliut, the major port in the Marshalls, was the turnaround point for the *Tambo*'s run 'along the equator'.

The Marshall Islands

The Marshallese, after migrating from Asia, had occupied the atolls for 2000 years. They were claimed by Spain, after several expeditions passed through in the sixteenth century, before being

---

272   The *Auckland Weekly News*, 10.4.1919, pp. 32–33; *Otago Witness*, 15.7.1920, pp. 32–33.

273   Eight of McMahon's published photographs of the Gilberts (mistakenly attributed to Maslyn Williams) are held by the Mitchell Library, State Library of NSW: Maslyn Williams, Gilbert Islands photographs, c. 1919–1970.

passed to German control from 1884 to 1914. The archipelago of 1156 islands and islets was under Japanese military administration in 1918 when McMahon visited, a prize awarded for their role in the Allied struggle against Germany. McMahon had already engaged in several polemical outbursts about the post-war fate of former German colonies in the Pacific, and now he confronted a strong Japanese presence, one he called a process of 'Japanning the Islands'. For a patriot like McMahon, confronting firsthand the developments and policies Japan was setting in place in its new island empire, created a dilemma. Why, he asked readers, was this development, efficiency and good colonial administration not a characteristic of Australian colonial rule?[274] The Marshalls were a great surprise to McMahon, as they probably were to audiences who saw his eighty photographs and eighteen articles published from 1919 to 1924. He visited Namorik Atoll as the *Tambo* headed towards Jaliut Atoll, the major port in the Marshalls, and made short visits to neighbouring Majuro and Arno Atolls, and north to Likiep Atoll.[275]

McMahon focused on the people and their culture far more than he had in Nauru, Ocean Island and the Gilberts. Two-thirds of the published images from this trip were portraits or tableaux depicting traditional and modern costumes, family or fishing groups, dancing, canoe making and neat progressive villages. Close-up portraits captured women making fans, dresses and Panama hats and using sewing machines. He highlighted the longevity and benevolent rule of the Marshallese chiefly families

274   For the Marshalls Islands, see Clyde, P.H. *Japan's Pacific Mandate*, New York, Macmillan, 1935; Purcell, D.C. 'The economics of exploitation', *Journal of Pacific History*, Vol. 11, nos. 3–4, 1976, pp. 198–211; Peattie, M. *Nan'yo: The rise and fall of the Japanese in Micronesia 1885–1945*, Honolulu, University of Hawaii Press, 1988; Hezel, F. *Strangers in their own land; a century of colonial rule in the Caroline and Marshall Islands*, Honolulu, University of Hawaii Press, 1995.

275   McMahon misspelt several names: Namedrick for Namorik, Liegeib for Likiep and Arhno for Arno.

and photographed a wealthy potentate tattooed in traditional marking. He claimed the Marshallese liked dressing up and were fond of hats, neckties, leather shoes and canes. With a slight nod towards tourist potential, McMahon photographed a lateen-rigged outrigger, lattice-work fish traps, scenic views and curiosities, including a signboard in several languages (as he had done in both Nauru and Ocean Island). The commercial, economic and industrial reportage that had dominated his early visits to New Guinea and the Solomon Islands, Nauru and Ocean Island had in the Marshalls been set aside while he presented a cultural window on the people of mostly unknown central Pacific atolls.

McMahon's commentary on Japanese influence in the Marshalls suggested he admired their colonial policy and economic success, stressing to readers the modernising impact of acculturation and the 'Japanning' of Marshallese culture. To emphasise the Japanese influence over the atolls, he published two photographs of a Japanese volunteer dental team at work in a village, with captions noting that Japanese trading vessels transported itinerant dentists who did a lively business around the atolls (see Fig. 24). Marshallese school children were shown in cadet uniforms and were 'perfectly drilled Japanese naval cadets'. Juxtaposed against images of disappearing traditional costume were images of Marshallese dressed in kimonos. Why, McMahon asked, had Australian colonial rulers in Papua, New Guinea and Nauru not followed similar welfare and educational policies? Praising the Japanese was contrary to McMahon's vilifying of the previous German rulers of the Marshalls, a repetitive theme following anecdotal evidence he had collected on brutal German behaviour in New Guinea and Nauru. Ultimately for Australian readers, McMahon was asking rhetorically whether Australian colonial rule would have equalled the progress he saw in the

Japanese-ruled Marshalls and whether Marshallese would have been better off culturally under Australian colonial rule. When it came to trade prospects, McMahon was on more confident ground, photographing the Jaliut harbour, stores and offices, outer island trade stores, traders weighing copra and portraits of the Japanese colonial officials who were supervising the developments they were bringing to the Marshalls.

Australian readers would have been somewhat confused by McMahon's admiration for Japan. He repeated phrases like 'wonderful work by the Japanese … building up a new Japan in the central Pacific … Japan is winning the trade'. He declared the Marshalls had benefitted from benevolent social and domestic policies, compared to what he called twenty-five years of German neglect. He praised the rapid success of Japan, who had quickly occupied the former German territories in the north Pacific at the start of WWI, and repeated an anecdote in several of his columns in which Marshallese chiefs and kings were taken to Japan and filmed, and when these films were later screened in the atolls, this added greatly to the chief's delight and Japan's prestige.

The theme of lost Australian opportunities due to Japanese expansion was visually highlighted through a series of photographs of Japanese trade stores, schoolteachers, dentists and hospital staff. A portrait of what he called 'high officials' of the Japanese administration was published several times, with and without McMahon posed among a group of Japanese naval officers. The accompanying text described at length how Japan had developed the islands and was increasingly capturing the export market and general goods trade that previously went to the US or Australia. McMahon used his photographs politically to warn British, American and Australian readers of this commercial encroachment, and the golden opportunity that had been lost by allowing Japan to take over the former German territories in the north Pacific.

Photomontage

Most of his Marshall Islands photographs were published in a collage or photomontage format, and the arrangement reveals that McMahon carefully and strategically positioned at the top of the page the initial visual message about Japan that he wanted to convey to readers. For example, he opened one photomontage gallery with a Marshallese 'belle' in Japanese costume and a hairstyle that was 'distinctly Japanese'. In *Stead's Review* in February 1919, the editors chose a portrait of four Japanese naval officers for the cover. McMahon's coverage was more about Japan than about the Marshall Islands,[276] making it clear to readers that the Marshalls were a Japanese colony, not German, British or Australian. A month later, this same group portrait of 'high officials' was published in *The Sydney Mail* but with McMahon in the centre of the back row. This was a composition he used in all the islands he visited, as a strategy to say to readers, 'I was there'.

His eighteen illustrated articles on the Marshalls appeared in Australia, New Zealand, Europe and America in *Stead's Review, Travel, Pacific Ports, Mid-Pacific, PLA Monthly, Boys Own Paper, The Wide World, The Bulletin, Empire Review, Dun's Review (International), L'océanie Française, Mid-Pacific Magazine* and *Sunset: The Pacific Monthly.* McMahon's trans-Tasman publishing in New Zealand also continued with a report on the Marshalls in February 1919 with six photographs including a Japanese dentist, a Marshallese in a kimono, hat makers, churches and village scenes.

---

276   *Stead's Review* (cover), Melbourne, 22.2.1919.

Audiences were informed that the Marshall Islands were 'freed from German Rule'.[277]

A few photographs of the Marshall Islands were published a second or third time or cropped to provide a different version. A portrait of King Jedrick appeared, for example, as a full body shot, and then as a head-and-shoulders-only portrait. Jedrick is not frozen, nor looking straight at the camera, but looking to the side, composed, assured and impressive. McMahon declared he was a 'powerful native potentate' and very wealthy from exporting copra.[278] One of the few photographs to be used on multiple occasions was a scene of Japanese dentists operating in the open air with a crowd of villagers posed in the background (see Fig. 24). This appeared in *The Sydney Mail*, *Stead's Review* (Melbourne), *The Wide World* (London), *Travel* (New York) and *Sunset: The Pacific Monthly* (San Francisco), demonstrating again McMahon's efficiency in getting material quickly to editors and his keen sense of worldwide publishing opportunities.[279]

His efforts to gain global circulation can be seen in the tactic of sending a story using the same title but with a rearranged text to editors in both New York and London. For example, 'The land of model husbands' appeared in *Travel* in New York in November 1919 and *The Wide World* in London in February 1920.[280] McMahon used twenty photographs with only four repeated: dentists at work in a village, King Jedrick's body tattooing, and

---

277   McMahon, TJ. 'Formerly under German Rule', *Otago Witness*, 27.2.1919. p. 34.

278   See *The Sydney Mail*, 1.1.1919, p. 9; *Travel*, Nov. 1919, p. 8; *The Wide World*, Feb. 1920, p. 277.

279   Several of McMahon's photographs of Ocean Island, and the Gilbert and Marshall Islands were made into postcards. He was not acknowledged; see Max Shekleton Postcard Collection, Noumea, New Caledonia.

280   McMahon, TJ. 'The land of model husbands' in *Travel*, Vol. 34, Nov. 1919, p. 59; *The Wide World*, Vol. 44, no. 262, Feb. 1920, pp. 273–80.

portraits of the 'royal' families of Queen Luato and King Tobo.[281] The photomontage layout in *The Wide World* was not created by McMahon but was a standard format in *The Wide World*. It presented readers with a kaleidoscope of the Marshalls and was primarily an ethnographic window for readers.[282]

The categories that dominated were the Marshallese people, costume, families, villages, canoe building and tattooing. A series of photographs depicted the general cleanliness of villages. The photographs, for example, of King Jedrick of Majuro Atoll and other Marshallese in both traditional and borrowed Western attire revealed to readers a range of detail about cultural changes occurring in the Pacific as the world recovered from the war. The impression for readers was overwhelmingly ethnographic – villages, portraits, costume, canoes and tattooing – with Japanese influence and general scenery limited to only five photographs.

A series of portraits was used to depict the clothing of pre-Japanese times, called their 'national costume' by McMahon, with men and women shown wearing woven pandanus mats as lower body covering and carrying spears and paddles.[283] The men were depicted as stocky, with a proud countenance, and usually wore mats and fibre waist covering and were sometimes tattooed. Three impressive group portraits depicted Marshallese dressed in full dance costume.[284] A second series of portraits depicted Marshallese in Japanese kimonos and carrying a Japanese parasol, or dressed formally in European attire with long dresses, suit and

---

281   Captioned as 'King Lobo' and 'King Tobo'.

282   *The Wide World* was also publishing other illustrated stories on the Pacific such as WN Beaver's 'Among the head-hunters of New Guinea' (Nov. 1920) and CA Monckton's 'British drive into darkest Papua' (Sept. 1921). McMahon would certainly have been following illustration trends in these popular magazines.

283   These appeared in *The Sydney Mail, Mid-Pacific, The Wide World, Sunset: the Pacific Monthly* and *Travel* in 1919–1924.

284   For the dance groups, see *Mid-Pacific*, Vol. 127, 1924, pp. 175–6.

tie and Panama hats or carrying a cane or umbrella. These were portraits taken in atolls influenced by a hundred years of European contact and with regular links to the outside world. While full-length 'Mother Hubbard' dresses were common for all adult females, only Marshallese in paid employment in administration, shipping and the export of copra could afford the formal suit and tie and Paris fashions that McMahon photographed. A third series of portraits focused on women making Panama hats, dresses and fans and using sewing machines. These were staged compositions. McMahon noted that an American mission teacher had introduced sewing machines in the mid-nineteenth century, but that machines were now being obtained from Japan.

McMahon only published one photograph of mission activity and only one directly on the copra industry, although two scenes at the harbour could have been interpreted by some audiences as being related to shipping and trade. McMahon never ventured far from the main wharf or trading enclaves and was constrained by short stays, tight shipping schedules and his own predilections about the message he wanted to take back to Australian readers. He was correct in noting that in the central Pacific in 1918, indigenous costume and dress, political structures and material culture were being maintained but were changing as new ideas and technologies swept the region. His photographs reveal a Westernisation of dress, the reshaping of settlement patterns, the creation of mining enclaves, an imported labour economy and familiarity with tourists and visitors carrying cameras. These changes had been evolving for a considerable time, at least over the previous half-century. McMahon's images record this process of change, but he seemed unaware of the longevity of the adaptations and adoptions of Island peoples. He photographed quirky and unusual customs and clothing for readers back home, but this evidence does not support the claims in his text of a social and physical reordering of Island lives and Island peoples. Viewers of his photographs would have noted the industrialisation of the landscape on Nauru and Banaba, the trains and bicycles, but at the same time, they would have appreciated, for example, the retention of traditional dance and performance among the Banabans, Nauruans, Gilbertese and Marshallese.

The visual evidence in group portraits of dancers suggested to readers that Marshallese danced in lines, were partially naked, that men and women danced together, both sexes carried clubs or short spears, and that mats, shells, necklaces, and fibre skirts were worn for decoration. Readers would have nodded in agreement, acknowledging that this was the normal dance attire in the South Seas. But the captions countered this visual record, noting this was a pre-colonial form of dress and that men dominated women's lives. The captions therefore served to direct readers to know the Marshallese in different ways compared to the knowing offered within the frame. Guided by McMahon's accompanying text, audiences were told that 'national costume' had been abandoned just a few years previously and was now seldom seen, that tattooing was reserved for chiefs and kings, and that men (and, by implication, women) were awakening to a sense of their own importance because of a new, Japanese, colonial government.[285]

Because McMahon's photographs were published with a caption and an accompanying text that often contradicted the indexical evidence within the frame, a photograph of a building in a coconut grove with a large crowd gathered in front and a Japanese man wearing a white suit and Panama hat in the foreground only took

---

285   For example, see *The Wide World*, 1921, pp. 275 and 277; *Travel*, Nov. 1919, pp. 8 and 17; *The Sydney Mail*, 1.1.1919, p. 9; *Mid-Pacific*, 1927, p. 17; *Sunset: The Pacific Monthly*, June 1919, p. 31; *Auckland Weekly News*, 27.2.1919; *The Queenslander*, 5.7.1919; 4.10.1919; 29.11.1919; 8.5.1920; and 29.5.1920.

on meaning when McMahon's caption declared, 'every lagoon in the Marshalls has a store like this'.[286] A maritime panorama of a mundane harbour scene with two canoes, a three-masted trader and a smaller steamer took on a patriotic message when McMahon's caption declared, 'the extensive lagoon is nowadays invariably full of Japanese shipping.'[287] When looking through the lens at this quiet waterfront and harbour scene, McMahon saw Japan, a trading competitor and Imperial rival, and this was the message he wanted viewers to confront. The caption merely rammed home the point and left little room for alternative readings.

While in the Marshalls, McMahon visited Likiep Atoll and reported his surprise in finding Joachim de Brum, an enthusiastic photographer who had a well-fitted-out dark room. They chatted about plates, developing and the difficulties of obtaining photography supplies, and McMahon reported that he was 'an old customer of Kodak's Sydney branch', a link maintained by Burns Philp's 'island run' to the Marshalls.[288] Likiep had been purchased in 1877 by Georg Eduard Adolph Capelle and Jose Anton de Brum and they had remained through the transfer from Spain to Germany in 1885 and the Japanese administrative takeover in 1914. Capelle and Company were a well-known Pacific trading firm.[289] In a caption to a family portrait of de Brum with his wife and seven children with McMahon, de Brum was described as a 'well-to-do half-caste ... a striking personality' who had a 'splendid library in a comfortable elegant bungalow'. McMahon noted that de Brum had arranged for two resident English schoolteachers

---

286   *The Sydney Mail*, 12.3.1919, p. 8.

287   McMahon, TJ. 'Japanese trading vessels, Jaluit harbor', *The Sydney Mail*, 1.1.1919, p. 9.

288   *Australasian Photo-Review*, Vol. 15, no. 3, 1919, p. 214. De Brum was misspelt as de Broom in this article. De Brum House on Likiep is listed on the US's National Register of Historic Places.

289   See Firth, S. 'German firms in the Western Pacific Islands 1857–1914', *Journal of Pacific History*, Vol. 8, 1973, pp. 10–28.

and an artist and musician from San Francisco to live on Likiep. [290] Joachim de Brum, a descendant of the founding family, left behind an amazing photography collection. [291]

The ethnographic photographs reveal McMahon's quickly acquired admiration for Marshallese people, and their adaptability in handling successive foreign rulers from Spain, Germany and now Japan. McMahon never referred to the Spanish period, which had ended four decades earlier, and only briefly, and negatively, referred to the German period that had ended in 1914, five years before he arrived.

Having visited four central Pacific territories and witnessed the impact of industrial mining on Nauru and Ocean Island and the comparative impacts of British and Japanese colonial administration on the Gilbert and Marshall Islands respectively, McMahon returned to north Queensland. He immediately sent away prints and accompanying texts and captions to editors while also earning casual income from his back-country reporting role with the *Northern Herald* and *The Cairns Post*. His main concern in mid-1919 was a preoccupation with the planning of his next major adventure – a ten-month-long trip to England that he hoped would cement his career and bring attention to his recently acquired firsthand knowledge of the Pacific.

After his return to Australia in June 1920, he headed to the New Hebrides and in 1921 to Fiji. His photography output from these visits is covered in the next two chapters.

---

290   McMahon, TJ. 'A modern arcadia: the half-caste settlement of Leigieb, Marshall Islands', *The Queenslander*, 29.5.1920, p. 11.

291   See Petrosian-Husa, Carmen CH. *The De Brum Photo Collection – Memento Mori Alele* Report 2005/1, Historic Preservation Office, Majuro, Marshall Islands, 2005.

New Hebrides:
a lost opportunity

After returning from a two-month visit to the jointly governed British and French condominium known as the New Hebrides (now Vanuatu), McMahon promptly posted off to the editors of *The Telegraph* in Brisbane a five-part series of full-page features, each with three or four photographs and a short accompanying text. These were published in November and December 1920, suggesting that McMahon had been writing drafts while away, and then immediately developed the prints, in multiples, on return. He used the same format in *The Telegraph* as he had in 1918 for his features on the central Pacific islands, relying again on iconic representations and easily deciphered images to suggest a nearby territory under colonial control (the courthouse), missionary influence (a church or mission launch) and commercial export prospects (copra, cotton, labour, plantations and processing plants).

The underlying message intended by McMahon was that Australian readers should be aware of the political situation in the archipelago, governed under an unusual colonial apparatus known as a joint-rule or condominium form of administration, with neither French nor British willing to give the other an untrammelled authority over the islands. His criticism of this system was clear in the caption for a photograph of the courthouse

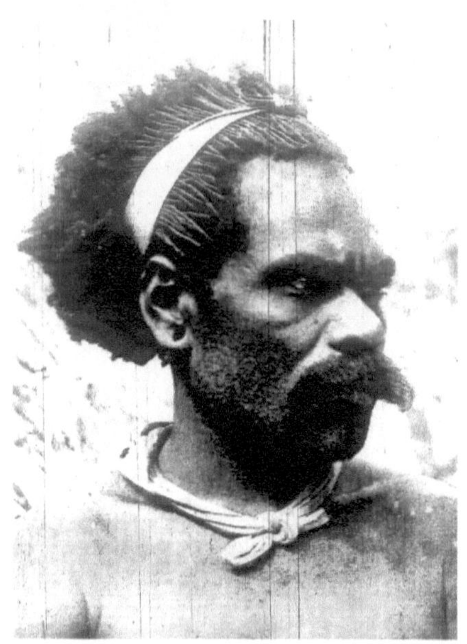

Fig. 25 'With coconut fibre in his hair; a savage
native of Tanna Island', 1921

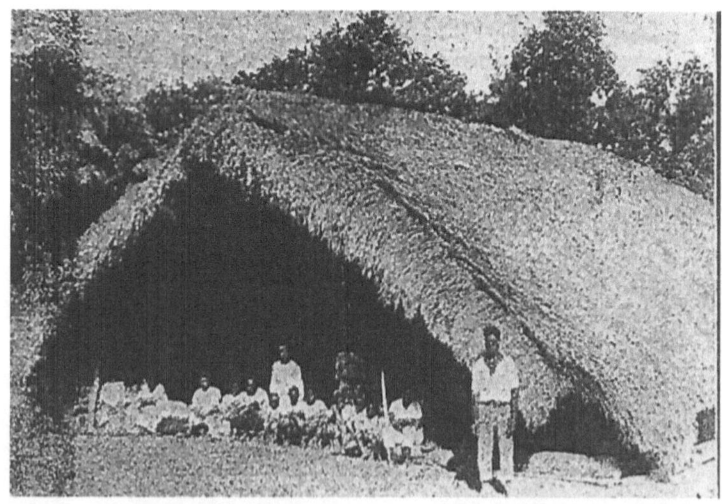

Fig. 26 '*The house of talk, or native senate*',
Efate Island, New Hebrides, 1919

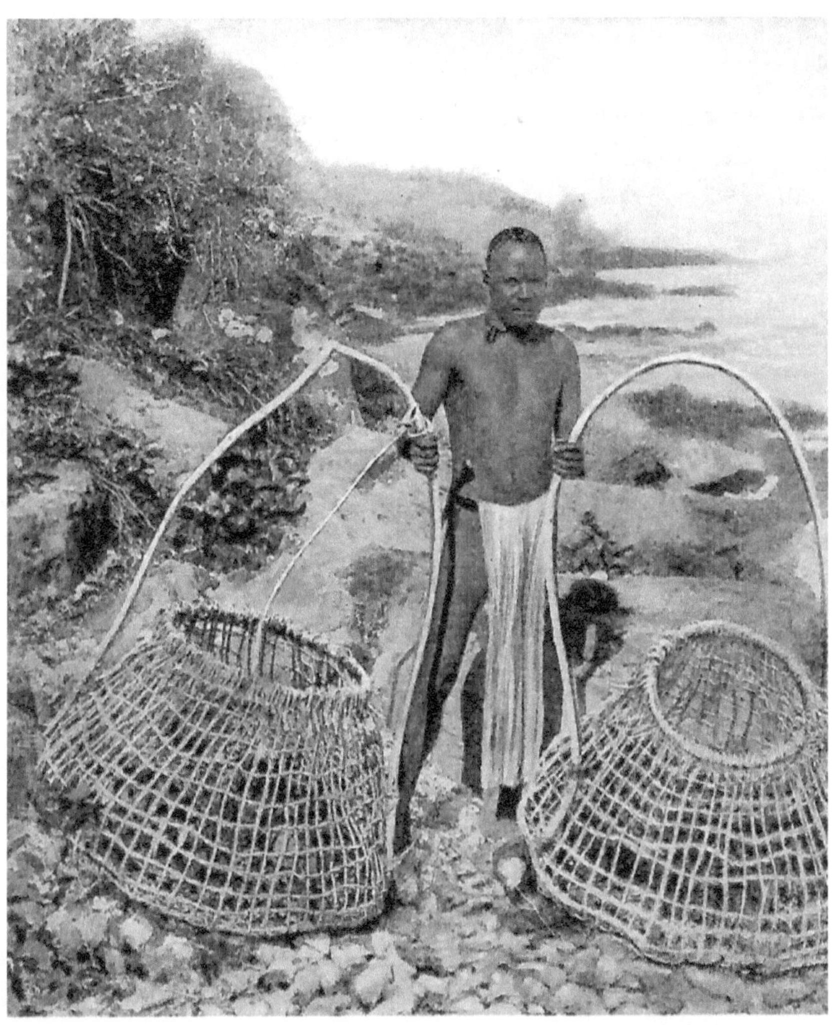

Fig. 27 Fish traps, Tanna Island, New Hebrides, 1923

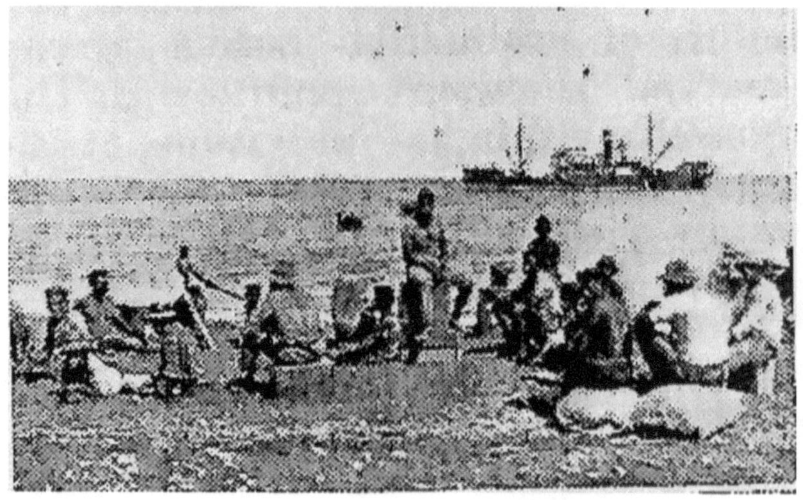

Fig. 28 'An Australian trader leaving supplies
at a British cocoanut plantation', 1921

in Port Vila. He declared the legal system in the condominium
was considered a 'comic opera rather than a serious court of justice'.
He repeated this phrasing several times, claiming elsewhere that
'wiser settlers are loudly demanding the abolition of a government
that is more comic opera in its style'.[292] In an introduction to
McMahon's article on the New Hebrides in *Stead's Review* in
July 1921, the editor informed readers that McMahon had just
returned from the New Hebrides and that he was able to reveal
the 'failure of the condominium'. The editor argued that the
example of Australia's success in governing Papua, which many
others decried, was enough reason to hand the New Hebrides
over to Australian control.[293]

---

292   *Pacific Ports*, July 1921, p. 164.

293   McMahon, TJ. 'New Hebrides', *Stead's Review*, 23.7.1921, pp. 75. The editor's claim
       of successful rule in Papua was controversial, and McMahon personally had already
       been criticised over his exaggerated and overly enthusiastic reporting on Papua.

McMahon's other message was economic, shown by the banner headline in a feature in *The Sydney Mail*, 'Where Australian trade is dwindling'.[294] In *The Sydney Mail* features of March and April 1921, he made several references in the text and captions to Australians in the New Hebrides, citing trading and plantation concerns on Tanna, Efate and Erromanga Islands, claiming they have done remarkably well. One photograph in *The Sydney Mail* was spread across two pages, depicting a scene on a beach with a freighter lying offshore with fifteen labourers surrounded by boxes of supplies and bags of copra. They were, McMahon declared, loading supplies for Australians employed on a British plantation. In the caption for the same photograph used in an American magazine, he noted that 'it is one of the tragedies of our national administration that Australian trade throughout the whole of the South Seas is dwindling away whilst the United States and Japan are forging ahead'. He used the same photograph for articles in *Pacific Ports* and *Stead's Review*, where he made the message more dramatic by declaring in a caption that 'Australian trade is quickly disappearing in the New Hebrides'.[295] One photograph in his *Pacific Ports* feature emphasised the American connection with a caption claiming New Hebridean labourers were 'loading copra on an American steamer at Vila, New Hebrides for shipment to San Francisco'.[296] This was a message McMahon had been pushing for several years. He had previously visited Papua, German New Guinea, Solomon Islands, Nauru, Banaba, the Gilbert and Marshall Islands, had seen how other colonial administrations operated – British, German, French and Japanese – and he had now spent five years boosting greater Australian interest in the commerce and trade of the region.

---

294 *The Sydney Mail*, 20.4.1921, pp. 18–19; 2.3.1921, p. 17.

295 *Stead's Review*, 23.7.1921, p. 76; *Pacific Ports*, July 1921, p. 53.

296 *Pacific Ports*, July 1921, p. 52.

Of interest to Australians

In his private papers, McMahon's campaign to promote Australian trade can be seen on a copy of his *Pacific Ports* article on which he scribbled changes in preparation for republishing elsewhere. He changed 'the advent of American trade' to the 'advent of British and Australian trade'. In another correction, he scribbled over 'of special interest to Americans' and changed it to 'of interest to Australians'.[297]

Prime Minister Billy Hughes and other patriots had suggested a greater role for Australia in the New Hebrides in the post-war realignment of colonies, but the joint British and French condominium remained in place. McMahon noted there was domestic discontent over policies within the condominium. He told readers that although relations were generally friendly, tensions existed between the French, British and Australian settlers. He failed to mention in his columns there had been a scheme promoted by Burns Philps and the Australian government to entice Australian settlers to take up land in the New Hebrides that Burns Philps owned, partly as a counter to an increasing French presence. This scheme had run intermittently from 1902 to the beginning of the Great War but had never attracted large numbers of settlers, despite being written up by the famous Australian poet, story writer and journalist, Andrew 'Banjo' Paterson.[298] Referring to a French settlement scheme, McMahon

---

297   Copy in McMahon papers, Royal Geographical Society (Qld).

298   See, Halter, N. and Quanchi, M. 'Boosting the Frontier: Australian Settler Colonialism in the Pacific 1860s–1900s', *Australian Historical Studies*, 2021, Vol. 53, no. 3, 2022, pp. 415–32; and Halter, N. *Australian travellers in the South Seas*, Canberra, ANU Press, 2021, pp. 196–216.

claimed France had resettled many returned WWI soldiers on plantations in the New Hebrides.[299]

The reluctance to refer to Paterson, whom McMahon had probably read in newspapers and magazines circulating in rural Australia, was professional jealousy. He also ignored the publications of the well-known Douglas Rannie, writing at the same time in Australian newspapers about the New Hebrides[300], and he did not acknowledge rural newspapers that had published on the New Hebrides, such as a five-part series on 'A trip to the New Hebrides: Contents of a diary' by a Mrs Lan Anderson in *The Gundagai Times* in 1914.[301] He had probably read Louis Becke's Pacific tales such as the popular *By reef and palm* (1894) and *Ebbing of the tide* (1895). Only once, in an article on phosphate mining in 1919, did he briefly mention Becke, the 'writer of delightful island tales'.[302] In Papua, McMahon had ignored the presence of Beatrice Grimshaw despite visiting the China Strait and Samarai Island in 1915, 1917 and 1921. Like Paterson, she was a famous fiction writer who had also done commissioned work for Burns Philps. McMahon had possibly read her most recent and popular non-fiction books, *From Fiji to the Cannibal Islands* (1907), *In the Strange South Seas* (1907) and *The New New Guinea* (1910) but in his quest for personal fame as an Islands expert, he was reluctant to acknowledge other writers.[303]

The period after 1900 had seen a flowering of literature,

---

299 *The Sunday Times* (Sydney), 10.10.1920, p. 5. The fate of Australia's soldier settlement scheme was covered at greater depth in his back-country reporting in Queensland (see below, ch. 14).

300 Rannie, D. 'The New Hebrides,' *The Queenslander*, 12.6.1915, p. 8.

301 Anderson, L. 'A trip to the New Hebrides: Contents of a diary,' *The Gundagai Times*; the five-part series concluded on 29.9.1914, p. 2.

302 *The Telegraph* (Brisbane), 3.2.1919, p. 13.

303 Grimshaw had also just published several works of fiction: *Vaiti of the islands* (1907), *Guinea Gold* (1912), *Red Bob of the Bismarcks* (1915) and *Coral Queen* (1919) among others.

travelogues and reports on the Pacific and McMahon would have noted these being reviewed in capital city and provincial newspapers. Before visiting the New Hebrides, McMahon could have read several recently published books such as Douglas Rannie's *Notes on the New Hebrides* (London, 1912) and two works by Frank Paton, *Glimpses of the New Hebrides* (Melbourne, 1913) *and Australian interests in the New Hebrides* (an eight-page pamphlet, 1919). Other recent books included JMH Abbott, *The South Seas: Melanesia* (London, 1908) and Florence Coombes, *Islands of enchantment: Many-sided Melanesia* (London, 1911) as well as others on the wider Pacific such as Frank Fox, *Problems of the Pacific* (London, 1912), Robert Brummitt, *A winter holiday in Fiji* (Sydney, 1914) and William Lees, *Around the coasts of Australia and Fiji Illustrated,* (Brisbane, 1916). Being determined to elevate his own career as the expert on the Islands, he relied instead on information gathered firsthand, usually anecdotal evidence from planters and traders. His hosts were occasionally mentioned not as a source but for having fine commercial prospects or a substantial plantation house. There is no record of McMahon having a personal library. By the time he visited the New Hebrides in late 1920, he had already visited London and had failed to attract enough attention to win the sought-after appellation, FRGS.

Rural newspapers often reprinted the McMahon features that had appeared in city newspapers. So, McMahon's arguments for greater Australian involvement in the New Hebrides must have surprised readers, for example, of Urana's tiny, four-page *Independent and Clear Hills Standard* on a Friday in October 1920, in which McMahon was identified as the 'well known traveller and lecturer'. In his article, he regaled its country New South Wales readers with claims of how the condominium was failing and that the Presbyterian Mission was approaching Prime Minister

Billy Hughes to act in the New Hebrides. He praised cotton, promoted the possibility of sulphur mining (in the Banks Islands) and deplored the loss of 7000 New Hebridean labourers who had gone to work in New Caledonia's nickel mines. He declared that he was satisfied that 'there is a great commercial future before the group'.[304] What wool and meat graziers in this small Riverina town, 550 kilometres south-west from Sydney, thought of McMahon's posturing and boosting of an island territory they might have known only through mission work remains unknown.

Perfect for cotton, cocoa and coffee

McMahon opened his article in *Stead's Review* in 1921 with the claim that the New Hebrides had perfect conditions for copra but also for products such as cotton, cocoa and coffee. Photographs supported this argument, such as a freighter waiting offshore to load copra. He noted that copra was sent direct to Japan and the United States of America, and that the proportion exported to Australia was falling; a fall, he declared, caused by Australia's 'perverse' shipping regulations. Boosters like McMahon ignored trade statistics, actual export figures and world commodity prices and were often weak on detail but attracted attention because of their panegyric promises.

Cotton attracted McMahon's interest, and for Australian readers, it was perhaps an unexpected economic activity to find in the tropical south-west Pacific. He photographed field workers in several locations, the picking and bagging of the cotton in the processing plant and the bagged cotton awaiting export. In an accompanying text, he noted that cotton exports in the New Hebrides had risen from 600 tons in 1914 to 2000 tons in 1920. Cotton, he declared, was grown on a British-owned plantation on

---

304 *Urana Independent and Clear Hills Standard*, 8.10.1920, p. 4.

Epi Island, and he provided readers with a series of photographs depicting the fields, picking, the ginning mill, sorting and baling cotton. He noted that sea-island cotton was being grown on 'very fine plantations' but admitted it was second to copra in terms of production and there were problems developing the export trade because of competition between rival ginning mills on Epi Island and in Noumea in nearby New Caledonia. He highlighted in a caption that the Epi mill was British-owned and the mill at Noumea was a French-backed enterprise. The pro-British connection was stressed even further when he claimed that bales of sea-island cotton sent to Liverpool had 'topped the market' and generated further large orders. His photograph of the substantial ginning mill at Epi was carefully composed with a pile of cotton bales in the foreground waiting to be exported. These images appeared widely in 1921–1922 in Australia in the *Importer and Exporter Journal of Australia*, *Sea Land Air* and *The Sydney Mail*, and overseas in *Pacific Ports*, *The Far Eastern Review* and the *London Illustrated News*.

He also photographed the even more unusual spectacle of a sheep farm on the high inland plateau of Erromango Island, managed by Australians who were selling their wool in Australia and the mutton to local planters. McMahon added to the caption that 'the natives make excellent shepherds'.[305] He published this photograph only once. The merino flock was still producing wool and mutton in the 1950s when Brett Hilder visited as captain of Burns Philp's inter-island trader, the *Muliama*.[306]

A short column on Vanua Lava Island, in the Banks group in the north of the archipelago, in *The Queenslander* in October 1920, was not illustrated. McMahon noted Vanua Lava was rich in sulphur and

---

305   *The Sydney Mail*, 20.4.1921, p. 19.

306   Hilder, B. *Navigator in the South Sea*, London, Percival and Marshall, 1961, p. 145.

of possible interest for mining extraction.[307] He had sent this column back to Brisbane from the New Hebrides. He repeated this story, in a full-page feature with three photographs, a few months later in *The Sydney Mail*, titled 'Vanua Lava: a great sulphur mountain'.[308] He patriotically declared this sulphur deposit was 'a commercial asset of the first importance to the Commonwealth', stressing that a French company had invested heavily in mining, aerial railways and wharf facilities, but had then failed due to the oppressive impact of malaria. He declared the vegetation and waterfalls were brilliant and described at length the river of gold, a sulphur-affected watercourse that flowed to the coast. Three different photographs of the 'river of gold' appeared in publications between 1921 and 1922.[309] McMahon stressed in each article the commercial possibilities of extracting the sulphur, calling it the 'most needful of modern commercial commodities'.[310] This sulphur story was repeated verbatim in *Pacific Ports* and in provincial newspapers, with a few editorial changes and different illustrations.

Missions

As he had done during visits to the other territories and islands, McMahon mostly ignored missionary activities. Missions from several denominations had been in the New Hebrides since 1839 (the London Missionary Society) and by the 1860s were well established.[311] New Zealand missions had been active in

---

307   McMahon, TJ. 'Vanna Lava Island' (misspelling of Vanua Lava), *The Queenslander*, 16.10.1920, p. 38.

308   McMahon, TJ. 'Vanua Lava: a great sulphur mountain', *The Sydney Mail*, 2.3.1921, p. 17.

309   *The Sydney Mail*, 2.3.1921, p. 17; *Importer and Exporter Journal of Australia*, 24.6.1922.

310   McMahon, TJ. 'Vanua Lava: a great sulphur mountain', *The Sydney Mail*, 2.3.1921, p. 17.

311   Mission history has an extensive literature, going back to Forman, Charles W. 'Missions and colonialism: the case of the New Hebrides in the Twentieth Century', *Journal of Church Studies*, Vol. 14, no. 1. 1972, pp. 75–92.

the archipelago since 1868. The major early evangelical impact in the New Hebrides was from French Catholic missions, so McMahon, as an Australian patriot, refrained from writing about their efforts. For McMahon, the mission field was not a new frontier, not topical and was not purely Australian enough to attract Australian readers' interest. He published only one full-page feature in *The Telegraph* in Brisbane. This was printed on a 600 by 700 mm broadsheet size page, with four photographs and five columns of text. The photographs included a church at Dillon's Bay, two of missionaries posing with their families and congregations (Rev. Milne and Rev. Macmillan), and a class portrait from the Model Village school on Mele Island.[312] The accompanying text was devoted to schools, training colleges, bans on alcohol, treatment of women and village hospitals. McMahon refrained from his usual rant about French officials or the alleged failings of the condominium administration. McMahon did take photographs of missionaries, churches and schools and had taken advantage of mission launches to visit outer islands, but mission hagiography was not on his agenda.

The New Hebrideans

His repetition of images of both economic development and ethnographic subjects showed his acquired understanding of readership – an armchair fascination with 'natives' and other, distant cultures parallelled with patriotism and support for greater Australian regional involvement. Nearly fifty per cent of his published images of the New Hebrides were portraits, depictions of coiffure and dress, canoes and fishing and material

---

312   *The Telegraph*, 27.11.1920, p. 11. Mele is a small islet just off the southern coast of Efate Island and close to Port Vila. The sloping sandy beach of Mele Bay was used to train US marines for the invasion of Tarawa in 1943.

culture related to funeral rites and ancestor worship.[313] McMahon had clearly been fascinated by the people, customs and cultural artefacts he saw on Rano, Malo, Aoba, Malakula, Tanna, Efate and Espiritu Santo Islands, a reasonable representation from a much larger and diverse archipelago.[314] This new interest was signalled to readers in 1922 with a headline that read, 'South Sea Way: Natives of New Hebrides, Old customs change'.[315] The three supporting photographs did not necessarily illustrate his claim of a cultural transformation. Instead, the photograph of slit-gong drums, a woman carrying a child, and a dugout canoe seemed to suggest old ways were continuing. His published photographs of the New Hebrides included fish traps, canoes, ceremonial practices and slit-gong ancestor figures. New Hebrideans were depicted as labourers, converts or merely going about their normal daily business. This emphasis on depicting indigenous people and cultures, visible in some of his earlier publications, was maintained in a subsequent trip to Fiji.

The slight change of emphasis away from boosting, polemical writing about Imperial opportunities and commercial opportunities also suggests he saw in the New Hebrides the benefits that might arise from fame as a traveller and reporter on human-interest topics. McMahon took on this persona for some features he published on the New Hebrides, being introduced to *The Sydney Mail* readers as 'the well-known traveller and explorer'. The former was accurate as he had spent five years travelling around the Islands, but the latter was not. McMahon

---

313   The inability of editors to accurately spell island names recurred with two photographs published in May 1921 captioned 'Aitchen Island', but this was probably Ambrym: *The Telegraph*, 6.5.1921, p. 11.

314   McMahon did not mention the Polynesian 'outlier' populations on the islands Emae, Mele (Ifira-Mele) and Futuna-Aniwa.

315   McMahon, TJ. 'South Sea Way: Natives of New Hebrides, Old customs change', *The Telegraph* (Brisbane), 6.5.1922, p. 11.

only attracted the label 'explorer' in the New Hebrides because of several articles he published on volcanoes.[316] He had focused on Yasur volcano on Tanna Island, first recorded by Europeans when James Cook visited in 1774, with different illustrations, in articles for *Sea Land Air* and much later in 1927 in *The New Nation Magazine*.[317] He also published an account of Tanna with the headline, 'Living on the edge of eternity: Tanna and its volcano' in *The Sydney Mail,* with five photographs of the volcano, local scenery and an unrelated photograph of cotton cultivation.[318] McMahon also photographed the tropical vegetation, bird life and the behaviour of the Tanna Islanders including what he called 'some weird native superstitions'.[319] This focus on the culture and customs of local people was a major change away from the visualisation of economic opportunity and Australian expansion that had dominated his photography for the previous five years. This change was most noticeable in the last article he published on 'Tanna and its interesting volcano' in which the illustrations were not of the volcano but of a group of portraits of Tanna men and boys under a giant tree and a picturesque bay on the coast. The switch from imperialist rhetoric to travelogue-style literature was obvious in the accompanying text which described Mt Yasur but was devoted mostly to Tanna's 'scenic charms', lakes, legends, earthquakes, birds and magic.[320]

---

316   McMahon had probably seen an illustrated article published on Ambrym's volcano in *The Wide World* in October 1915. Photographers certainly copied earlier framing and composition but, like McMahon, always added their own emphasis.

317   McMahon, TJ. 'Tanna Island: Its interesting volcano', *The New Nation Magazine*, Dec. 1927.

318   McMahon, TJ. 'Living on the edge of eternity: Tanna and its volcano', *The Sydney Mail*, 27.4.1921, pp. 3, 37.

319   All this was captured much later in a motion picture film, '*Tanna*', nominated for best foreign language film at the 2015 Academy Awards.

320   McMahon, TJ. 'Tanna Island: Its interesting volcano', *The New Nation Magazine*, Dec. 1927.

Early in 1921, McMahon continued with a human-interest theme when he presented readers of *The Sydney Mail*, the illustrated weekend news review magazine of the *Sydney Morning Herald*, with an impressive double-page spread of thirteen photographs of 'the New Hebrides and their picturesque people'.[321] Eight were portraits or village scenes from Espiritu Santo, Tongoa, Erromanga, Tanna, Rano and Efate Islands and offered Australian readers an appropriately varied glimpse of New Hebridean people, customs and culture. McMahon acknowledged the religious beliefs, reverence of ancestors, dress fads and concept of consensus decision-making in a visual lesson on a people whom Australians knew little about, despite New Hebrideans forming the main component of the Kanaka, or South Sea Islander, indentured labour in northern New South Wales and Queensland sugar plantations from the 1860s to 1906. McMahon did not reveal he was offering only a restricted view. He omitted to tell readers he had visited only a couple of the thirty inhabited islands in the New Hebrides archipelago, where more than seventy languages were spoken by 100,000 people in independent and autonomous tribes not overseen by an indigenous or colonial centralised authority. This diversity was not highlighted. Even more confusing for readers was that the banner headline read, 'Where Australian trade is dwindling', but the thirteen supporting photographs were all on the culture and traditions of the New Hebrideans.

McMahon's published gallery on the New Hebrides included many close portraits of individuals and groups, a composition he had rarely used in the previous five years. For example, a standard head-and-shoulder framing of a chief from the Big Nambas, a large tribal and language group on Malakula Island, was a sensitive,

---

321   McMahon, TJ. 'Where Australian trade is dwindling', *The Sydney Mail*, 20.4.1921, pp. 18–19.

intimate and very close-up portrait. Other portraits included a 'savage native' from Tanna, a chief with elaborately carved headwear and a young boy from Malo Island (off Espiritu Santo Island), which highlighted the shaved, elongated head caused by binding and a hairstyle leaving only a shaped tuft on top.[322] The emphasis on culture and customs continued with publication of photographs of the Erromango Island practice of women wearing multiple petticoats of fabric and pandanus leaf, said by McMahon to indicate 'high-caste'. One of the most repeated of McMahon's ethnographic photography was a scene on a beach with a man displaying two basket traps, to be left overnight with a lure to catch fish on the reef (see Fig. 27). A caption noted they looked like Western-style lobster pots. One caption identified this location as Tanna Island, in the south of the archipelago, but in another caption as Aoba Island in the north, off Espiritu Santo Island. This photograph appeared in *The Telegraph* in late 1920 and then in 1921 in *The Wide World* and the *Illustrated London News*, and in the illustrated serial encyclopedia, *Countries of the World* in 1923 and in *Lands and People* in 1929. McMahon also photographed canoes, a ceremonial graveyard (which he noted was related to ancestor and shark worship) and an unusual stone trilithon-shaped altar 'to the Gods'.[323] McMahon's reporting on New Hebrideans also included an albino female and more prosaic compositions such as a group of men under a huge tree, a man blowing a conch shell, a man pointing to a taro plant and a group selling coral to tourists.[324]

The most published ethnographic composition was the

---

322 *The Sydney Mail*, 20.4.1921, p. 18; *The Wide World*, Aug. 1921, pp. 287, 389; *Illustrated London News*, 1.10.1921, p. 444. His article in *The Wide World* included ten photographs of the New Hebrides.

323 Canoes in *The Wide World*, Aug. 1921, p. 389, *Countries of the World*, Vol. 6, p. 3781; ancestor/shark grave in *The Wide World*, Aug. 1921, p. 387, *The Sydney Mail*, 20.4.1921 p. 18; stone trilithon in *The Wide World*, Aug. 1921, p. 387.

324 These were each used only once by McMahon.

depiction of slit-gong drums – upright, two-metre tall, hollowed out logs decorated with spiritual imagery. McMahon staged several photographs of a group of men sitting, posing or pretending to beat the slit-gong drums, probably on Malakula as there is no record of McMahon visiting Ambrym. Malakula's slit-gong drums and ancestor figures were photographed by the anthropologist John Layard in 1914, but those from Ambyrm Island and elsewhere are equally famous.[325] McMahon noted they were able to produce the deafening boom of a bass drum. A caption in *The Wide World* noted that the drums 'contain the spirits of famous men and are beaten by skilled young men during ceremonies'. However, some captions were added by editors far away, the fate of many photographs from the Pacific that were published in Europe, the US and Australasia.[326] For example, the captioning of one photograph varied, in one publication being called 'sing-sing grounds', in others labelled as a memorial to warrior chiefs or the site of annual shark rites or a man-only dancing ground.

A photograph, used three times in 1921, sums up McMahon's new-found interest in indigenous culture. It depicted a large, thatched roof building, the size of a tennis court, on Efate Island, home to the condominium capital at Port Vila. McMahon called it the 'native parliament house' or 'house of talk' or the 'native senate'.[327] It functioned as a place where elders could meet and discuss matters of importance to New Hebrideans across the archipelago and the policies being imposed on New Hebrideans by the French and British administrations. He was alert to the changes underway in the modern twentieth-century Pacific and photographed the 'house of talk' as a positive move, attributing

---

325   Gesimar, H. and Herle, A. *Moving images; John Layard, fieldwork and photography on Malakula since 1914*, Honolulu, University of Hawaii Press, 2010.

326   McMahon, TJ. 'Life in the New Hebrides', *The Wide World*, Aug. 1921, p. 391.

327   For 'house of talk', see *The Sydney Mail*, 20.4.1919, p. 19.

it perhaps more to colonial motivations than to its indigenous purposes. The 'house of talk' appeared in 1921 in *The Sydney Mail, The Wide World* and *Stead's Review*, but was not picked up for use in serial encyclopedias that were concerned more with showing the exotic 'other' and a so-called traditional native life.

Several of his photographs were made into a TJ McMahon series of postcards, possibly by a photography studio in Port Vila. They had been purchased, or perhaps swapped, when McMahon was visiting Port Vila, the capital of the condominium.[328]

Number	Caption
27	Cotton pickers, Malo
28	Canoes, Aitchen
37	School, Mele
141	Native house, Santo
273	Tanna, bushmen
0	Shark's grave, Rano
0	Trader's home, Efate

Table 2: McMahon's photographs published as postcards in Port Vila

McMahon also lent or sold several photographs of the New Hebrides to the Australian writer Jack McLaren, and they subsequently appeared as illustrations in McLaren's long-running weekly serial, 'On the fringe of the law', in *The Sydney Mail* in late 1920 and early 1921.[329] *The Telegraph* also published single photographs randomly as illustration 'fillers' over the following

---

328   Max Shekleton Postcard Collection, Noumea, New Caledonia. Not all cards were numbered. The publisher was not listed.

329   For New Hebrides photographs, see *The Sydney Mail*, 12.1.1921, p. 26; 19.1.1921, p. 25; 9.2.1921, p. 25; 2.3.1921, p. 25.

years.[330] Several of the photographs from *The Telegraph* series were used by McMahon elsewhere in 1921 in *The Wide World*, *The Sydney Mail*, *Pacific Ports* and the *Illustrated London News* and later in the serial encyclopedia, *Countries of the World*, demonstrating again his eagerness and ability to distribute his photography quickly and widely.

McMahon did not publish as extensively about the New Hebrides as he had for earlier islands and territories, perhaps because it was a joint French and British colony, and there were also fewer Australian connections to report on compared to Papua, the Solomon Islands and the central Pacific phosphate mining islands. The emphasis in McMahon's New Hebrides photography therefore changed from the strident boosting of economic activity and trade potential that had dominated reporting on the earlier islands he had visited. The ethnographic emphasis in his New Hebrides photography also illustrates his growing understanding of the complex relationship between indigenous people, settlers and colonial administrations and how fame might be achieved in different ways by human-interest reporting on the people of the islands as much as by polemic boosting of Australia's involvement and Imperial status.

After returning from the New Hebrides, he developed and printed multiple copies of prints, wrote accompanying columns, and posted away packages about the New Hebrides, while at the same time earning a regular income by continuing in his casual, paid reporting and photography of back-country topics with *The Cairns Post* and the *Northern Herald*. He also started planning his next venture – to the Fiji Islands.

---

330   For example, a river scene on Malakula Island, *The Telegraph*, 16.5.1920, p. 6; Tanna fish traps, *The Telegraph*, 16.4.1921, p. 11.

Chapter 10

Fiji: wonderful development

Fiji was on the cusp of change when McMahon arrived in August 1921.[331] An Indian indentured labour scheme, known as Girmit, that provided the workforce for Fiji's sugar industry since 1879, had ended in 1916. A small quota was allocated to females, but the majority of the 62,000 who came were men. In 1920, all Indians in Fiji could either return to India or stay as free people.[332] This created a problem for McMahon as he had to decide how much relative coverage to give to trade and economic matters, to the indigenous Fijians (called ITaukei) or to the expanding, formerly indentured, immigrant Indian community, known as Girmitya. After a disappointing trip to England in 1919, and then going to the New Hebrides, McMahon had been active, arguing visually and in accompanying columns and public speaking engagements, that the British, and therefore Australia, should be proactive in the Islands. This was a persuasive argument in relation to the former German territories redistributed after the War but carried less weight regarding established British colonies such as the Solomon Islands, Tonga, the GEIC and the jewel in the crown, Fiji.

---

331   I would like to thank noted Fiji scholar and friend Brij Lal (1952–2021) for comments, advice and criticism of this chapter.

332   The Fiji scheme was part of the two million indentured Indians who served around the world between 1834 and 1920. See Tinker, H. *A New System of Slavery: The Export of Indian Labour Overseas 1820–1920*, London, OUP, 1974.

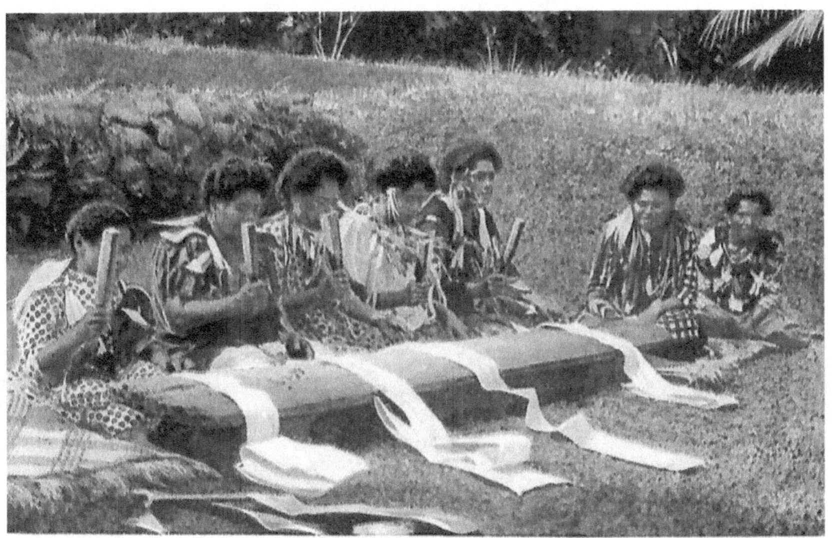

Fig. 29 *Masi* (tapa) making in Fiji, 1923

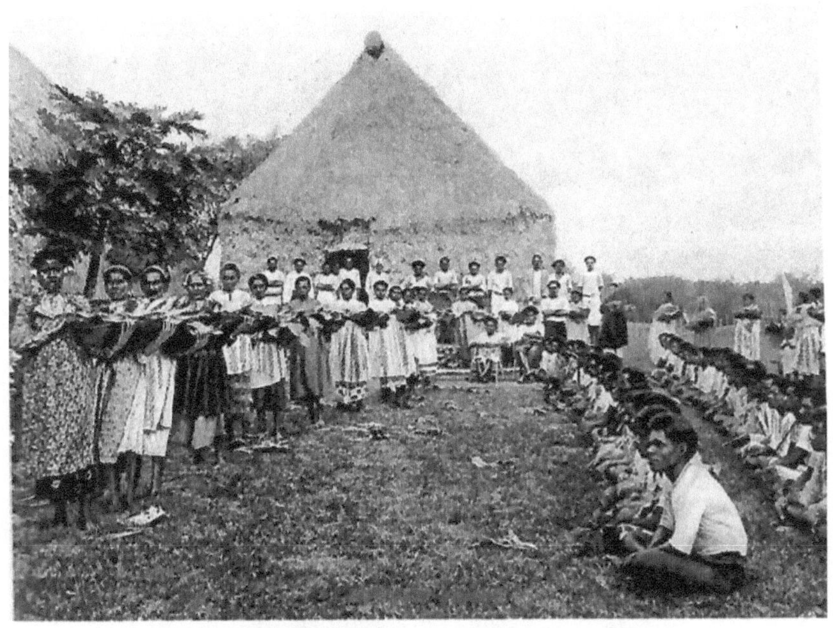

Fig. 30 Preparations for a Fijian feast, 1928

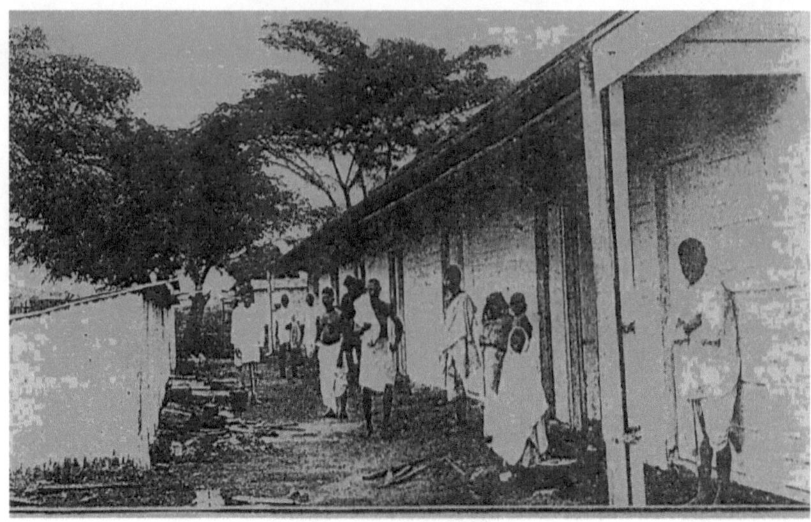

Fig. 31 'Native labour lines', Fiji, 1922

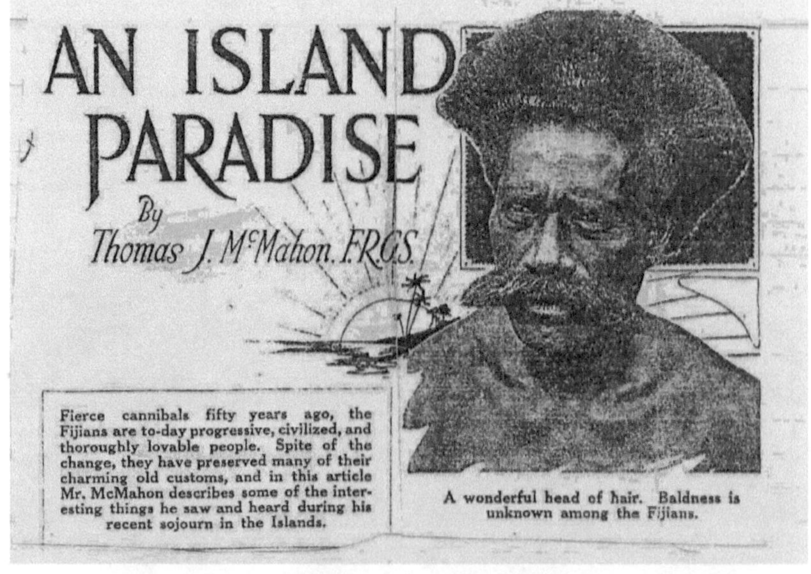

Fig. 32 Typical banner in a pictorial magazine, 1923

Fiji consists of two big islands, Viti Levu and Vanua Levu, and 330 smaller islands, with only 110 inhabited, including Ovalau Island where the former capital, Levuka, was located. Britain had annexed the Fiji Islands in 1874 to establish control over Britishers involved in the indentured labour trade, land purchases and trade generally. Fijians prefer to call this a 'cession', arguing that thirteen great chiefs had ceded Fiji to Britain. Under a series of governors, a policy was developed to protect the indigenous Fijian way of life, keeping Fijians in their villages, and included a ban on their employment in the sugar industry. The protection of Fijian indigenous people and their village way of life and the use of imported indentured labour was known as the Gordon-Thurston Orthodoxy, after two of the early governors.

In 1881, the newly proclaimed British Crown Colony made Suva the capital due to its large harbour and role servicing the Rewa and south coast plantation districts. The Polynesian island of Rotuma, 400 kilometres to the north was also included by the British in the Crown Colony of Fiji. Levuka and Rotuma had been significant ports in the whaling era and during the China trade in island resources. They were port towns where new crew could be signed on, provisions taken, and goods off-loaded to smaller coastal craft for local distribution.

Fiji, a secure Crown Colony, was the headquarters of the Western Pacific High Commission which oversaw all British domains in the Pacific, and its economy was already dominated by an Australian company, the huge sugar monolith, the Colonial Sugar Refining Company, known simply as CSR or 'the company'. Fiji's second major industry, gold mining, was also dominated by an Australian company, the Red Emperor Gold Mine near Ba. The Bank of New South Wales was well established in Fiji and Suva Grammar School followed the Victorian curriculum. In the 1860s, it had been Victorians who numbered highly in the 3000 or more optimistic settlers in the so-called 'Fiji Rush', migrating to Fiji in the hope of becoming cotton planters.[333] In the 1880s, there had been a campaign for Victoria to annex Fiji or for Fiji to possibly join a confederation of Australian States and New Zealand, called the Federal Union.[334] Fijians had also demonstrated admirable loyalty and service to Britain during the 1914–18 War.

During his three months' stay, he took a ten-day cruise to Levuka, Mokagai Island, Taveuni Island, Somo Somo and the Macuata Province on Vanua Levu. He tried hard to photographically capture this diversity for distant audiences who were limited to knowing Fiji had previously been called the 'Cannibal Isles'.[335]

The land of sugar

Sugar, an indigenous plant to the Pacific, was tried at Suva in the 1870s as a substitute export crop for the failed cotton industry, but the industry soon moved to richer river flats and then to the drier coastal plains in the west. CSR started operations in 1882 with a mill at Nausori, another at Rarawai at Ba in 1886 and then at Labasa in 1894. CSR took over the privately run but failing Penang mill at Rakiraki in 1926.[336] At the same time, the

---

333 See Quanchi, M. *Glorious Company: The Polynesia Company in Melbourne and Fiji*, Suva, Pacific Studies Press, 2022.

334 See Quanchi, M. 'Fiji sixth star for the Australasian Federation', *Pacific Islands Monthly*, Aug. 1976, pp. 37–8.

335 For Fiji, see Burns A. *Fiji*, London, HMSO, 1963 (part of the Colonial Office's 'Corona' library on British colonies); Lal, BV. *Broken Waves: A history of the Fiji Islands in the Twentieth Century*, Honolulu, University of Hawaii Press, 1992; Quanchi, M. and Shekleton, M. *An ideal colony and epitome of progress: Colonial Fiji in picture postcards*, Suva, USP Press, 2019.

336 For sugar, see Lowndes, AG. 'The sugar industry of Fiji', in *South Pacific Enterprise: The Colonial Sugar Refining Company Limited*, edited by AG Lowndes, Sydney, Angus and Robertson, 1956, pp. 67–90; Lal, BV. *Girmityas: The origins of the Fiji Indians*, Canberra, Journal of Pacific History, 1983.

landscape was changing as CSR was about to transition from large plantation cropping and company-owned sugar farming to small tenant farms taken up by Indians as their indentures were cancelled. Fiji was also hit by strikes and industrial disputes over wages, rents and crop prices. So-called 'Gandhi followers', or agitators, were arriving from India and were allegedly stirring up dissent by challenging the authoritarian rule imposed by Britain over its colonies. Moreover, the sugar industry had undergone a huge slump and two of Fiji's mills, the Penang mill at Rakiraki and the Tamanua Sugar Mill at Navua, were heading for closure.

The sugar industry that dominated the Fiji that McMahon found on arrival was located mainly on the west coast of Viti Levu and the north coast of Vanua Levu, the respective 'dry' coasts. The biggest mill was in Lautoka with smaller mills at Rarawai (Ba), Penang (Rakiraki), Nausori on the southeast coast of Viti Levu, and Labasa in Vanua Levu. Hundreds of kilometres of railway linked the sugar-producing districts to the mills. Lautoka, on the west coast of the main island of Viti Levu, was known as the 'sugar port' and was regarded as a powerful influence on the economy, equal to the capital, Suva, located on the south-east coast. The giant Lautoka mill commenced operations in 1903. This type of industrial activity – centred on mills, railways, and export crops – was familiar to McMahon, as he had photographed sisal, rubber and tobacco plants in Papua, sulphur mining in the New Hebrides and phosphate mills on Nauru and Ocean Island. As sugar was already a substantial industry, with strong government support and established markets, there was little boosting to be done, so McMahon briefly documented the field gangs, rail lines and mills for the interest of distant audiences.

The context for McMahon's portrayal of Indians in Fiji was concern over the sugar industry, which up until 1920 had relied on the indentured labour of Indians for its profits and success. He published photographs of Indians cutting cane, loading light rail trolleys at Navua and Nausori, the wharves and mill at Lautoka from several angles[337] and the former 'coolie lines'.[338] To an American audience, he reported there were 8000 labourers employed by CSR, 2000 horses, 4000 rail trolleys and forty English-built locomotives. He noted the recent opening of the Panama Canal in 1914, and that Suva was destined to be 'the great half-way house of South Pacific shipping'. This article was accompanied by three photographs: the mill at Lautoka, field workers cutting cane and an Indian housing settlement. The text was revised slightly in *Empire Review* later in the year.[339]

McMahon visited Suva and then toured the sugar districts at Tailevu, Navua, and Rewa near Suva and photographed the CSR mill at Lautoka on the west coast. His photographic coverage of the sugar industry was slight, and this might seem surprising considering the importance that sugar played in Fiji's economy and in the daily life of nearly half its population. But McMahon was an Imperialist and opportunist and determined to establish a reputation as a patriot. The sugar industry was safe and profitable under Australian control so, other than a few general interest views, there was little purpose for a booster like McMahon in photographing an established industry. This meant that, in Fiji, he lacked a platform on which to reiterate the sub-Imperialism

---

337   For Lautoka, see *The Telegrap,* (Brisbane), 26.11.1921, p. 11; *The Louisiana Planter and Sugar Manufacturer,* 29.4.1922, p. 272; loose prints, McMahon Collection, Royal Geographical Society of Queensland.

338   For cane fields, see *The Telegraph* (Brisbane), 29.10.1921, p. 11, 26.11.1921, p. 11; *The Sydney Mail,* 1.3.1922, pp. 16–17; *The Louisiana Planter and Sugar Manufacturer,* 29.4.1922, p. 273; *Auckland Weekly News,* 5.7.1923, pp. 422–43. The *Otago Witness* (6.7.1920), for example, had already published an anonymous report on sugar in Fiji with seven photographs not by McMahon.

339   McMahon TJ, 'The sugar industry of the Fiji Islands', *The Louisiana Planter and Sugar Manufacturer,* 29.4.1922, pp. 272–74.

agenda and economic boosting role he had been playing for the previous six years.

As there was no expansionist platform or glowing commercial opportunity that he could boost, his 150 published photographs of Fiji are evenly divided between four fields he hoped audiences would relate to – the Fijian people, the formerly indentured Indian population, the sugar industry and glimpses of expatriate life.

McMahon was not the only journalist publishing on Fiji's post-*Girmit* future and the efficacy of Britain's policies on self-rule. Others were calling for the protection of the indigenous Fijian way of life, while others, supporting CSR, made insistent demands for changes to the workplace, tenancy and landholding. McMahon would have seen illustrated articles, for example, in *The Sydney Mail* in 1911–1912 on the 'coolie question' and the copra and the cattle industry. Three months before McMahon's Fiji features began to appear, the readers of *The Sydney Mail* had seen Phyllis Clark's 'Four months in Fiji', accompanied by eight of her pen and ink sketches.[340] The similarity between the subject matter and composition of her sketches and McMahon's later gallery of photographs of Fiji suggests there may have been borrowing back and forth between the genres. Her sketch of a male dancer, a woman holding a pandanus mat and a panorama of an Indian 'village' could easily be mistaken as prototypes for McMahon's photographs of the same subjects. McMahon may have also read the recent publications on Fiji such as a small official sixty-eight-page pamphlet, *Colony of Fiji; land and resources*, in 1919 and WA Chapple's *Fiji – Its problems and resources* in 1921.[341]

A month after returning from his visit, McMahon's Fiji

---

340   Clark, P. 'Four months in Fiji', *The Sydney Mail*, 31.8.1921, pp. 12, 27.

341   See Quanchi, Max. 'Photography, capitalism and empire: a case study of the Handbook of Fiji', *Journal of New Zealand and Pacific Studies*, Vol. 12, no. 1, 2024, pp39-54.

photographs began to appear in *The Telegraph* and *The Week* in Brisbane and *The Sydney Mail,* and then in magazines globally such as *Empire Review* and *The Wide World* and in specialist publications like *Dental Science Journal of Australia* and the *Louisiana Planter and Sugar Manufacturer,* and later in the 1920s in serialised pictorial encyclopedias.

'Wonderful development': *The Telegraph, The Week* and *The Sydney Mail*

McMahon's first presentation about Fiji was an impressive ten single-page features, each with two or three photographs, that ran from October to December 1921 in *The Telegraph* in Brisbane. The visual impact was spread across European industrial impact, indigenous peoples and Indians. The headline banners for *The Telegraph* series revealed McMahon's message to his Australian audience.

Date	Number of photos	Banner headline
29 October	3	Wonderful development
5 November	2	A colony of islands; Australia's relationship
12 November	2	Government Institutions: Suva; The capital
19 November	3	Picturesque Suva; Indians much in evidence
26 November	3	Trade Resources and Industries
3 December	2	Prolific in Products; Indian Agriculturists Fail.

Date	Number of photos	Banner headline
10 December	3	Decline of Native Civilization; Success of British administration
17 December	2	Kava; The national drink
24 December	3	The failure of the Indians: Agitation, Strikes, Riots
31 December	3	Helping the Indians

Table 3: The Fiji Islands series in *The Telegraph* in 1921

McMahon's headlines and photographs offered readers evidence of success, as well as problems and failures. It was an expansive visual reportage of Fiji in a time of change, highlighting European development, commerce and administration, demographic changes and the maintenance of Fijian custom.

Running parallel to this coverage in a daily newspaper (*The Telegraph*), McMahon also published a nine-part series in *The Week*, a weekly summary of news, from early November 1921 to early January 1922. The photographs in *The Week* were accompanied by columns using the same text and headlines as *The Telegraph*. He also contributed features to the daily newspaper, *The Brisbane Courier*, and to its weekend magazine edition, *The Queenslander*. It seems strange today that McMahon would have been published in four of Brisbane's newspapers at the same time; this suggests that weekend readers of *The Queenslander* and *The Week* would not have been deterred by the similar material appearing in the daily newspapers, *The Telegraph* and *The Brisbane Courier*. McMahon's photographs of Fiji were also appearing concurrently in Sydney in *The Sydney Mail*. Editors in the 1920s clearly did not mind that their photographic coverage overlapped with opposition publications, but it also shows how McMahon astutely and carefully varied the content he was sending to editors.

His Fiji series in *The Week* contained twenty-four photographs. Seven of these appeared only in *The Week* and some later in *The Wide World, Auckland Weekly News* and the *Louisiana Planter and Sugar Manufacturer*. McMahon presented *The Week*'s readers with three windows on which to view Fiji – Indians, Fijians and European activities or developments – but excluded the sugar industry.[342] Fijians dominated as a subject, being double the number of photographs of Indians. Fijians were shown making *kava* and presenting it to chiefs and having meetings in villages and outside their homes, called *bure*, made of local materials. One large *bure* was miscaptioned a 'native parliament', a political aspect of Pacific life that he had previously photographed in the Gilberts and the New Hebrides. One portrait depicted a female's braided hair. European influence was depicted by photographs of Carnegie Library, the public bandstand and police brass band, a vista along Victoria Parade, a school and the leprosy station on Makogai Island. Sugar and bananas, the two staple export industries, were not featured, with only a cattle ranch at Tailevu to suggest there were other potential economic activities.

At the same time as this series appeared in Brisbane in *The Week* and *The Telegraph*, McMahon published a nine-part series in *The Sydney Mail* from November–December 1921. His *Auckland Weekly News* and *Otago Witness* in New Zealand features appeared later, at intervals from November 1921 through to November 1923. For his New Zealand publications, he used several photographs that had not appeared in *The Week, The Telegraph* or *The Sydney*

---

342   On Fijians, see *The Week*, 4.11.1921, 16.12.1921, 23.12.1921. On Indians, see
        25.11.1921, 9.12.2921, 30.12.1921. For European activities, British administration
        and Suva, see 11.11.1921, 25.11.1921, 18.11.1921.

Mail, demonstrating again his tactic of spreading his portfolio astutely and sparingly.

The twenty-nine photographs in *The Sydney Mail* were dominated by three human interest subjects – Fijians, Indians, expatriate life – with the sugar industry given marginal attention. A full-page feature headlined 'The Fijians: A virile and interesting race' had photographs of the making of *kava,* a male sitting dance and musical performance, a chief's house (*bure*), a young female serving *kava,* a kindergarten class for Fijian children and a portrait of the *Roko,* or district chief of Somo Somo.[343] He called Suva a picturesque city, a term he had rarely used over the preceding six years, and highlighted the Carnegie Library, town hall, Botanical Gardens, post office, Government House, bandstand, goal, the police brass band and the iconic arched promenade along Nabukalou Creek.[344] This Suva gallery of nine photographs, spread over two pages, also included a portrait of a Fijian male showing his trimmed, fuzzy hairstyle and a prominent expatriate, the Hon TF Fell, Colonial Secretary and Acting Governor during McMahon's visit. McMahon was very impressed with Suva. He rarely mentioned or provided photographs of smaller towns in Fiji such as Levuka, Nausori, Sigatoka, Savusavu, Labasa, Ba or Tavua.

Bananas, leprosy and missions

The absence of mission activities was noticeable. Missionaries had been in Fiji since 1835, and after the conversion of major chiefs in 1855, churches and schools had sprung up all over Fiji. By the time of McMahon's visit in 1921, the Methodist Wesleyan

---

343 McMahon, TJ. 'The Fijians: A virile and interesting race', *The Sydney Mail,* 28.12.1921, pp. 9, 35.

344 These arches along the creek remain as the facade for a modern building. They were pictured many times in postcards and tourist literature. For Suva, see *The Telegraph* (Brisbane), 19.11.1921, p. 11; 3.12.1921, p. 11; 10.12, 1921, p. 11; *The Sydney Mail,* 16.11.1921, p. 17.

Mission had its own training college, orphanages and schools and was closely linked to the British administration. Compared to other territories he had visited, the difference in Fiji was that McMahon did not have to rely on missions to facilitate visits to plantations, mines, villages or outer islands. In Fiji, he could travel independently using existing roads, motor cars, the sugar railways and an extensive local coastal shipping network, all options less available on his visits elsewhere. In his first Fiji feature in *The Telegraph,* he did include one photograph of Baker College at Davuilevu, the Methodist enclave near Nausori,[345] but this was less about missions and more about European architecture and the cosmopolitan nature of the European presence in Fiji. He took a group portrait of fourteen students and two teachers at Davuilevu, but it was never published. In *The Sydney Mail,* he included a photograph of a Methodist kindergarten class for Fijian children taken at Davuilevu, and he mentioned he had been impressed by the 'finest qualities' of Fijian singing at a Catholic Mass he attended, but otherwise readers would have thought there was negligible mission influence in Fiji.[346]

McMahon published very few photographs of the banana industry, then a thriving part of the colonial economy. There were none included in *The Sydney Mail* series and only one in *The Telegraph.*[347] A feature specifically on 'The banana industry in Fiji' in the *Auckland Weekly News*, with four photographs, was a recognition that New Zealand dominated the export trade for Fijian bananas, and McMahon judged that this was a topic of

---

345   *The Telegraph,* 19.11.1921, p. 11; loose print, McMahon collection, Royal Geographical Society of Queensland.

346   McMahon, TJ. 'The Fijians: A virile and interesting race', *The Sydney Mail,* 28.12.1921, pp. 8–9.

347   *The Telegraph,* 29.11.1921, p. 11.

interest in Auckland but not in Brisbane or Sydney.[348] McMahon announced in *The Telegraph* on his return from Fiji that banana growers were 'exasperated' by the Australian tax on imported bananas and that New Zealand had captured the trade. The next day, a Mr Scott, a member of Fiji's Legislative Council who was visiting Brisbane, commented on McMahon's views in *The Telegraph*. Scott asked whether Australians understood where Fijian growers sold their bananas. He noted that taxes prevented Fijians from selling their bananas in Australia, and this meant Fijians imported their considerable trade in consumer goods from New Zealand, not Australia. He declared, 'It's not philanthropy. It is business.' An editor at *The Telegraph* added that Scott and McMahon should address their remarks to the federal parliament, then sitting in Spring Street in Melbourne.[349]

McMahon visited the island of Makogai, a leper colony started in 1911, and published an article in *Dental Science Journal of Australia* in which he took the opportunity to play the sub-Imperial booster role by stressing that 'British administration has glorified itself in its dealings with all native peoples of the South Pacific'. He declared the treatment of leprosy (now called Hansen's disease) was 'one of the wonders of the age'.[350] He noted there had once been 300 Indians on Makogai but that most had been repatriated to India. At the time of McMahon's visit, there were 200 patients from various Pacific Islands. The leprosy station closed in 1969. He published only one photograph from this visit,

---

348   For bananas, see *The Telegraph*, 29.11.1921, p. 11; McMahon, TJ. 'The banana industry in Fiji', *Auckland Weekly News*, 2.2.1922, p. 37.

349   *The Telegraph* (Brisbane), 5.10.1921, p. 4; 6.10.1921, p. 4.

350   McMahon, TJ. 'The lepers of the lonely isle', *Dental Science Journal of Australia*, 2.10.1922, pp. 470–73. See also Buckingham, J. 'Indenture and the Indian Experience of Leprosy on Makogai Island, Fiji', *Journal of Pacific History*, Vol. 52, no. 3, 2017, pp. 325–42.

a panorama of the men's ward with a large group of patients and officials in the foreground.[351]

Fijians

Fijians dominate McMahon's published Fiji gallery, comprising fifty per cent of all photographs. Three subjects captured the most attention: *bure,* Fiji's unique house architecture; *kava,* the use of a Pacific-wide drink made from yagona, a root plant; and *meke,* music and dance. McMahon did not use the term *bure* but used 'house' or 'palace' to describe the large dwellings with high-pitched, thatched roofs and distinctive gables. The houses on raised mounds were reserved for chiefs, and McMahon noted this distinction. He also photographed panoramic views of villages. In a historically valuable piece of evidence, he also photographed an Indian family who used a classic Fijian *bure* as their home, demonstrating the cultural mixing of Indian and Fijian ways of life in Fiji.[352]

McMahon published several different *meke,* or dances; these were not *in situ* but posed shots with dancers arranged for the camera. He noted the *meke* used song and dance to tell a story of past great battles and traditions. At Somo Somo on Taveuni Island, he took both a single male portrait and a group photograph of what he called 'spear' dancers. The full body portrait was of a man dressed elaborately, posed in the act of throwing a spear at the photographer, a pose that appeared in many Fiji postcards at this time. The group photograph of dancers or warriors was also a composition used widely and which McMahon would have seen in several of Suva's studio and postcard outlets. He also photographed

---

351   *The Week* (Brisbane), 18.11.1921, p. 16. There may have been other photographs published of Makogai but not found in searches so far.

352   *The Telegraph,* 3.12.1921, p. 11. For other *bure* photography, see *The Sydney Mail,* 28.12.1921, pp. 8–9; *The Wide World,* May 1923, p. 16; *Louisiana Planter and Sugar Manufacturer,* 29.4.1922, p. 273.

what he called the 'Fijian piano', in which one Fijian held a small solid piece of wood while a second Fijian drummed out a beat using two wooden drumsticks. On two occasions, he photographed a Fijian beating a large hollow log known as a *lali*, noting that bells were never used, and that the *lali* could be 'heard for miles'. These photographs appeared in *The Telegraph, The Sydney Mail, The Wide World* and the *Auckland Weekly News*.

McMahon photographed several scenes of preparing and presenting *kava*, noting it was used for both 'important public ceremony' and that it was non-intoxicating and the 'national drink'. He claimed that in Suva, Fijian workers gathered daily at 11 o'clock to have a bowl of *kava*, and that it was important to make a visible sign of appreciation by clapping one's hands after being given a bowl. Despite Fijians now being famous for the construction of *drua, takia* and smaller canoes, he only published one photograph of what he called 'a picturesque island sailing vessel'. He mostly bypassed *tapa* or bark cloth fabric making, another distinctive Fijian custom, known in Fiji as *masi*, although one photograph of a line of seated women beating the bark to make *masi* was later colourised and used in the serial encyclopedia, *Countries of the World* (see Fig. 12).[353]

McMahon had not taken many close-up photographs of males and females during his previous visits around the islands, but in the New Hebrides and in Fiji he posed several head-and-shoulder portraits, in each instance with the subject looking away from the camera. These compositions or framing were specifically directed at the unique Fijian hairstyles with shaped, braided and exceptionally large dimensions. These portraits included a police bandsman, a young girl and an older man.

---

353 *Countries of the World*, Vol. 6, p. 3754. A black-and-white print was also published in the *Auckland Weekly News*, 3.11.1921, p. 33.

Another aspect of Fijian culture and society that attracted McMahon's camera was the role of chiefs. He photographed several *bures* and arranged several posed single and group portraits of men of chiefly rank, known as *Ratu* in Fiji. He also noted that local Fijian chiefs appointed for a district under the British provincial administration were known as *Roko* or *Roko Tui*. McMahon's poor understanding of the role of chiefs meant he lazily relied on the term 'prince' to describe these important men. His portraits include Ratu Pope and Ratu Joni Antonia Rabici.[354] McMahon wanted to acknowledge that these were distinguished Fijians within their own social, cultural and political world, but primarily he wanted to assure audiences that they represented the success of the British administration in corralling and promoting their leadership. Continuing his new-found interest in photographing indigenous culture and society, in Fiji, McMahon photographed indigenous Fijians proudly and comfortably maintaining their language, customs and village-based lifestyle.

Indians

McMahon also had to decide how he would depict the Indian population of Fiji and how to acknowledge their unique integration into Fiji's population and workforce, expanding past 65,000 in 1921, against the indigenous Fijian population of 85,000. Indians had just been released from indenture and were now free to stay in Fiji and continue in self-employed small businesses or become tenant farmers when CSR introduced a change away from large plantations and company production of sugar. India, their homeland, was in turmoil with the boycotting

---

354   See *The Telegraph*, 29.10.1921, p. 11; *The Sydney Mail*, 28.12.1921, pp. 8–9; *The Wide World*, May 1923, p. 14; *Auckland Weekly News*, 20.11.1923, pp. 422–3.

of British goods and a non-cooperation movement launched by Mahatma Gandhi.

In a long column in *The Telegraph,* reprinted in the *Northern Herald* and *The Cairns Post,* he added a short final paragraph declaring that Fijians 'despised the Indians', claiming that in fifty years, only three Fijian women had married Indian men and only one Fijian man had married an Indian woman.[355] He claimed, without offering any evidence, that venereal diseases were rife among Indians and that the Fijian chiefly class in particular shunned Indians. These were claims based on hearsay and not on official statistical evidence. He also claimed so-called 'agitators' were coming to Fiji and spreading news about self-government, independence and human rights and were the cause for agitation, strikes and riots. What would become of Fiji's Indians, McMahon asked, now no longer bound by indenture? McMahon was covering a story that had already attracted attention worldwide, with feature articles on Fiji's Indians in *Empire Review, Sea Land Air, The Lone Hand, The Sydney Mail* and *The Wide World.*[356] CF Andrews and WW Pearson also published an influential pamphlet in 1916 on the indenture system in Fiji and Florence Garnham had published a critical review of the social and moral conditions of Indians in 1918.[357] She had toured Fiji for three months on behalf of the Combined Women's Societies of Australia and spoke in

---

355   *Cairns Post,* 29.12.1921, p. 3; *Northern Herald,* 11.1.1922, p. 8.

356   For example, *The Lone Hand* had published 'Fiji; Eastern Outpost' in April 1913, *The Sydney Mail* on 'Where revolt has been crushed' on 17.3.1920 and *Sea Land Air* on 'Life and work in Fiji; Two races' in May 1922. McMahon published in all these publications and probably monitored other writers who were covering the places he was visiting.

357   Andrews, CF. and Pearson, WW. *Indian indentured labour in Fiji,* Delhi, 1916, reprinted in Perth, 1918; Garnham, F. *A report on the social and moral condition of Indians in Fiji, being the outcome of an investigation set on foot by the combined women's organizations of Australasia,* Sydney, Kingston Press, 1918.

Sydney before returning to India.[358] It is likely that McMahon read these articles and reports prior to his visit to Fiji.

In 1921 and 1922 in his extensive photographic coverage in the *Telegraph* and *The Week*, Indians featured in only four photographs: an Indian home, a 'town' (McMahon noted that Fijians lived in villages and Indians in towns), children playing skippy and a rare photograph of a group of Indians sitting on the ground about to be repatriated, said by McMahon to be going home to India. A feature on Indians titled 'Fiji: a big problem' contained ten photographs but depicted none of the so-called problems noted in the text: industrial disputes, speech-making, strikes, troublemakers and agitators. Instead, McMahon provided an ethnographic gallery of Indian life: a hawker, a barber, a jeweller, a temple, a bejewelled woman, well-established labourers housing, Indian graves, children and an Indian school.[359] This was another instance in McMahon's publications where readers were confronted with contradictory images and text.

In London's *Empire Review*, under the banner, 'The problem of the Indians', McMahon wrote that there were persistent strikes, agitation and riots and alleged that Indians in Fiji were trying to bring European enterprise, namely the sugar industry, to a state of chaos. He claimed 'the Indians remain aggressive, sullen, intent on hampering the progress of the colony' but then contradicted himself by declaring the situation was not serious and had been exaggerated as part of anti-British propaganda originating in India. His view of Indians as a 'problem' was contradicted a second time by his own published photographs of happy, hardworking, educated, well-housed and free Indians. Photographs of hawkers, barbers, coir mat makers and Indians cutting cane challenged

---

358   *Sydney Morning Herald*, 26.11.1918, p. 4. See Mishra, M. 'Between Women: Indenture, Morality and Health', *Australian Humanities Review*, 2012, p. 52.

359   McMahon, TJ. 'Fiji: A big problem', *The Sydney Mail*, 1.3.1922, pp. 16–17.

the allegations cited in his text. Photographs of Indian temples and graves, women bedecked in jewellery and 'crowds of healthy happy children' at school in the Indian settlements suggested to audiences that, rather than being a problem, Indians were well entrenched in Fiji and were maintaining their Indian customs and traditions. His commentary became more confusing when he declared Indians were among the richest in the colony and that 6500 adults and children had sailed for India in 1920 and 1921, taking with them jewellery and cash worth £145,000.[360] It remains unknown what audiences made of McMahon's text and photographs, with a sympathetic, respectful human-interest reportage contradicted by criticisms of the Indian presence in Fiji.

An island paradise

McMahon's popularity with the editors of *The Sydney Mail* led to his being asked in December 1922 to submit a page for the extremely popular annual Christmas edition of *The Sydney Mail*. His half-page photomontage titled 'In the Fiji Islands' was purely ethnographic, depicting a Fijian male beating a *lali* drum, a Fijian male dressed for the 'spear dance,' an Indian 'monkey' temple at Navua and a Fijian child sitting in a *kava* bowl. McMahon added that children bathed in coconut oil every morning because it made 'their bodies very glossy which is considered beautiful'.[361] There were no photographs of Suva, missions or the sugar industry. This choice of photographs by McMahon, two years after his visit, demonstrates how his photography had the power to influence public opinion, in this instance away from acknowledging the complex relationships between Fijians and Indians to seeing Fiji

---

360   McMahon, TJ. The problem of the Indians; Position in Fiji', *Empire Review*, Vol. 36, 1922, pp. 117–21. *Empire Review* was a monthly journal published in London from 1901 to 1942.

361   *The Sydney Mail*, Christmas edition, 13.12.1922, p. 55.

as simply a Fijian entity. It also reflects his switch away from political posturing and Australian sub-Imperial boosting and why he chose in 1923 not to include Fiji in his McCarron's set of eight Pacific Islands albums/booklets.

In 1923, towards the end of his career photographing the Pacific, McMahon contributed a single feature in *The Adelaide Chronicle* titled 'An island paradise; the story of Fiji', with ten accompanying photographs. Assuming he had free range to choose from the several hundred photographs taken during his three-month visit, it is revealing to see what he included and what was omitted. His selection, three years after his visit, was overwhelmingly ethnographic. There were no photographs of Indians, missions, Suva, the sugar industry or the leprosy station on Makogai. In his selection process in 1923, Fijians were depicted serving *kava,* playing the *lali* drum, attending a village council meeting, making music, dancing and sailing canoes. The interior of Government House was shown decorated in Fijian style. A portrait of a *Roko* standing with a British District Commissioner was the only reference to colonial rule, although audiences probably saw this portrait as a typical example of the well-built, sturdy and confident-looking Fijian male. McMahon declared that 'despite the remarkable progress they have made during the last 50 years under British administration, the Fijians cling to many old customs, especially in their love of ceremonial'.[362]

With several month-long series published in Brisbane, Sydney, Auckland and Dunedin newspapers, McMahon's published photographic coverage of Fiji was impressive. He no doubt hoped, after a disappointing trip to England, that his Fiji publications would restore his reputation as an Islands expert. The noticeable difference between his Fiji coverage and other islands he visited

---

362   *Adelaide Chronicle,* 25.11.1923, pp. 32, 52.

between 1915 and 1920 is that he only published four illustrated articles on Fiji in magazines and journals outside Australia. He had realised that Fiji was an established and settled colony safe in British hands with historical connections to New Zealand, Victoria and New South Wales and was of little interest to American or British audiences. It possibly explains why discussion of Fiji was omitted from his longer opinion pieces on the rise of German, Japanese and American trade in the Pacific. The results of his Fiji visit appeared in publications globally in late 1921 and 1922 and some in 1923, but by then he had abandoned the Pacific and decided to take a trip through Asia and gain attention as an expert on China. Fiji was the last of McMahon's adventures in the Pacific and was his final adventure in the Islands in the hope of gaining fame as an Islands expert.

The next three chapters survey his published photography from the Northern Territory, the Torres Strait Islands, Lord Howe Island, Norfolk Island and Queensland's 'back-country'. This role had been his bread-and-butter employment and had financed his Island trips and publishing endeavours. Ironically, he perhaps became more well-known, certainly in Queensland, for back-country reporting in *The Brisbane Courier* and *The Queenslander* than for his photography of the Pacific Islands.

Chapter 11

Torres Strait, Northern Territory, Norfolk Island and Lord Howe Island

From 1915 to 1922, McMahon visited the nearby south-west Pacific Island colonies and territories on self-funded trips. To pay for these photography and information gathering adventures, he acted back home as a freelance back-country photographer and reporter, visiting rural Queensland, the Torres Straits, Northern Territory and Australia's two offshore dependencies, Norfolk Island and Lord Howe Island. He then sold these illustrated features to Australian, New Zealand, American and European publishers. How much he earned from this prodigious output globally is not known but it must have been substantial, allowing him to travel around the south-west Pacific on month-long or longer voyages and support his expensive printing and developing and postage costs. His archive of published photographs is today a significant repository and a fascinating window on life in out-of-the-way early twentieth-century Australia and on places otherwise regarded as on the edge or fringe.

Torres Strait Islands

McMahon's first published photograph of the Torres Strait was in August 1916, a year after changing careers from being a tutor on

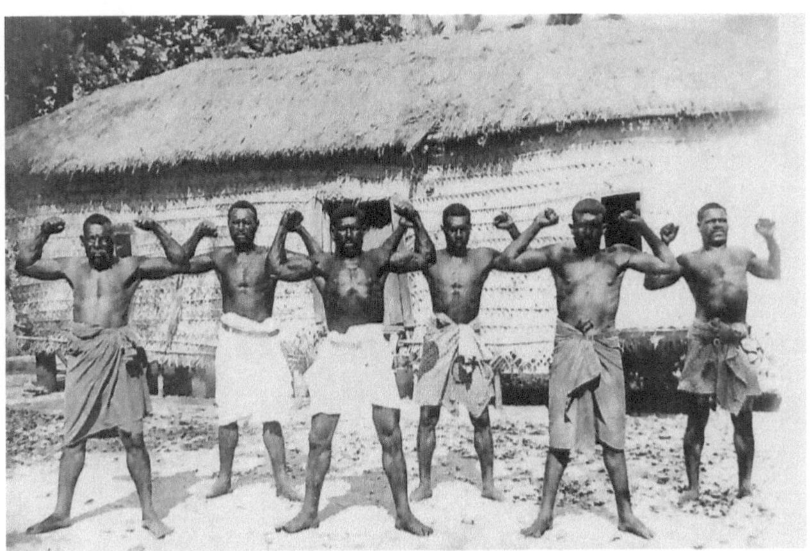

Fig. 33 'Pearlers of Yama Island, Torres Strait', 1917

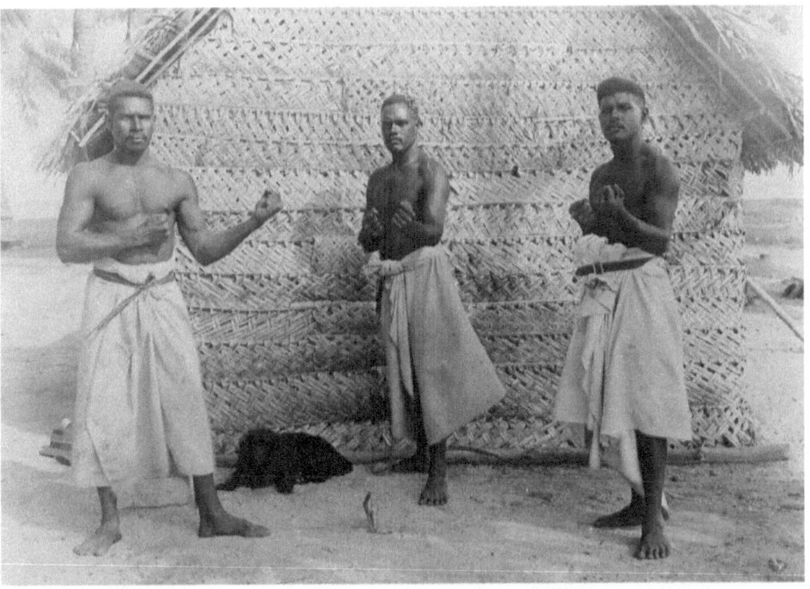

Fig. 34 'Three boys boxing (Yama Island)', 1917

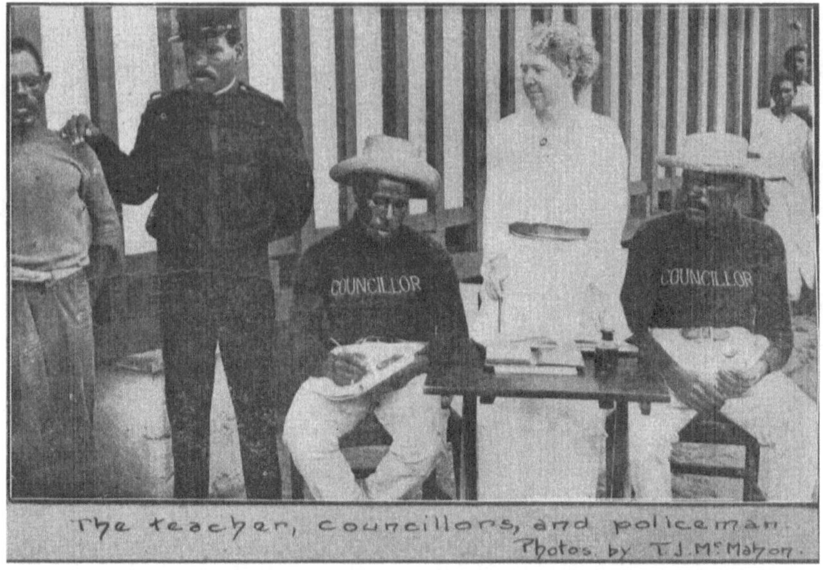

Fig. 35 Mrs ME Zahel, Administrator and teacher, Badu Island, 1916

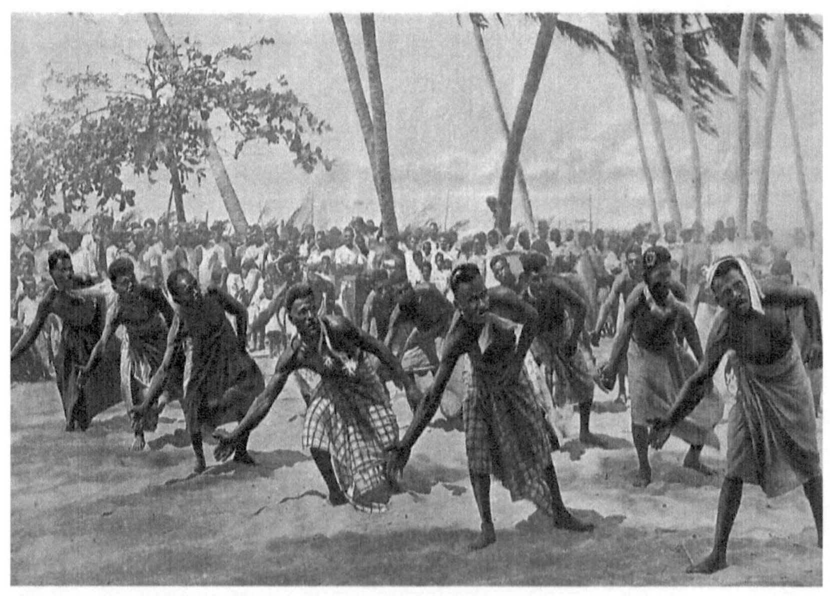

Fig. 36 Pigeon dance, Mabuaig Island, Torres Strait,
The Queenslander, 1916

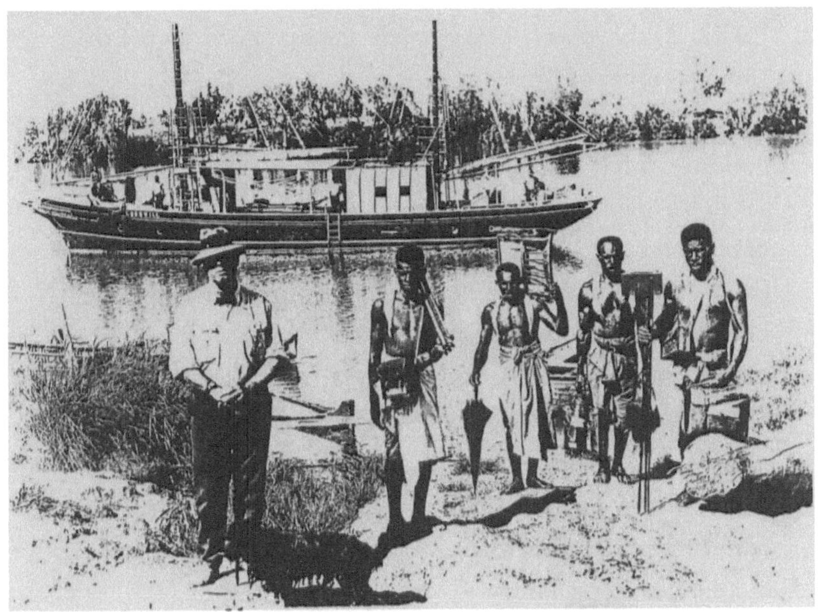

Fig. 37 McMahon and his camera crew, Roper River

pastoral properties. He was now touring the outback country of Queensland and the Torres Strait and was referred to as a reporter for *The Cairns Post* and the *Northern Herald*. He was also sending his Torres Strait photography to *The Sydney Mail* and *Sunday Times* in Sydney, *The Queenslander* and *The Week* in Brisbane and the *Australasian* in Melbourne. Even though he made two trips to Papua and German New Guinea, the Solomon Islands and elsewhere, he continued sending Torres Strait material to capital and provincial city illustrated newspapers and to overseas journals and magazines, with some not appearing until 1928.[363] He also published several Torres Strait photographs in his own book, *The Orient I Found*, as well as lending some to the author Jack McLaren for a popular account of McLaren's travels in the

---

363   For example, *The Lone Hand*, Aug. 1917, pp. 443–5 (five photographs); *Auckland Weekly News*, 19.2.1920, p. 34 (eight photographs); *The World Today*, Vol. 51, 1928, pp. 304–10 (eight photographs).

Pacific, *My Odyssey* (1923).[364] McMahon published more than 130 images of the Torres Strait and they might be regarded as his bread-and-butter income, providing expenses for his career-building trips to the Pacific.[365]

Badu, Mabuiag and Murray Island (Mer) were the major sites of his photography, but he also visited Yorke (Masig), Adolphus (Mori), Yam (Yama or Iama) and Darnley (Erub), leaving behind an important photographic record of life in the Torres Strait in the war and immediate post-war years. He visited the Torres Strait on commission but he also called at Thursday Island, a major port, garrison and communication centre, during his three trips to Papua and New Guinea. He also made photography and reporting trips to the Northern Territory, which meant making more stopovers on Thursday Island.

McMahon's photograhic reportage on the Torres Strait was comprehensive, and although only focusing on a few of the 242 islands in the Torres Strait, it gave viewers and readers a good sense of what, to most audiences, was a remote, hardly known corner of Australia. Torres Strait Islanders had been part of the later waves of migration out of Asia through New Guinea 3,000 years ago and this created five distinct groups of people and two main language groups with hundreds of dialects. The strait was first explored by Europeans in 1606 when the Spaniard, Luis Vaez de Torres, proved New Guinea and Australia were separated. Australia's eastern seaboard was claimed 164 years later by Captain James Cook for Britain. By the nineteenth century, the strait had become a major shipping channel linking the east coast of Australia and the Pacific to Batavia (now Jakarta), Singapore and on to Europe.

---

364   McMahon's photographs were not mentioned in reviews of McLaren's book; for example, *The Queenslander*, 9.2.1924, p. 3.

365   His TSI photographs appeared on at least 200 separate occasions. Further searching might reveal many more uses.

The London Missionary Society (LMS) arrived in the Torres Stait in 1871 and at the time of McMahon's visit, the Anglicans, Catholics and Methodists were also present. The Rev. Frederick Walker, formerly of the London Missionary Society, was based on Badu and had just created Papuan Industries Limited, which encourged Torres Strait Islander participation and ownership in the pearling industry. Another industry in the Torres Strait was bêche-de-mer fishing but McMahon only published one photograph of a group of workers, under a tree.[366]

Between 1872 and 1879, Queensland added all the islands to the colony of Queensland, including Boigu and Saibai adjacent to the coast of New Guinea, and retained control after federation. In 1904, the infamous, discriminatory and restrictive 'dog act' was legislated, placing Torres Strait Islanders under the *Aboriginals Protection and Restriction of the Sale of Opium Act*. At the time of McMahon's first visit, the revision of the Act was being debated in Queensland parliament. The proposed transfer of control of Badu from the LMS to the Queensland government was also being proposed by Queensland's Home Secretary.[367] In 1912, the islands had been placed under a system of Queensland government control called 'reserves' which involved curfews, restricted travel and set wages. The Queensland government had also just amended the *Pearl-shell and Beche-de-Mer Fishing Act 1881*. The amendments created reserved fishing grounds for 'Aboriginals' and introduced a new licensing system.[368] Islanders had also been encouraged to join island councils created by Resident Magistrate John Douglas. These were the men, wearing shirts with the word 'Councillor' embroidered on the front, whom McMahon photographed several times in 1916.

---

366   For bêche-de-mer, see *The Queenslander*, 28.10.1916, p. 24.

367   *Northern Herald*, 5.5.1916, p. 6; *The Queenslander*, 6.5.1916, p. 39.

368   *The Week* (Brisbane), 9.11.1917, p. 17.

McMahon's imagery captured the diversity of life in the Torres Strait, noted later by the artist, Ray Crooke, during his WWII military service. Scott Bevan's description of Crooke's period on Thursday Island notes that the islands

> had been attracting people to seek to enrich their souls or their material well-being. It was a dry place but hardly barren, possessing a particular beauty. Cultures and peoples had washed up on its shores from other islands and from throughout Asia and Europe. Trading and passenger ships nuzzled into the bays ... Asian divers plunged for pearl shell and beche-de-mer helping to build the fortunes of white traders who lounged in the shade of stately homes on shore'.[369]

This description could apply equally to McMahon's visits two decades earlier.

Audiences perusing McMahon's published photographs were not informed of this long and complex history. Instead, they saw indigenous people busily going about their daily lives, adapting to Western presence and being guided benevolently and patronisingly by Europeans. This relationship was signalled in his very first photomontage on the Torres Strait in which Islanders are depicted inside a workshop repairing boats, but looming to the left and right of the image are two Europeans wearing ties, suggesting to audiences quite clearly that Europeans were managing and in control of the operation of the workshop.[370]

McMahon was not the first to report using photographs on the Torres Strait but he was the most persistent in sending material to editors. For example, *The Sydney Mail* had published two illustrated stories on pearling in the Torres Strait before it published McMahon's features in 1917. One of these was by the famous author,

---

369   Bevan, S. *Battles Lines: Australian artists at war*, Milson Point, NSW, Random House, 2004, p. 173.

370   'Boat repairing', *The Queenslander*, 12.8.1916, p. 22.

AB (Banjo) Paterson, using nine photographs he purchased from RJ Nicholas's Austell Photography Studio on Thursday Island.[371]

Our northern outpost

McMahon opened his series in *The Queenslander* in 1916-17 with two double-page photomontages with thirty photographs. A month later, the series continued with thirteen more features with another seventy photographs. The popularity of this subject matter is indicated by the choice of the editors on four of those occasions to feature his Torres Strait photographs on the opening page of the 'Queensland Pictorial', the illustrated section of *The Queenslander*. The message he was offering was partly admiration for the traditions and customs of Torres Strait Islanders and also acknowledgement that they were playing an active role in commercial operations, mission life and self-government. This would have been enlightening for Brisbane readers who were not accustomed to such sympathetic treatment of indigenous peoples, either Indigenous Australians, or South Sea Island *kanakas*, most of whom had been deported just a decade earlier. McMahon used the racist terms 'black' and 'nigger' in these articles, but audiences in 1916 may not have been as shocked by that word as we are today. In 1917, in the final six images in his *The Queenslander* series, McMahon chose to emphasise the people and culture of the Torres Strait. This emphasis can be seen in his choice to include portraits and scenes of a woman and child, muscular workers, a boat crew (carrying McMahon ashore), a woman carrying

---

371   Paterson, AB. 'Pearling industry at Thursday Island: a day on a lugger', *The Sydney Mail*, 2.5.1902, pp. 1240–1242 (with nine photographs spread over three pages). This was during his trip to the New Hebrides; see Paterson, AB. 'New Hebrides; The pilgrim's progress; experiences of the settlers', *The Sydney Mail*, 2.8.1902 (with thirteen photographs, photographer not shown). See also anon., 'A pearling expedition to the South Sea Islands', *The Sydney Mail*, 25.5.1904, p. 1311 (with seven photographs).

bananas, and a local house. A European presence – visible only in a photograph of Councillors and the ketch *Herald* – was swamped by images of Torres Strait Islanders making lace and baskets, at school, in villages, weddings, games like tug-of-war, Island festivals and traditional and contemporary dances.

The Torres Strait Island Councillors were a popular subject for McMahon. He widely published one portrait with Mrs Zahel and Councillors, and in a separate formal setting, arranged four seated Councillors with four policemen in the rear row (see Fig. 35). This appeared in *The Queenslander* and in *The Sunday Times* in 1917 and in *Sunset: the Pacific Monthly* in 1918. The ethnographic and 'popular anthropology' approach in the Torres Strait gallery contrasts dramatically with his photography in the south-west Pacific where he mostly focused on European enterprise, plantations, mining, towns and wharves. McMahon's first publication on the Torres Strait was an impressive, seven-month-long series titled 'Around the Torres Strait Islands' in Brisbane's *The Queenslander*. It offered readers a comprehensive window on island life.

Date	Pics	Banner headline
12.8.1916	14	Badu (Mulgrave Island); An interesting community (over four pages)
16.9.1916	16	A quaint Torres Strait festival: Merry making on Mabuiag (double page)
14.10.1916	3	A Badu Island wedding
21.10.1916	0	Success of the Aboriginal Act; Isolation of teachers[372]

---

372   *The Queenslander*, 21.10.1916, p. 8. The Pictorial section that weekend was mostly WWI portraits.

Date	Pics	Banner headline
28.10.1916	7	Murray Island; Torres Strait
4.11.1916	9	Yorke Island; Torres Strait (double-page)
11.11.1916	2	Among the islands of Torres Strait
18.11.1916	6	The Guard at our Northern Outpost (Thursday Island)
2.12.1916	10	The ten little nigger boys
9.12.1916	6	Our Northern Outpost
6.1.1917	4	Darnley Island, Torres Strait
20.1.1917	6	Across the Gulf of Carpentaia; From TI to the Roper River
17.3.1917	6	The Roper River Mission
17.3.1917	5	The Juvenile section of the Roper River Mission
27.10.1917	6	A cruise around the islands of the Torres Strait

Table 4: *The Queenslander*'s Torres Strait series by McMahon

The final in this series on the Torres Strait was a summary statement with photographs carefully selected to be representative of the Torres Strait that McMahon had wanted to offer audiences.[373] This photomontage included pearling, portraits, villages and a classic boxing pose of three men on Yama Island and a group of six muscular men showing off their physique (see Fig. 34). McMahon's caption claimed, 'this type of men seen on all the islands'.[374] The line-up of muscular young men was a much-used composition in all his visits around the Pacific Islands; it

---

373   *The Queenslander*, 27.10.1917. p. 24.

374   *The Queenslander*, 27.10.1917, p. 24; and *The Australasian* (Melbourne), 21.4.1917, p. 5.

was not about boxing, but suggested the availability of fit, sturdy men as indentured labourers. He was to take many similar posed group portraits of muscular Islander men around the Pacific in the next decade, evidence for his claim, falsely, that there were plenty of labourers available in the Islands waiting to be employed in expansionary Australian enterprises.

Across *The Queenslander* series, McMahon was also keen to show how Australians were involved in the commerce, evangelism and administration of faraway places, so he included Mrs Zahel, the administrator and teacher on Badu, two European overseers in a boat repair business on Badu, a group of missionaries having afternoon tea, a group of twenty European visitors at a Mabuaig dance festival, and the training of Torres Strait Islanders as naval signallers. As he did not have to rely on the missions for housing, transport or guides, he included only four photographs of mission activity, a marginalisation of mission activity found in all the islands and territories he visited.

Pearling

Thursday Island, known as TI, was a significant port situated on several major shipping routes, but if the region was known at all 'down south', it was for the pearling industry. This had begun in the 1860s and it brought trading companies, hundreds of luggers, onshore jobs and a sizeable Asian and Pacific Islander population to the Torres Strait, right across northern Australia and down to Broome in the west. The pearling industry was a major focus for McMahon. He photographed several pearling stations, European managers, boat repairing, an Islander pearler's wedding and even a rough bush shack used a 'pearler's weekend resting place'.[375] He published several group portraits of the

---

375   'Boat repairing', *The Queenslander*, 12.8.1916, p. 22; *The Australasian*, 21.4.1917, p. 5.

pearling crews[376] but many more of luggers anchored offshore or beached at low tide. His favourite subject was a motor auxillary schooner, the *Goodwill,* owned by Papuan Industries Limited and he photographed Rev. Walker with the crew and later joined a supply run to the Roper River.[377]

McMahon's comment that pearling had been characterised by the behaviour of unsavoury types in the 'bad old days' attracted a letter to the editor from a Mr James Clark of Queen St, Brisbane, who challenged McMahon's account as 'libellous'. Clark cited many Europeans of a 'good class', some who were now fighting for the Empire. McMahon in contrast had referred to 'the orgies of the pearlers of former days … and the vile exploitation of the unfortunate natives'. The editor of *The Sydney Mail* agreed with McMahon, adding a comment that 'men of every class and colour from every part of the globe rushed to the new fortune-hunting rendezvous as the pearling industry boomed … many of whom led wild and desperate lives, made and lost fortunes'. The editor also noted that McMahon could not answer these criticisms as he was away in the Pacific, and defended McMahon by noting he had a fulsome knowledge of past and present pearlers, and that Mr Clark's rash generalisations about good types on the basis of one or two characters was inappropriate. The editor concluded that 'perhaps Mr McMahon was unnecessarily trenchant or was misinformed but on his part he is entitled to fair criticism'.[378]

In the accompanying text to *The Queenslander* series,

---

376   For the crew, see *The Orient I Found*, p. 40; *The Australasian*, 21.4.1917, p. 5; *The Queenslander*, 27.10.1917, p. 24, 22.9.1919, p. 23; *The Sydney Mail*, 16.5.1917, p. 16; *Auckland Weekly News*, 19.2.1920, p. 34.

377   For the *Goodwill*, see *The Queenslander*, 12.8.1916, p. 24; *The Sydney Mail*, 24.7.1918, p. 1; loose prints, McMahon Collection, Royal Geographical Society of Queensland. McMahon captioned it as both a ketch and a schooner.

378   McMahon wrote in *The Sydney Mail*, 24.7.1918, p. 19 and Clark to the editor on 21.8.1918, p. 22.

McMahon made assumptions and predictions in a journalistic style that he was to repeat often in the following decade as he sought fame as an Islands expert. On Badu, he praised the success of Papuan Industries Limited, declaring, 'this company have [*sic.*] built up a fine trading station, with stores, slip, loading jetty and a private residence, in fact everything for the complete working and handling of sea products such as trochus shell, turtle shell, beche-de-mer and before the war, pearl.' He also raised the possibility of increased scientific and scholarly interest, a topic on which he rarely commented, by saying of Murray Island that it will 'attract many travellers from all countries of the scientific world'. He had previously noted that the famed Cambridge University Expedition to the Torres Strait had studied the islands during 1898–1899. He also mentioned a theme that later became his dominant platform – commercial expansion and opportunities. He suggested that Darnley Island offered the Queensland government, as the controlling authority, 'an opportunity of starting cocoanut plantations on up-to-date and profitable lines ... that would not only benefit the natives but must from the start bring in a return'.[379] McMahon highlighted two industries that were 'of great commerical value and in constant demand ... I refer here to the collecting of trochus shell so useful in the making of pearl buttons and many other common articles, and beche-de-mer which is much prized as a food by the Chinese.' He noted that hundreds of tons of both items were leaving Thursday Island every month for China and Japan.[380]

---

379   For predictions, *The Queenslander*, 28.10.1916. p. 8; 12.8.1916, p. 8; and 6.1.1917, p. 6.

380   McMahon, TJ. 'Collecting Trochus shell and bêche-de-mer', *The Sydney Mail*, 1.8.1917, p. 14.

The *Sydney Mail*

Early in 1917, McMahon published twenty-eight photographs of the Torres Strait in *The Sydney Mail*. Some were in feature articles, some used by editors as a filler and some used in a general feature articles on Papua and the regions. He repeated some photographs from *The Queenslander* series but used others for the first time. The titles of his *The Sydney Mail* articles carried a similar message to those in *The Queenslander* eight months earlier.

Date	Pics	Title
28.3.1917	1	Native Signallers at Badu (a filler)
28.3.1917	1	Native Signallers at Badu (a filler)
16.5.1917	4	Native life on the islands of the Torres Strait
30.5.1917	5	Travel in Papua and Northern Australia (one pic on TSI)
1.8.1917	6	Collecting Trochus Shell and Beche-de-mer
24.10.1917	6	Industries of Papua and the Torres Strait (one pic on TSI)
24.7.1918	8	Torres Strait story of regeneration (double-page feature)
16.4.1921	1	Mrs Zahel on Badu (a filler)
6.7.1921	6	Badu Island (but photographs wrongly attributed to a distribution agency, PICA)

Table 5: McMahon's Torres Strait photographs in *The Sydney Mail*

The most spectacular feature in *The Sydney Mail* series focused on what McMahon called 'the story of regeneration'. It was a double-page spread, with eight photographs of a church, a large bible class, the Rev. Walker and his boat crew, dancers, barbers and market gardeners. The regeneration to which McMahon was referring was the transformation occurring in the Islands as industries, schooling and a cultural revival were taking place. It was a positive statement of success by the Islanders themselves, with support from missions and the Queensland government. McMahon, in an overly eulogistic manner, declared, 'the islanders … are thriving and unoppressed, their intelligence is remarkable and their usefulness is beyond question'. McMahon had been led to this conclusion after attending a remarkable cultural festival on Mabuiag Island early in 1916.

The festival had been in planning for several years until it was decided by the Islanders to combine the opening of a new Anglican church on Mabuiag with the proposed revival of play-acting, old dances and songs. Islanders came from other islands and many Europeans travelled to Mabuiag with McMahon claiming thousands of expatriate and Islander spectators had joined the 500 inhabitants on Mabuiag to attend the four-day festival. He declared that 'a more joyous, happy crowd one cannot hope to see'. As well as many photographs published in *The Queenslander* and *The Sydney Mail* series, McMahon also published a long report in *The Wide World* in 1918, titled 'Reviving an Aboriginal festival'.[381] It was about the Torres Strait Islanders, not Indigenous Australian Aboriginals. This article included ten photographs of the Mabuiag festival, including a war dance, pigeon dance (see Fig. 36), tennis dance and children's action songs, as well as feasting and a display by the Thursday Island naval signallers. McMahon indicated an empathy that he rarely displayed in his later travels

---

381   McMahon, TJ. 'Reviving an Aboriginal festival', *The Wide World*, Dec. 1918, pp. 15–56. These photographs also appeared in *The Queenslander*, 19.9.1916, p. 25.

round the south-west Pacific by declaring, 'it is to be earnestly to be hoped [*sic.*] that they never be robbed of that individuality of character which is at present one of the charms of these interesting and intelligent island races'. This phrase was repeated in both *The Queenslander* and his *The Wide World* article six years later.

McMahon's series of seven feature articles on the Torres Strait in *The Sunday Times* in Sydney did not appear until July 1920. The opening Torres Strait feature gave readers no chance of mistaking the economic value of the 'prolific isles of the Torres Strait'. The banner headline, with multiple by-lines typical of the day, declared:

THE PROLIFIC ISLES OF THE TORRES STRAIT
VAST RESOURCES OF WEALTH OF OUR NORTHERN ISLANDS
FAMOUS PEARL FISHING
GOVERNMENT OF NATIVE WORKS

The opening photograph was of local Councillors and police, and two of the six images depicted pearling.[382] Superlatives such as 'prolific', 'vast' and 'famous' were littered across McMahon's publications, starting in 1915 and continuing into the 1930s.

As well as the thirty features in *The Queenslander*, *The Sydney Mail* and *Sunday Times* (Sydney) McMahon published features from 1917 to 1920 in *The Australasian*, *The Week* and the *Northern Herald*, and newspapers occasionally used single photographs as fillers. One filler was a photograph of a large school group with their Torres Strait Islander teacher standing to the side, which appeared in *The Queenslander*, *The Australasian*, *Northern Herald* and *Sunday Times*. McMahon astutely guarded

---

382 *The Sunday Times* (Sydney), 18.7.1920, p. 18.

his portfolio, and of the twenty-two photographs used in these one-off filler or single appearances, ten had not previously been published. McMahon's Torres Strait articles also appeared in *The Lone Hand* in 1917 (Badu Island, with five photographs), in *Sunset: the Pacific Monthly* in 1918 (Murray Island, with four photographs), *The Geographical Review* in 1920 on the pearling industry (two photographs), in *Sea Land Air* in 1922 on Murray Island (two photographs) and in *Overland Monthly* in 1922 on the Torres Strait generally (no photographs).

When McMahon was revising an article he had published in *Sunset: the Pacific Monthly* in 1918, for publishing in *Sea Land Air* in 1922, he changed the title from 'The hiding place of thunder; Next door to utopia in the South Seas' to 'The hiding place of Thunder; Murray Island'. He added 'FRGS' to the version in *Sea Land Air*, and added a third and fourth by-line: '*Interesting native pearl fishers; Unique system of self-government*'. For *Sea Land Air*, the four photographs in the *Sunset: the Pacific Monthly* edition were replaced by photographs of dancers on Mabuiag Island and naval signallers demonstrating their signalling techniques. The text of the two articles differed slightly but retained the same line of argument that the progress, harmony and development in the Torres Strait relied on the provision of a good Australian administration.[383] In his private papers, there is an annotated copy of the *Sunset: the Pacific Monthly* article with numerous deletions and places where he intended to add new text. He changed the closing paragraph from 'what can be accomplished among black people through the paternal interest of a white government' to conclude four years later in *Sea Land Air* with,

---

383   *Sunset: the Pacific Monthly*, September 1918, pp. 33–34; *Sea Land Air*, Apr. 1922, pp. 249–51.

'what can be accomplished amongst black people by a humane white government'.[384]

Torres Strait: 1916–1923 compared

The diversity of McMahon's photography and its careful use for publishing can be seen by a comparision of his first feature in August 1916 with features over the next seven years. In *The Queenslander* in 1916 he began with a spectacular four-page photomontage with fourteen photographs. It was simply titled, 'Badu: Mulgrave Island'.[385] Two years later, ten photographs appeared in *The Wide World*, eight more in the *Auckland Weekly News* in 1920 and twelve more in McCarron's album on the Torres Strait in 1923. Of these later thirty photographs, only five had been published in his 1916 feature – making baskets, the battle dance, tennis dance, pigeon dance and Mrs Zahel posing with three Councillors. A village scene with forty Islanders sitting in the foreground of the Yorke Island Anglican church that had first appeared in *The Queenslander* in 1916 was also repeated later in *Northern Herald* and in McMahon's book, *The Orient I Found*. This suggests that McMahon had a large portfolio of prints made from glass plates and had so many to choose from that only five from the 1916 gallery were used again.

The photograph most used in these four publications between 1916 and 1923, was of Mrs ME Zahel, the administrator and teacher on Badu Island. McMahon also used it for features in *The Lone Hand, Illustrated London News, The Sydney Mail, The Week* and *Northern Herald*. Mrs Zahel was also one of his 'notable women of the Pacific' in an essay he published in *The*

---

384   McMahon Papers, Royal Geographical Society of Queensland.

385   McMahon, TJ. 'Badu Island (Mulgrave Island)', *The Queenslander*, 12.8.1916, p. 22–23.

Week in 1921.[386] The most noticeable emphasis in the forty-four photographs he published between 1916 and 1923 was that a third were ethnographic – portraits, dances and villages. There was only one in the picturesque category, four of mission activity, two related to administration and five of the pearling industry. Audiences distant from the Torres Strait and with little knowledge of its history probably read this visual record either as an accurate window on Indigenous life or as a sign that changes were having an impact – women making baskets and lace for sale, men repairing European boats, children attending school and local leaders serving as Councillors.

The most unexpected Torres Strait photographs that McMahon published were about turtles, demonstrating an interest in flora and fauna that he did not show elsewhere in his travels. He offered audiences photographs of turtle eggs, baby turtles and a huge 1.5-metre-wide turtle caught on a pearling lugger, and twice posed photographs of Torres Strait Islander children riding on the back of a turtle on a beach. These appeared in *The Queenslander* and many years later were used in 1928.[387] His Torres Strait photographs in *The Queenslander* series are an important historical archive as they document boat building, dance, housing, costumes and industries in the second decade of the twentieth century.

During his trip photographing and reporting on the Torres Strait, McMahon also travelled across the Gulf of Carpenteria (known as 'the Gulf') to Darwin to document the inland development of cattle stations, pastoral properties and missions.

---

386   McMahon, TJ. 'Notable women of the Pacific', *The Week*, 25.3.1921. p. 26.

387   Islanders had traditionally used turtle shell for fishhooks, needles, awls, spoons, combs, masks and ornaments. Historical records show that Islanders had traded turtle shell for iron and steel products during early European contact. It later became a major trade to Japan and the US for buttons and adornment.

The next section looks at his visual reportage on the Northern Territory.

The Northern Territory

The Northern Territory was in controversy at the time of McMahon's visit, with accusations of low levels of Commonwealth expenditure, or alternatively that funds had flowed into the Territory but with little development or impact. The Commonwealth had assumed control of the Territory from South Australia after federation, in 1911. Further debate surrounded the fate of Indigenous Australians, whether 'white men' could work in the tropics and whether the pastoral, agriculture and mining industries could survive high wages, unionism and a high cost of living. Commonwealth control was judged by many to be 'inimical to the welfare of the Territory ... bound up in momentuous questions of race deterioration, effective occupation and the very existence of the Commonwealth itself'.[388] McMahon commented on these issues in his text, but audiences perusing his photographs were not given any visual clues on these problems.

There had been several unsuccessful attempts to colonise the Northern Territory in the nineteenth century. By 1916, Darwin was a busy port, pastoral properties had expanded into remote areas, missions were active in Indigenous communities and the final 234-kilometre section of the Adelaide to Darwin railway was soon to be completed. McMahon photographed various scenes in Darwin but these did not give a sense of the uneven development and straggling existence, described by EJ Brady in 1918 as 'the unfinished metropolis of an empty country.'[389] The Northern Territory, commonly referred to as 'NT' or the 'Top End', was

---

388 Brady, EJ. *Australia Unlimited*, Melbourne, Robertson, 1918, p. 522.
389 Brady, EJ. *Australia Unlimited*, p. 540.

little known or understood down south, a silence in Australia's history that has been highlighted by Price, Cole, Hall, Reynolds and others.[390]

The Commonwealth's failings in the territory and its allegedly ill-directed expenditure were the subject of debate in federal parliament and a constant topic for Territorians. In an article in *The Lone Hand*, with five photographs, McMahon declared, 'there is nothing to show for that money and population is not steadily but quickly disappearing'. He was referring to failed pastoralists and agriculturalists who had quit the Territory. He added that 'the emptiness of the great vast north of Australia is one of the Commonwealth's greatest weaknesses'. It could be solved he suggested if the Territory's mineral wealth was developed, but overall he despaired of 'complete failure through the Commonwealth's indifference and incompetence'. He suggested that a Royal Commission should be called to inquire into these failings.[391] In 1920, after seeing a wide range of administration in colonies and territories around the nearby Pacific Islands, McMahon returned to this old theme. He had now heard the grumbles of settlers in Papua, the Solomon Islands and the New Hebrides where similar controversy raged about government policy, untrammelled access to indigenous labour, taxes and freight costs, and these were much the same complaints he heard in the Northern Territory. In an article in *The Wide World* magazine in 1920, primarily about the 'Never Never Land' and the Roper River mission and cattle properties, he again lamented that 'despite the

390   This silence is also covered later in ch. 13. Price, AG. *The history and politics of the Northern Territory*, Brisbane, University of Queensland Press, 1930; Hall, E. *The Territory; The classic saga of Australia's far north*, Sydney, Angus & Robertson, 1951; Cole, T. *Hell west and crooked*, Sydney, Angus & Robertson, 1988; Reynolds, H. *North of Capricorn; The untold story of Australia's north*, Sydney, Allen and Unwin, 2003; Mullins, S. *Octopus Crowd: Maritime History and the Business of Australian Pearling in its Schooner Age*, Tuscaloosa, University of Alabama Press, 2019.

391   McMahon, TJ. 'The Northern Territory', *Lone Hand*, 2.7.1917, pp. 388–90.

efforts of the government to develop it, and for a half-century at least, it will remain the strange weird Land of Loneliness'.[392]

His first contact with the Northern Territory was along the Roper River on a supply run by the *Goodwill*, involving a 160-kilometre trip up-river to pastoral properties and a mission station. He published photographs of the Anglican mission, the 'most isolated Police station in the British Empire' and the wreck of *Young Australian*, a victim of floods for which the Roper River was notorious. Well up-river at Paddy's Lagoon cattle property, he met Mrs Warrington Rogers and took several photographs of her posed with groups of Indigenous Australian workers who helped her run the property while her husband was away for six months each year driving cattle to market.[393] He later included Mrs Warrington Rogers as one of the 'Notable women of the Pacific' in the feature he published in 1921. He published two photographs of alleged 'murderers' who were being sent to Darwin for jail or to be trained as 'Black Trackers' used for capturing other wanted Indigenous Australians. McMahon noted the policeman who had captured them had fought at Gallipoli in 1914.[394] Referring to men who had fought in the war still raging in Europe was a common and noticeably popular journalistic approach and continued well after the war ended.

He also published photographs depicting Indigenous Australian culture and customs, including posing a large group of dancers for a portrait, body painting, *gunyahs* (huts), women carrying their children and a cave painting said to be a burial site.[395] In a tactic he was to use later in the Islands, he took a posed

---

392   McMahon, TJ. 'The land of loneliness', *The Wide World*, Sept. 1920, p. 476.

393   For Mrs Warrington Rogers, see *The Northern Herald*, 17.8.1917, p. 27; *Overland Monthly*, Apr. 1918, p. 286; *The Wide World*, Sept. 1920, p. 475.

394   For the two alleged murderers, see *The Sydney Mail*, 18.4.1917, p. 17; *The Wide World*, Sept. 1920, p. 475. For a modern treatment of this era, see the award-winning film, 'Sweet Country' (1917).

395   For the burial site, see *The Wide World*, Sept. 1920, p. 477.

portrait of a large group of men, and then a second photograph with himself in the middle of the group.[396]

The Roper River was said to be one of the Territory's richest assets, a great inland waterway and allegedly soon to be home to a Commonwealth-funded experimental sheep station. McMahon also had a self-portrait taken with four Islanders carrying his photographic equipment with the *Goodwill* anchored behind in the Roper River (see Fig. 37). This was widely published, appearing in *The Lone Hand, Overland Monthly, The Wide World* and *The Sydney Mail* from 1917 to 1920. This is a rare example that allows historians today to access McMahon's photography practice and the assistance he received locally wherever he visited. Another widely reproduced photograph featured the *Goodwill* pulled up along the banks of the Roper River with the crew unloading. A children's band on the bank had instruments made from old oil tins.[397] In 2021, Wikipedia used this McMahon image for its entry on the 'Roper River, Northern Territory'.[398]

McMahon's reportage of his expedition up the Roper River on the *Goodwill* highlighted the Christian mission and its surrounding Indigenous Australian people. In the seventh instalment of his *The Queenslander* series, McMahon devoted a whole page and accompanying text to the mission, which was an unusual level of emphasis for McMahon. His photographs included a general view of the mission, the rectory, the missionary's residence and a bedroom. A portrait of Rev. and Mrs Warren and

---

396   For a male dance group, see *The Wide World*, Sept. 1920, p. 475; *Overland Monthly*, Aug. 1918, pp. 283–9. It was also mistakenly published in an article on Papua: McMahon, TJ. 'Mists of Mafula,' *Overland Monthly*, Aug. 1919, pp. 83–5.

397   For the Roper River unloading and children's oil tin band, see *The Queenslander*, 20.1.1917, p. 21; *The Lone Hand*, 2.7.1917, p. 388; *Overland Monthly*, Apr. 1918, p. 289; *Otago Witness*, 26.7.1917, p. 36, *The Wide World*, Sept. 1920, p. 475.

398   The Oxley Library, Brisbane, was cited as the source. McMahon was not acknowledged as the photographer.

their baby included four of their mission helpers. Mrs Warren, who had ventured to the Territory as a young woman and had given birth without outside help, was later highlighted by McMahon as a notable woman of the Pacific.[399] In a group portrait of Indigenous Australians who lived at the mission, McMahon used terms today considered racist but in use at the time. This group portrait was captioned, 'Mission Blacks and Half-castes'.[400] He also published a group portrait of two Indigenous women and two children, captioned 'A happy family'.[401]

Darwin had been a brief visit and he only published photographs of the Commonwealth Hotel, Government House and a portrait of Judge Bevan, Vesty's payday and an Asian wood carter. The operation of supplying alcohol and hotel facilities in the Territory was a Commonwealth responsibility, and McMahon devoted a whole instalment in *The Queenslander* to the failure and resulting iniquities of this 'Commonwealth Hotel' system. He declared, 'not one word can be said in their favour'. The accompanying photographs for this long tirade against Commonwealth policy included one of a hotel. To provide context, he included photographs of a shipwreck, policing, the Pine Creek–Katherine railway and a self-portrait with his camera crew.[402] It was an unusually diverse gallery not obviously related to the hotel question. His trip south along the Pine Creek–Katherine railway only produced three photographs. He photographed a Royal Mail coach, claiming it 'makes the longest and loneliest journeys in the world'.[403] McMahon was never short of superlatives.

399   For Mrs Warren, see McMahon, TJ. 'Notable women of the Pacific', *The Week*, 25.3.1921, pp. 16, 26; *The Queenslander*, 17.3.1917, p. 8.

400   *The Queenslander*, 17.3.1917, p. 8.

401   This was the opening page of *The Queenslander*'s Pictorial section, 20.1.1917, p. 21.

402   McMahon, TJ. 'Government hotels in the Northern Territory', *The Queenslander*, 18.4.1917, pp. 17, 31.

403   For the Royal Mail, *The Wide World*, Sept. 1920, p. 477.

McMahon gave an address to the Royal Geographical Society (Queensland branch) in Brisbane in January 1917, attended by the governor. The *Northern Herald* noted that his recent articles on the Northern Territory had appeared in *The Brisbane Courier* and *The Queenslander*. Later in the year, McMahon gave another lecture and lantern slide presentation in Melbourne to a meeting of the Australian Natives Association. *The Age* in Melbourne reported that McMahon, 'in a chatty humourous style, described a number of excellent views illustrating a trip made from Thursday Island to the Roper River and Darwin'. In this talk, McMahon criticised current policies in the Territory and the failure to promote 'white men' in the development of the Territory. The Administrator of the Northern Territory, Dr Gilruth, was in the audience and *The Age* reported that he responded with comments of a 'non-controversial nature'. McMahon then travelled north to Cairns and gave a similar illustrated lecture for a Red Cross charity event.[404]

The Queenslander series on the Northern Territory started with 'On the Roper River' in January 1917 and ran for ten instalments with seventy-five photographs. Four instalments were devoted to the Roper River trip, mission and 'Aboriginal' culture, three to Darwin and one article each to Vesty's meat works, Commonwealth-owned hotels and the Pine Creek–Katherine railway. Some photographs also appeared in a feature in the *Northern Herald* and many appeared as single fillers in *The Sydney Mail* in the 1920s, including one portrait of a seven-foot-tall (213 cm) pastoral worker and another of giant ant hills.[405] Another thirty-three photographs appeared later in illustrated articles in *The Lone Hand, Overland Monthly, The Wide World* and

---

404   *Northern Herald*, 26.1.1917, p. 31. *The Age* report was published in the *Northern Herald* on 18.5.1917, p. 31.

405   *The Sydney Mail*, 3.3.1926, p. 35 (man), 10.3.1926, p. 12 (ant hills).

Mid-Pacific. Although he had visited the Roper River and Darwin and travelled on the Darwin–Pine River–Katherine railway line, this was a limited contact considering the size of the territory. Although a small gallery compared to the deluge on Papua he was publishing over the same period, these NT photographs form a valuable archive.

Norfolk Island and Lord Howe Island

McMahon briefly visited Lord Howe Island and Norfolk Island on the regular Burns Philps run while en route from Sydney to the New Hebrides in September 1920. *The Sydney Mail* reported his departure, noting 'his articles on Pacific questions have established him as an authority and his remarkable photographs have been published in many countries'.[406] This would have been a pleasing acclamation of his efforts over the previous five years.

The two-day stopover in Lord Howe Island was brief, and he only published nine photographs in two articles. The first was in the *Auckland Weekly News* in 1921, titled 'Glimpses of life and industry on Lord Howe Island'. It offered readers six scenes: a general view of the island, two of kentia palms, a settler's home, an old cannon and the landing of stores on the beach.[407] The second feature appeared a year later in *The Telegraph* in Brisbane, titled 'The land of the Kentia palm', with three different photographs: a horse dragging a bag of kentia nuts to the jetty, a kentia palm grove and a group of residents. McMahon noted the residents were all 'white people', just in case audiences might be confused by it being a Pacific island 779 kilometres north-east of Sydney. It had 130 residents when McMahon visited and had just been moved to the jurisdiction of New South Wales in 1913. McMahon noted the

---

406   *The Sydney Mail*, 28.7.1920, p. 7.

407   The cannon was rumoured to have been from HMS *Supply*, en route with convicts to Sydney in 1788.

kentia palm industry had started in the 1870s but had only been put on a sound commercial footing in 1906, which slumped during the war but had revived and was now exporting direct to Sydney. Kentia palm seeds and seedlings were then a boom industry, as a 'palm court' was a feature in the foyer of the world's top hotels, royal palaces and the homes of the wealthy. Visiting ships at Lord Howe Island had to stay offshore as there were no harbours and winds swirled around the island. With little produce to unload or take on as cargo, this was a short visit. With a small population, limited commercial opportunity and being safely in the British Empire, there was little to interest McMahon.

The Burns Philp run then headed further north-east to Norfolk Island, 1600 kilometres from Sydney. It had been mapped by James Cook in 1774, who noted the potential of its unique pine trees for shipping spars and masts and its flax for making sails. It then became a settlement for recidivist convicts from New South Wales in two phases: from March 1788 to February 1814, and from 1825 until closing in 1855. In 1856, the entire population of Pitcairn Island, the descendants of the HMS *Bounty* mutineers, was relocated to the vacant Norfolk Island due to overcrowding on Pitcairn. Although small groups returned to Pitcairn in 1858 and 1863, others stayed on Norfolk and made it their new homeland. McMahon related most of this story to his readers and accompanied this text with photographs of the physical evidence of the prison era, picturesque scenery and the lemon peel and juice industry. He noted that on the return leg of the trip, they had delivered 1600 cases of lemon peel and lime juice to Sydney.[408] He failed to mention the export of bananas to Australia or oranges to New Zealand. He commented on Norfolk as a 'honeymoon island' with possible tourist potential, an aspect of development in the

---

408   The *Urana Independent and Clear Hills Standard*, 8.10.1920, p. 4.

Islands he rarely commented on. The visit to Norfolk was only slightly longer than at Lord Howe Island, but McMahon managed to take portraits of some of the *Bounty* descendants.

Five of his Norfolk Island photographs appeared in *The Sydney Mail* in a feature devoted to the lemon juice and peel industry. This was said to be booming, with thousands of casks of juice and peel being shipped out to Sydney and an extraordinary harvest of lemons still waiting. He declared, 'there is no doubt a future for this industry and the Norfolk people look to Australians to encourage their enterprise'. This was classic McMahon, always searching for the expansionary commercial hook on which to make his reputation as an observer and expert. A single photograph of children playing by the walls of the convict ruins, used as a filler, appeared in *The Sydney Mail* in 1921 and another of a horse and cart carrying supplies down to the landing appeared in the *Importers and Exporters Journal of Australia* in 1922.[409] McMahon's reliability as a supplier of illustrations also led to several of his Norfolk Island photographs appearing in pictorial and serial encyclopedias, including the landing at Cascade, an impressive facade or arches in the convict ruins and an avenue of Norfolk Island pines.[410] He also published articles on Lord Howe Island and Norfolk Island, without illustrations, in *Chamber's Journal*.[411] After these two short visits, he continued on to Port Vila in the New Hebrides (covered in chapter 10).

The visits to Lord Howe Island and Norfolk Island were brief compared to his longer visit of two months to the New Hebrides and three months in Fiji. If his trips along the equator to Nauru,

---

409   McMahon, TJ. 'Lemon juice and peel industry of Norfolk Island; *The Sydney Mail*, 12.1.1921, p. 12; *Importers and Exporters Journal of Australia*, 24.6.1922, p. 57.

410   *Countries of the World*, Vol. 6, pp. 3785–86; *The New World of Today*, Vol. 8, 1922, p. 123.

411   McMahon, TJ. 'Lord Howe Island', *Chamber's Journal*, Apr. 1923, pp. 255–6; and 'Norfolk Island', Jan. 1926, pp. 39–41.

Ocean Island, the Gilberts and Marshalls and return trips to Papua and German New Guinea are added, there was certainly no other Australian journalist or photographer who could claim such an extensive itinerary, but travel did not necessarily make him an expert commentator, analyst or reporter. It might also be noted that his Torres Strait, Northern Territory, Norfolk Island and Lord Howe Island photographs, while prolific and wide-ranging, followed a familiar compositional format and conformed rather than challenged current visual practice, popular reporting conventions and aesthetic tropes. But taking into consideration his seven-year campaign, across a wide and diverse region, with thousands of photographs published and hundreds of articles, he indeed was without peer as an photographer and journalist.

Chapter 12

Empire, expansion and Australia's role in the Pacific

McMahon's illustrated articles over a decade, as the war ended and the superpowers realigned former colonies, promoted three lines of nationalist and sub-Imperial argument. The first was that Britain should be praised for its fine work in administering and developing its colonies but now should take a more dominant position in the post-war Pacific. The second, and more widely applied argument, was that Australia should take advantage of opportunities for trade and commerce and possible colonial rule over territories either formerly belonging to Germany, held by Britain or jointly held by Britain and France. The third was that Australians should, and had, migrate and settle successfully in the Islands. He maintained these three lines of argument for a decade even when the region's fate had been settled with Australia being awarded control over German New Guinea and given joint control over Nauru with New Zealand and Great Britain.[412] Neither Britain nor France had shown any inclination to change the status of the British Solomon Islands Protectorate nor the condominium arrangement in the New Hebrides. Despite this, he embarked on a journalistic campaign to publish opinion pieces on a range of topics linking Australia to the Pacific.

---

412   See Thompson, RC. 'Making a Mandate: The Formation of Australia's New Guinea Policies 1919–1925', *The Journal of Pacific History*, Vol. 25, no. 1, 1990, pp. 68–84.

McMahon's three-pronged strategy to attract fame began in late 1915 with a visit to Papua and the sending of photographs to Australian illustrated newspapers. The first tactic adopted was as a photographer, to publish, unsolicited, the photography of the islands he visited. His second tactic was to offer himself as a travelling expert and speaker on the public address circuit. Thirdly, as a journalist he wrote small supporting commentaries to embellish the images. In all three approaches, his main target was to become known as an expert not only on Australia's future role in the Pacific in commerce and trade but also as a colonial governing authority. In April 1916 in one of his earliest publications, McMahon used the banner headline 'Our new possession: German New Guinea'. This was not true as the war was still in progress, and although an Australian military force had occupied the former German colonial territory in 1914, it was not until December 1920 when Britain, for Australia, was granted a mandate. Calling German New Guinea 'our new possession' was his first foray into political posturing and boosting of a sub-Imperial role for Australia.

McMahon's obsession with fame caused him to have a myopic view of what was of national economic, political and strategic importance, and this prevented him from providing an objective reading of the post-war scene. However, he did update his rhetoric and boosterism to accord with the changing situations. For example, a feature in 1917 in *The Telegraph,* repeated in *The Week* in Brisbane, had a headline that boldly stated, 'Australia's concern; Retrospect of German trade and methods in the Pacific; Possibilities of German New Guinea'. This boosting, imperialist and expansionary argument regarding Germany's role in the region was repeated three years later in a feature in the *Northern Herald,* titled '*Watch on the Pacific: A traveller's worry; Australia's neglected opportunity*'.[413] But in 1920, he acknowledged that there were new threats on the horizon as he had just visited the Solomon Islands and Marshall Islands and noted the increase in Japanese trade with the Pacific. Countering Germany now changed to a platform of alarm and being wary of a new threat - Japan - alongside criticism of the USA for 'stealing' trade that otherwise should have come to Australia.

Germany was McMahon's first target. In December 1917, *The Week* noted a public address and lantern slide show by McMahon in Brisbane and declared, 'McMahon has been reminding us in Queensland that Germans are still in the islands acquired many years ago'. *The Week* reminded readers that McMahon had often highlighted the plantation potential and trade success waiting across the region and an editorial noted that 'Mr McMahon's plantation pictures were really the most suggestive and gratifying of his gallery'. A few weeks later in January 1918, he gave a public address and lantern slide show in Sydney on the fate of nearby islands in the post-war world. This talk was published between 10 January and 19 March in the *Daily Commercial News and Shipping Lists* and *Sydney Morning Herald* in Sydney, *The Capricornian* and *The Morning Bulletin* in Rockhampton, *The Age* in Melbourne, *The Cairns Post*, *The Daily Telegraph* in Launceston, *Northern Herald* in Cairns and in the *Papuan Courier* in Port Moresby.[414] This was an impressive level of public access across the Australian states. It suggests that what McMahon had to say about the Pacific was of national interest and topical. In January 1918 when he spoke in Sydney, the war in Europe was unresolved and General

---

413   McMahon, TJ. 'Australia's concern: Retrospect of German trade and methods in the Pacific', *The Telegraph*, 15.12.1919, p. 3 (with two photographs), repeated in *The Week*, 21 Dec. 1917, p. 20 (with four photographs); McMahon, TJ. 'Watch on the Pacific; A traveller's worry; Australia's neglected opportunity', *Daily Telegraph* (Sydney), reprinted in *Northern Herald*, 30.6.1920, p. 49.

414   Thanks to Trove, this type of republishing network can easily be traced.

Monash's stunning victory at Hamel was still months away, but the Islands nearby were open for trade and commerce and were clearly a matter of public interest. McMahon was arguing that the Pacific had been thrust into 'greater prominence' by the war and would become a magnet for trade and 'wonderful commercial activity'. McMahon called for 'one flag over these scattered territories ... with Australia as the crowning territorial jewel'. In a flourish, he concluded this article by suggesting 'the future of the Pacific should march with the future of Australia and with the future of the British Empire'. [415] This was boosterism and grand Imperial expansionism of the first degree.

He stressed in New York's *Dun's Review* in 1918 that 'the short space of thirty years has made investors and traders of other nations more keenly alert to the amazing prospects' of the Islands.[416] In 1919, in London's *Empire Review*, he repeated his main argument, highlighting the advances made by Germany and Japan in terms of trade but now argued that expansion was being held back by the 'strange and unpardonable ignorance of English people'. This, he claimed, was allowing other nations like Japan and the US to forge ahead in the Pacific and take the major share of a trade that in ten years 'should be worth fifty million a year'.[417] These concerns were perhaps lost in a Britain that was still engaged in a costly war in Europe.

In August 1918 as the war was ending, he published a long essay (of 2521 words) in *The Sydney Mail,* without photographs, titled 'The fate of Australia: German trade and methods in the Pacific'. This repeated his previous arguments that Germany had prospered

415   McMahon, TJ. 'The Pacific Islands', *Sydney Morning Herald*, 12.1.1918, p. 8. See also Strating, Rebecca and Wallis, Joanna. *Girt by sea: Re-Imaging Australia's security*, Melbourne, Black Inc, 2024, chapter 6.

416   McMahon, TJ. 'The islands of the South Pacific', *Dun's Review*, 29.3.1918, pp. 48–49, 51.

417   McMahon, TJ. 'The South Pacific Islands: Their resources and prospects', *Empire Review*, Aug. 1919, pp. 249–51.

and developed the Islands and that now it was Australia's turn to reap the commercial rewards and Imperial acknowledgement.[418] This was fine rhetoric and probably attracted applause from viewers and audiences at a public address and nods from newspaper readers, but when McMahon penned these phrases, the region was undergoing a post-war economic slump.

McMahon continued this same line of expansionary argument when he travelled to London in 1919. His speeches were printed in London newspapers and were later republished across the east coast of Australia. His article in late 1919 in the *London Mail*, 'Advance of the Jap; Command of the whole Pacific trade', was republished in the *Daily Herald* in Adelaide, *Kalgoorlie Minor* and *the Western Argus* in Kalgoorlie and *The Cairns Post* and *Northern Herald* in Cairns. He declared, 'this Japanese grip of the Pacific trade – not worth a Japanese toothpick five years ago – is especially significant', and he cited the Marshall Islands as an example of Japanese trade penetration 'where every article of trade ... is Japanese'. In London, he promoted the idea of British expansion and the British dominance of Pacific trade as a counter to the German trade presence and the more recent advances made by Japan. At three lectures at the Royal Photographic Society and then at the Royal Colonial Institute, McMahon argued that while the threat of German control of trade had diminished when they lost their Pacific colonies, Britain now had to step up rather than be uninterested in the Pacific.[419] He repeated much the same phrasing as he had been using in Australia, stressing that the value of South Pacific trade was ten million pounds annually and that it might grow to fifty million annually. McMahon rarely cited official sources and was rather loose with his predicted

418   McMahon, TJ. 'The fate of Australia: German trade and methods in the Pacific', *The Sydney Mail*, 13.8.1918, p. 17.

419   Reprinted in the *Northern Territory Times and Gazette*, 15.7.1920, p. 6.

trade figures. He highlighted the existence of major trading ports such as Suva, Port Moresby and Rabaul, noting they 'are in close touch with the outer world by telephone and wireless (and had) botanical gardens ... streets, tradesmen, fresh-water systems and other conveniences'.[420] To English audiences, he repeated an anecdote in which the King of Nauru petitioned King George to maintain the British protection and administration that had been in place since the removal of the Germans in 1914. This was the same argument that he just published in *The Sydney Mail*.[421] His London campaign was being followed in Australia, for example, with the *Examiner* in Launceston and the *Daily Commercial News and Shipping List* in Sydney reprinting his London talk on the value of the islands to the British Empire.[422]

While in London, McMahon replied to an article that had appeared in *The New York Times* and had been read at the Royal Colonial Institute in London. The topic was 'Problems of reconstruction in the Pacific' by Guy H Scholefield, a New Zealand journalist, historian and war correspondent.[423] McMahon wrote a letter to the editor of the *United Empire*, and declared,

> it is a great mistake to continue to suppose that the South
> Sea islands are any longer mere regular groves of cocoanut
> or pandanus palms and the haunts of naked and aggressive
> savages. British missionaries, traders, officials, investors and
> traders have all done splendid work and it is not fair that
> their energies should go unrecognised'.

---

420 McMahon, TJ. 'South Pacific Islands: Value to the British Empire, *The Daily Telegraph* (London), 16.10.1919.

421 *The Sydney Mail*, 29.10.1919. p. 17.

422 *Examiner* (Launceston), 29.12.1919, p. 6; *Daily Commercial News and Shipping List*, 29.12.1919, p. 3.

423 Scholefield had published *Who's who in New Zealand and the western Pacific* in 1908 and had just published *The Pacific: Its Past and Future*, London, 1919 and 'Problems of reconstruction in the Pacific', *United Empire*, pp. 326–9, 1919.

He had used this phrasing several times in articles published in London and in Australia, and when his letter to the editor of *Empire Review* was republished in *The Sydney Mail,* some readers might have noticed the repetition.[424]

By 1920, a lost opportunity caused by Japanese expansion of trade became his new platform. In Adelaide, on his way home from England, he gave an illustrated public lecture on the commercial possibilities of the Islands and the effect in Australia if Japan kept expanding its trade in the Pacific. This was covered in May 1920 in length by Adelaide's five newspapers: *Adelaide Advertiser, The Mail, The Express and Telegraph, The Register* and *The Observer.*[425] McMahon stressed again that the Islands were an attractive field for investment, that trade was valued in millions of pounds, and that if Britain was not awake to the possibilities waiting in the Pacific, then Australia should step in and reap the benefit.

He then travelled to Sydney and spoke at the Millions Club in June 1920, warning that 'Asia was waking from her sleep of ages'.[426] His talk was headlined 'Watch the Pacific: A traveller's warning; Australia's neglected opportunity'. McMahon stressed in this speech that industrial strikes, taxes and regulations on maritime shipping were strangling Australia and preventing it from becoming 'the mistress of the South Seas'.[427] The level of public or political party agreement with his arguments is unknown, but

---

424   *The Sydney Mail,* 29.12.1919, p. 17; same phrasing in *The Daily Telegraph* (London), 16.10.1919. Scholefield's article had appeared in *The New York Times,* 21.3.1920 and earlier in the *Otago Daily Times,* 22.5. 1919, p. 6 .

425   *The Adelaide Advertiser,* 4.5.1920, p. 6, 13.5.1920, p. 6; *The Mail* (Adelaide), 8.5.1920, p. 2; *The Express and Telegraph* (Adelaide), 12.5.1920, p. 1; *The Register,* 22.7.1920, p. 7; and *The Observer* (Adelaide), 24.7.1920, p. 20.

426   *Northern Herald* (Cairns), reprinted from the *Sydney Daily Telegraph,* 30.6.1920, p. 49.

427   *Daily Telegraph* (Sydney), 4.6.1920, p. 5. The Millions Club had been formed in 1912 to promote Sydney as a major city. It became the Sydney Club in 1963.

this speech was republished in the *Daily Telegraph* (Sydney), *Tweed Daily* (Murwillumbah), *The Northern Miner* (Charters Towers), *The Cairns Post, Townsville Daily Bulletin* and *Northern Herald*. In outback Queensland, the *Western Star and Roma Advertiser* noted his Sydney talk and declared, 'the eyes of the world were on the Pacific, which would become the amphitheatre of international interest before long'.[428] His views might have been alarmist and based on generalisations, but they were getting a wide distribution among capital city and provincial audiences.

McMahon had generated much of the Australian general public's understanding, albeit limited, of the neighbouring south-west Pacific Island region. He had been reporting on both what he saw in the post-war decade and on the thirty years of European contact before the war, beginning with German copra plantations and trade established in New Guinea since 1884, on the Solomon Islands where more than a hundred British plantations were well-established and on mining for phosphate that had started in 1900. He had reported on Fiji, where CSR had started operations in the 1880s. McMahon had also written on specific new industries such as phosphate, sisal and tobacco and the opportunities that existed for Australian investors if there was government support. He was writing in an era of post-1900 colonial expansion when New Zealand had taken control of the Cook Islands, Niue and Tokelau, Japan had expanded in the north Pacific, Britain had created colonies in Tonga and the GEIC and in the New Hebrides in a condominium with the French, and the USA had taken eastern Samoa, Hawaii and Guam.

McMahon was in full expansionary mode in 1920 when

---

428 *Western Star and Roma Advertiser*, 5.6.1920, p. 2. The paper did not mention that he was a local boy, born nearby at Mount Abundance in 1864. Mount Abundance Homestead is a heritage-listed homestead built in 1860, on the Warrego Highway at Bungil near Roma in the Maranoa region of Queensland. Wikipedia uses McMahon's photograph of the station, unattributed and wrongly dated.

he published in the *Sunday Times* in Sydney, extolling the opportunities that were awaiting Australia in Papua, German New Guinea, the Gilberts and Nauru. He alerted readers to Australians' potential benefit, and loss, in the scramble for post-war trade that included the Germans, Americans, French and Japanese. An editor's introduction to the third feature in the series declared that, after a trip to the New Hebrides, McMahon had, 'returned to Sydney to prepare a series of lectures and articles on the information he gleaned. He has come back filled with a desire to let Australians know what a chance they are missing in not taking more interest in the South Pacific Islands. He believes it is Australia's destiny to be trustee of all lands in the South Pacific'.[429]

Date	Pics	Headline
18.7.1920	6	The prolific isles of the Torres Strait
8.8.1920	6	Romantic treasure island of the Pacific (Nauru)
10.10.1920	1	Reflections from the South Pacific
17.10.1920	8	The gateway of the Pacific (Gilbert Islands)
24.10.1920	0	Trade buccaneers in the South Pacific; Will Australia beat them off?
14.11.1920	7	Big chance for Australia's energy; Papua's fertility
5.12.1920	6	The mandate over ex-German new Guinea

Table 6: McMahon's series in *Sunday Times* (Sydney) in 1920

McMahon presented an impressive expansionist, economically focused gallery on the Pacific to *Sunday Times* readers with

---

429   *The Sunday Times* (Sydney), 10.10.1920, p. 5.

thirty-four photographs. Five of these features were full-page collages with photographs cropped and presented in rectangular or oval framing, with some oblique or overlapping.[430]

In 1921, with the war over and German territories already redistributed, he returned to the same theme in *Empire Review*, but now the bogeyman was not British reticence but expansion by Japan and the USA. He also adjusted his timeframe by citing a twenty-year history of Pacific trade and growth and a much-reduced regional figure of £12 million sterling a year in trade. He repeated the ominous warning to Australia concerning, 'the astounding strides of Japanese trade and influence'. By this time, McMahon had visited the Japanese mandate in the Marshall Islands and seen firsthand the impact of Japan's presence. He repeated a criticism he had been making for several years, arguing that the failure of British trade to expand was caused by 'Australian industrialism' and the iron grip of Australian unionism.[431]

In 1921 before heading to Fiji, he published again about Japan, trade and commercial possibilities. The Japanese, he declared, were on a 'firm footing everywhere' and were now buyers of copra in places where seven years earlier they had not been known at all. He alleged the pearling industry in the Torres Strait Islands was 'now mainly controlled by Japanese', that the Northern Territory had become the magnet of Japanese ambitions and, incorrectly, that the nickel mines of New Caledonia were 'absolutely in Japanese hands'. He claimed that 6000 or 7000 Japanese had settled in New Caledonia. These were wild allegations, and while Japanese labour, traders and shipping were present in the Northern Territory, Torres Strait and New Caledonia, it was not as dramatic as McMahon alleged. He then gave a list of the

---

430   The series ran from July to December 1920.

431   McMahon, TJ. 'The South Pacific islands trade: Effect of Australian strikes', *Empire Review*, May 1921, pp. 164–67.

commercial and export potential of the Islands: copra, rubber, sisal, tobacco, cotton, cocoa, coffee, sugar, petroleum and phosphate. He had photographed all these industries and sent images around the world. He was on less sure ground suggesting that 'tea, rice, maize, spices and kapok' also had potential. In a rare example of citing published sources regarding trade, in *The Telegraph* and in *The Week,* McMahon provided a statistical summary of imports and exports for Pacific territories that he had borrowed from Stewart's *Handbook of the Pacific,* the standard reference on the Islands at the time, citing figures from 1920. His long commentary concluded in a typical McMahon flourish: 'Australia would be wise to take in a full recognition of the commercial possibilities of these islands and it will be a red-letter day in the commercial progress of the Commonwealth when once more its traders can command the trade of the South Pacific'.[432]

In a long essay in June 1922 in the *Importers and Exporters Journal of Australasia,* he repeated many phrases and paragraphs from earlier pieces but went into more detail on each potential item of trade: copra, cotton, sugar, rice, rubber, sisal and phosphates. He added a new category, marine products – pearl, trochus shell, bêche-de-mer, shark fins and turtle/tortoise shell – and revived an old claim from his publications on the New Hebrides, the sulphur industry. He also added ivory nuts to the list of potential export staples and suggested that cattle and sheep could be used effectively in plantations to keep vegetation down and supply a second stream of income. He claimed copper mining was about to begin at Laloki in Papua (it had already failed) and wrongly claimed Misima Island in eastern New Guinea was still a viable gold field. He concluded with the same appeal that he had been

---

432   McMahon, TJ. 'Pacific Islands trade; Japanese activities, development and progress in the South Pacific', *The Telegraph* (Brisbane), 26.2.1921, p. 11; also published in *The Week* (Brisbane), 4.3.1921, p. 26.

making for the past seven years – 'Australians particularly must arouse themselves to the commercial possibilities of the South Pacific'. The *Importers and Exporters Journal of Australasia* article was accompanied by ten photographs he had published several times previously: bales of sisal hemp ready for export, labourers, copra, cotton, rice and rubber plantations and, unrelated to the text of the article, a mission school and scenes at Suva, Vanua Lava and Norfolk Island.[433]

The visit to Fiji was his last venture in the Islands, and his final attempt to claim 'I was there' expertise as a booster of Australian interest in trade with the Pacific. After the trip to Fiji in 1921, he made a dramatic and remarkable (and brief) attempt at a new career by taking a voyage to China seeking fame as a photographer and reporter on East Asia.

The Orient I Found

In July 1922, McMahon departed on the Eastern and Australasian Steamship Company's *Arafura* on a long cruise through Asia, but his career as a patriot, Islands expert, booster of sub-Imperial expansion and British colonial expansion and photographer of the Pacific was not quite over. His boosting of Australian trade, investment and settlement of the Pacific continued. This was made quite clear in the report of his departure in *The Telegraph* in Brisbane.

> Mr Thomas J McMahon leaves today for a trip through China, Japan, Philippines, and Borneo. He will give a series of lectures before the commercial bodies in these countries and for the purpose is bringing with him sets of slides on Australian industries and his travels in the South Sea Islands. During his visit in the East, Mr McMahon will collect all the

---

433   *Importers and Exporters Journal of Australasia*, 24.6.1922, pp. 56–58.

information possible in reference to trade with Australia and on his return will travel through the states giving illustrated lectures on the subject.[434]

Immediately on his return to Australia, McMahon published a general commentary on his trip followed by a series of seven columns in Brisbane's *The Telegraph*, with an accompanying thirty-four photographs running through to January 1923.[435] The subject matter of these photographs of Asia reflects the choices he had been making in the Pacific Islands in recent years, wavering between commercial, trade and industrial imaging (banks, wharves, porcelain factories, quarry workers) and ethnographic or human-interest subjects (nursing children, shepherding ducks, junks, geisha, tea-houses, soldiers and meat sellers). The headlines for his articles suggest an emphasis on the former, the accompanying photographs on the latter. His series in *The Telegraph* began in November 1922.

Date	Pics	Headline
20.11.1922	0	Throbbing East; Australia's opportunities going to other nations
9.12.1922	4	Japan and China: Most fascinating travel
16.12.1922	6	Sandakan (British Borneo), the sea front and its people
23.12.1922	4	Manila (Philippines); a famous and beautiful city
30.12.1923	4	Modern Japan; a progressive people
6.1.1923	5	Modern Nippon: Australia and Japan

---

434   *The Telegraph* (Brisbane), 18.7.1922, p. 2. This notice was repeated the next day, p. 2.

435   These photographs appeared later, along with nineteen additional photographs in his book, *The Orient I Found*.

Date	Pics	Headline
10.2.1923	6	China: Cities of Swatow and Canton
17.2.23	5	Hong Kong; British energy and enterprise
24.2.23	7	Shanghai: The Paris of the East

Table 7: *The Orient I Found* series in *The Telegraph* (Brisbane), 1922–1923

The editor of *The Telegraph* called him a 'noted publicist' and a Queenslander who had made a name for himself for his photographs and descriptions of the Islands. The editor declared that McMahon was correct in 'at least two of his main propositions – namely, the greatness of the Eastern market, and secondly, the necessity for businessmen and not government agents attending to business there'. McMahon had stressed this second proposition with a subheading, 'Individualism and Commerce', suggesting that in the East, private commercial agents would achieve greater success than government appointees.[436] Strangely, he only sent one of these stories, 'Shanghai: The Paris of the East', to *The Sydney Mail*.[437]

By the early 1920s, McMahon's criticisms and Imperial posturing no longer attracted public attention as the world had moved on after the Great War. Australia had already assumed its new colonial responsibilities in Nauru and the former German New Guinea, aeroplanes were linking remote communities, soldier settlement schemes offered a new life for many, and the jazz era seemed to herald a period of progress and prosperity. Although prescient in his predictions about the rise of Japan as a trading

---

436   McMahon, TJ. 'Throbbing East; Australia's opportunities going to other nations,' *The Telegraph* (Brisbane), 20.11.1922, p. 2.

437   'Shanghai: The Paris of the east', *The Sydney Mail*, 28.2.1923, p. 15.

nation, this was still a long way ahead in the case of China. McMahon's predictions on Japanese expansion were ignored.

His book published in 1926, *The Orient I Found*, based on his trip to Asia, used many of the photographs published in *The Telegraph* in 1922. It sank without much comment. The photographs in *The Orient I Found* were considered by reviewers to be 'an admirable series of photographs' but the text was 'inclined to be rather alarmist of what the future may bring'.[438] It was considered a book of passing glances rather than a deep analysis of the turmoil in China due to the 1911 revolution, the end of the Manchu dynasty in 1912 and the armed conflict between warlords, revolutionaries, communists and nationalists that followed. He omitted to mention that the Communist Party of China had just been formed a year before his visit. He was criticised for being 'too prone to accept statements without verifying them' and providing information that was easily obtainable elsewhere and that was 'not only unreliable but definitely incorrect'.[439] His coverage was regarded as too superficial and merely anecdotal, being obtained hearsay or second-hand. A reviewer in *The Bulletin* declared, 'he saw no more than the ordinary tourist and has recorded his impressions fairly well though with a tendency into hasty generalizations'.[440] *The Telegraph* published a second review of his book four months later by 'EJ', who concluded that it was a 'well-written, splendidly illustrated book by a keen observer who knows what he is writing about but who has come to certain conclusions that are contestable'.[441] These were the same criticisms of his

---

438 *The Telegraph* (Brisbane), 25.9.1926, p. 11.

439 'OR', review of *The Orient I Found*, in *The Geographical Journal*, Vol. 68, no. 6, 1926, pp. 516–17. The reviewer thought his sixty-two photographs were 'excellent and well produced'.

440 Anonymous review in *The Bulletin*, 24.2.1927, p. 3.

441 *The Telegraph* (Brisbane), 13.1.1927, p. 4.

reportage that he had attracted throughout the decade following his first trip to the Islands in 1915.

On his return, he realised there were limited opportunities for being an expert on Asia and he took up a salaried position as a Brisbane-based photographer and journalist. The next chapter reveals another McMahon, quite different to the expansionary polemicist and Islands photographer in the chapters so far. Between 1923 and 1933, he became a popular back-country photographer and commentator on prize pigs, oil wells, rural shows, new bridges, railways and experimental farms.

The other McMahon: back-country photojournalist in Queensland

After a short break when he travelled unsuccessfully to Britain, McMahon focused his publishing mostly on the nearby Pacific Islands. In 1922, he was actively promoting his Pacific photography by sending articles to publishers worldwide while at the same time earning a livelihood by acting as a freelance back-country photojournalist.[442] Realising his search for fame in the Pacific was not going to lead to a Fellowship at the RGS, he made a short trip to east Asia in 1922, which led to articles and a book, but which he realised was also not a path to fame. So, his career took another turn and in 1923, he began full-time employment with the *Brisbane Courier* as a photojournalist covering the Darling Downs, Granite Belt, the south-west and Brisbane's hinterland. He also photographed out further west to Thargomindah, Charleville, Roma, Dalby, Warra and Cooyar and to the 'three corners', the junction of the borders of South Australia, New South Wales and Queensland. This was now a remarkably different Tom McMahon. His rural Australian photographs between 1915 and 1933 offer a gallery

---

442   A typical report in the *Northern Herald* by McMahon was on Mareeba, inland from Cairns, and Point Lucinda near Ingham in October 1915, with eight photographs in the *Northern Herald*, 8.10.1915, p. 27.

of photomontages on outback life and form an impressive visual archive of early twentieth-century rural Australia.

Phase 1: in North Queensland, 1915–1922

McMahon became well known to Queensland readers as a travelling back-country reporter visiting country shows, schools and new enterprises, sending in a photographic record of his visits accompanied by a column sometimes extending to a full newsprint page of text. Alongside *The Cairns Post* and the *Northern Herald*, he also published many of these stories in *The Bundaberg Mail*, *The Week*, *The Brisbane Courier*, *The Queenslander* and *The Telegraph* in Brisbane, *The Sydney Mail*, and *The Weekly Times* and *The Australasian* in Melbourne, where he was equally well-known. This was McMahon in the role we now know as a photojournalist, and in this role, McMahon's name was probably recognised as much by audiences as for his role as a photographer of the Islands and a polemicist for Australian expansion. Known to friends as 'Tom', he was comfortably employed but no doubt disappointed his Islands career had stalled.

In 1916, when he was living as a farmer at Malanda near Cairns and was a part-time roving rural photographer, he began sending illustrated features down to Brisbane, such as 'Mareeba: a northern town that is "smartening up"' (with four photographs) and on the Moravian Christian mission at Mapoon, with nine photographs.[443] Audiences were presented with a double-page feature on 'Mapoon Aboriginal Mission' with photographs of the old people's village, the playground, a staff member's house, the Mapoon band, girls at work sawing timber and displays of local produce including the 'staple industry – coconuts'. Three of the European missionary

---

443   McMahon, TJ. 'Mapoon', *The Queenslander*, 16.12.1916, pp. 8, 22–23. Mapoon later became infamous as a destination for the 'stolen generation'.

staff were featured in portraits. The associated text appeared in 'The Sketcher' pages elsewhere in *The Queenslander*.[444] A year later, some of these photographs appeared in the *Northern Herald* as 'fillers'.[445] McMahon did not show much interest in photographing Queensland's Indigenous population other than commenting on their role in articles on the cattle and pearling industries or in the craft industries they were taught while on mission reserves. In 1919, he published one commentary, without illustrations, titled 'Improving the Aboriginal'.[446]

In 1917, he published on Cooktown in *The Sydney Mail*, highlighting the Captain Cook memorial, the banana industry and Cooktown's proximity to Cape York,[447] and two articles in *The Queenslander* on Cape York called 'The tip-top of Queensland'. The Cooktown article included full-page collages with eleven photographs of local identities, the staff of the telegraph station, the abandoned jetty at Somerset, coconut plantations and an abandoned homestead, once 'the furthest northern cattle station'. Somerset, the subject of four of these photographs, had been established as a telegraph station, military outpost, customs house and residency in the 1860s but it was replaced by Thursday Island in the 1870s and had been long abandoned when McMahon visited. Frank Jardine, whom McMahon posed in a sitting portrait, was its most famous resident.[448] Several of McMahon's Cape York photographs were used later by John McLaren for an article in *The*

---

444   For Mapoon, see *The Queenslander*, 16.12.1916, pp. 22–23. The text was on p. 8.

445   *Northern Herald*, 10.8.1917, p. 27.

446   McMahon, TJ. 'Improving the Aboriginal', *The Telegraph* (Brisbane), 31.5.1919, p. 10. Indigenous Australian history and contemporary conditions did not attract McMahon's attention, as he was solely focused on the Pacific Islands and European-led commerce and expansion.

447   *The Sydney Mail*, 23.5.1917, p. 11.

448   McMahon, TJ. 'The tip-top of Queensland', *The Queenslander*, 10.11.1917, p. 23, 17.11.1917, p. 23.

Lone Hand on 'Utingu; The coconut plantation at Cape York', and by McMahon for his own book in 1926, *The Orient I Found*.[449] The photographs he sent down south to Melbourne included a full-page collage on 'North Queensland and the Islands', with four photographs of the Torres Strait Islands, the Mapoon mission and Indigenous men training as naval cadets.[450]

A boosting-type illustrated article, published in *The Cairns Post* and *The Sydney Mail* in June 1917, highlighted the local paper pulp and dyeing industry that was supplying southern states and New Zealand. It was widely repeated, appearing, for example, in *The Australasian* (Melbourne) and *The Evening Telegraph* (Charters Towers), again illustrating how authors and photographers were reaching a wide audience as both capital city and rural newspapers republished material from other districts, other states and overseas.

An illustrated feature in Townsville's *Northern Herald* on the Cairns hinterland had eleven photographs dramatically arranged across two pages; this included several street scenes, a dairy on the Atherton tableland, mills, bridges and vistas of tropical river scenery.[451] It was a format that he relied on many times over the next two decades. Although mining was a staple of the Queensland economy, it was not a major focus of his reportage. He did report briefly on the arsenic mines on the Granite Belt,[452] the gold, silver, lead and zinc mines at Chillagoe near Mareeba and the tungsten mining at Wolfram, west of Cairns in 1919, calling it a 'rich centre'. His eleven photographs of Wolfram certainly gave

---

449   *The Lone Hand*, 1.10.1917, pp. 545–46; McMahon, TJ. *The Orient I Found*, pp. 30, 32, 68.

450   The initial feature on the pulp paper industry, without photographs, was in *The Cairns Post*, 29.6.1917; it later appeared with five photographs in *The Australasian*, 7.7.1917, p. 25.

451   *Northern Herald*, 29.5.1919, pp. 30–31.

452   McMahon, TJ. 'The wonderful arsenic mines of Queensland', *The Sydney Mail*, 26.11.1924, p. 19.

an impression of a busy, working mining operation with aerial ropeways, processing plants, dams for water and a busy town servicing the miners. Mining at Wolfram had slumped after 1910, was closed during the war and collapsed in the 1920s. Audiences of McMahon's gallery were not alerted to this decline.[453]

McMahon's rural reportage was earning him a regular income and it financed his visits to the Pacific Islands. When he took a trip to London, this meant rural Queensland took a back seat in his publishing output in the 1919–1921 period while he focused on nationalist, expansionary material on the south-west Pacific.

Phase 2: magnificent achievement

McMahon returned to outback Queensland topics in 1922 with a series of articles on the Upper Burnett, inland from Bundaberg, where he had been a tutor in an earlier career. These appeared in *The Queenslander*, *The Telegraph* and *The Week*. He was critical of the close settlement scheme to develop the district known as the 'Burnett scheme' and noted the cattle industry was in a depression, and that despite being along the Burnett River, farmers were boring for water.[454] He then took an extended trip to the 'Great Southwest' that led to photographically illustrated articles on Goondiwindi and other centres. *The Telegraph* reported on his return to Brisbane in July 1922, noting McMahon's criticisms of the lack of government support for remote ventures. McMahon had listened to rural grumbles and then reported on crippling taxation rates, the failure to eradicate prickly pear, and transport

---

453   For Wolfram, see *Northern Herald*, 27.8.1919, p. 31 (illustrations), pp. 36–37. The Wikipedia entry on Wolfram uses a McMahon photograph of the main street: https://en.wikipedia.org/wiki/Wolfram,_Queensland. The Historical Towns of Australia website for Wolfram also includes many of McMahon's photographs (but not attributed): https://historicalaustraliantowns.blogspot.com/2018/07/wolfram-camp-remnants-of-mining-past.html

454   *The Telegraph*, 9.6.1922, p. 3, repeated in *The Week*, 16.6.1922, p. 5 and *The Telegraph*, 17.6.1922, p. 11.

and marketing struggles faced by the wool industry in the far west. In contrast, closer to home, in *The Telegraph* and *The Week*, he noted that on the Darling Downs, he was 'much impressed with the grand stretches of cultivation about Warwick, Toowoomba and Ipswich ... such evidence of rich soils and prosperous farmers is a magnificent advertisement for Queensland'.[455] This was the classic style of boosting that had characterised McMahon's reporting on the Pacific.

McMahon continued to extol the commercial potential of every rural district he visited. In the Great Southwest, while reporting on 'The progress of the famous sheep runs', he depicted substantial homesteads, railway lines and piles of wool bales ready for shipping to the coast.[456] He also wrote of troubles in the wool industry, including taxation. His North Queensland features included 'Go ahead Townsville – the capital of the North', Malanda, 'the heart of the tableland' and closer to Brisbane, Nambour, which he declared was 'rich and beautiful'.[457] In a brief diversion, he also reported on the scientific preparations at Goondiwindi for a solar eclipse.[458]

In 1923, in his new salaried career with *The Brisbane Courier* and *The Queenslander*, he published a feature on Gayndah, calling it the 'cotton metropolis of Queensland', but strangely the accompanying photograph was of the Gayndah butter factory. This would have been an editorial error, certainly not by McMahon. His Gayndah feature in *The Telegraph* was repeated in *The Week* in Brisbane and a year later in *The Sydney Mail*.[459]

---

455   *The Week*, 8.7.1922, p. 6.

456   *The Telegraph*, 'The Great Southwest', 8.7.1922, p. 6; 22.7.1922, p. 15; 29.7.1922, p. 11.

457   *The Telegraph*, 25.10.1922 (Malanda); 9.6.1923 (Nambour); 28.7.1923 (Townsville).

458   *The Week*, 15.7.1922, p. 11.

459   For Gayndah, see *The Telegraph* (Brisbane), 28.4.1923, p. 11; *The Week* (Brisbane), 4.5.1923, p. 25; *The Sydney Mail*, 7.5.1914, p. 30.

McMahon was perhaps confusing readers when he highlighted cotton, but then praised dairying, beef, timber, piggeries and butter factories as the main economic activity in the Upper Burnett. According to McMahon, Dalgangal House, Hillcroft cattle property and the self-proclaimed beef capital of Eidsvold were evidence of Queensland's rural prosperity.[460].

In 1925, McMahon published six photographs of the construction of the new Monto railway line in the Upper Burnett. Lines were also being planned to link Monto to Maryborough, Bundaberg and Gladstone. This was the type of economic expansion – in this instance based on cattle and mining – that McMahon loved and had been promoting all through his career and always wrote about with a great flourish, even if the photographs were often prosaic, depicting construction camps, rail laying and bridges. He also photographed Ceratodus railway station, named after the lungfish found in the Burnett River, one of only three rivers in the world that is a habitat for the *ceratodus*.[461]

In another diversion, he published a full-page collage in *The Telegraph* on 'Sydney; city of gaiety and enterprise'.[462] Audiences would have been impressed with the array of Sydney's multi-storied public buildings, bridges, the city, the Mint, Government House and Sydney's Union Club but perhaps wondered why no gaiety or private commercial enterprise was pictured.

Soldier settlers

In 1923, McMahon reported on another contentious issue – the fate of the Commonwealth soldier settlement scheme in which

---

460   For Eidsvold, see *The Queenslander*, 25.10.1924, p. 23, with eight photographs in a full-page collage.

461   *The Queenslander*, 18.7.1925, p. 26. Ceratodus station officially opened in October 1923.

462   *The Telegraph*, 14.7.1923, p. 11.

returning soldiers from the Great War could be given rural allotments as a means of starting a new life and concurrently adding to the nation's rural economy. This operated in all states. McMahon's feature with five photographs on El Arish (also known as Maria Creek), 100 kilometres north of Cairns, was republished by *The Week, The Telegraph* and *The Sydney Mail* depicting stability and progress.[463] When McMahon visited El Arish in 1923, three years after it had been declared a settlement, the first substantial homes were being built by the seventy men now engaged on their own land in the sugar industry. The railway to Innisfail and the school had also just opened. In 1924, he visited a soldier settlement scheme on the Granite Belt where 700 parcels of land known as the 'Pikedale Scheme' had been granted to 400 returned soldiers.[464]

McMahon visited the Granite Belt region again in 1930 and 1931 and reported on success rather than the failure of the scheme. He also reported on the soldier settlement scheme at "The Highlands" near Samford, noting there were now only twenty farmers remaining. The accompanying photographs depicted strawberry farms, barley, the local school and the Pine River. His text now reads as a sad comment on the scheme. He reported that,

> The soldier settlement known as The Highlands, situated twenty miles from Brisbane and six from Samford, is close to Mounts Nebo, Glorious and O'Reilly. Some twenty settlers are engaged in dairying, fruit growing, and market gardening in this picturesque area. About ten or twelve years ago the area was apportioned out to a number of returned

---

463   *The Telegraph*, 3.11.1923, p. 11; *The Week*, 2.11.1923, p. 3; *The Sydney Mail*, 28.11.1923, p. 29. The name El Arish came from a garrison captured by Australian forces from the Ottoman Empire in 1916; El Arish was featured on the ABC TV Landline series in 2012; see https://www.abc.net.au/news/2021-04-24/anzac-landline-soldier-settler-success-at-el-arish/100092126.

464   *The Brisbane Courier*, 8.3.1924, p. 15. Of those who started in 1917, only fifty remained in 1927.

soldiers, but from the first they were of the opinion that they were handicapped, as the class of country was not considered by them to be sufficiently productive from an agricultural point of view, the value of the land was high, and the holdings were too small. Finding it impossible to make a comfortable living a number of the settlers abandoned their holdings, which have since been taken up by the remaining settlers, some of whom now own up to 100 acres, which they have converted to freehold.[465]

McMahon also photographed WWI memorials, then being built in every country town, usually at a road junction, in a park or in front of a substantial public building. After visiting Goondiwindi in 1922, he reported on the opening of its new memorial. He wrote, 'this memorial will stand in the most prominent public place in the town at the junction of several streets and the way to the railway station. It is of marble and of striking dimensions and will ever be a splendid testimonial to brave men'.[466] At Maryborough and Stanthorpe, he also photographed the new local halls dedicated in the memory of soldiers.[467]

In Stanthorpe in 2017, a monument to local soldier settlers was erected, depicting a soldier settler, his wife, horse, plough and tools surrounded by logs, granite, and unfelled trees. The story of soldier settlement was told brilliantly by Marilyn Lake in *The Limits of Hope: Soldier Settlement in Victoria 1915–38*. Much of her analysis also applies to Queensland's experience.[468]

---

465   *The Brisbane Courier*, 13.9.1930, p. 9.

466   *The Week* (Brisbane), 8.7.1922, 15.7.1922.

467   For Maryborough, see *The Sydney Mail*, 6.8.1924, p. 38; for Stanthorpe, see *The Sydney Mail*, 24.9.1924, p. 43.

468   The history of rural, suburban and city war memorials in Australia was the subject of the award-winning book by Ken Inglis, *Sacred Places: War Memorials in the Australian Landscape*, Melbourne, OUP, 1998. For New Zealand, see Phillips, J. *To the memory: New Zealand's war memorials*, Nelson, Potton and Burton, 2016.

The north: prosperous and bountiful

McMahon's employment with *The Brisbane Courier* allowed him to freelance and use photographs taken from 1915 to 1922 for publication in other newspapers and magazines. In 1923, McMahon launched a four-month series with illustrated articles on 'The North' in both *The Telegraph* and *The Week* in Brisbane. To announce the start of this series, *The Week* declared it would provide evidence of 'problems both many and varied studied from week to week by Mr McMahon, our special correspondent'. It noted McMahon was an author and traveller and would provide fully illustrated articles.[469] *The Cairns Post* reported that McMahon was travelling on behalf of several metropolitan publications in Victoria and New South Wales and that his clear lucid descriptive style would be well illustrated.[470] For two weeks, *The Telegraph* repeatedly announced the promised series on 'The North' would begin soon, and this editorial was republished outside Brisbane, for example, in *The Bundaberg Mail* and the *Beaudesert Times*. In Brisbane, *The Week* repeated the notice of the forthcoming series, but rephrased the by-line to 'What the North needs'.[471] *The Cairns Post* and *Northern Herald* responded to this question with a controversial editorial – 'New state for Queensland and why'.[472] Breakaway movements had already tested the new federal structure with Western Australia also asking similar questions, so this type of journalism attracted readers' attention.

McMahon's series on 'The North' finally began in September 1923 with a feature on 'Innisfail; the gold land, surpassing fertility and beauty'.[473] This was classic McMahon, praising progress and

---

469 *The Week*, 21.9.1923, p. 3.

470 *The Cairns Post*, 26.7.1923, p. 4.

471 *The Week*, 21.9.1923, p. 3.

472 *The Cairns Post*, 22.10.1923, p. 9; *Northern Herald*, 28.10.1923, p. 29.

473 *The Telegraph*, 22.9.1923, p. 11 (with six photographs).

economic success but now adding the picturesque as a further lure to southern readers. Twelve feature articles with an impressive eighty-six photographs followed, running through to December 1923. Each feature appeared in both *The Telegraph* and its sister publication, *The Week*.

Date	Pics	Headline
22.9.1923	10	Innisfail: The Gold land; Surpassing fertility and beauty
27.9.1923	6	North Queensland: Richest and most resourceful portion of the Commonwealth
6.10.1923	6	Disabilities of Settlement: Commercial relationships of North Queensland to Southern states
13.10.1923	6	Go-Ahead Townsville: Capital of the North
20.10.1923	6	Chillagoe and district: The Mining smelters
27.10.1923	6	Bowen: Its resourceful district; Rich coal fields of Collinsville; Beautiful Sugar
3.11.1923	5	El Arish: Successful Soldier Settlement in North Queensland
10.11.1923	7	Babinda: A rich sugar district
17.11.1923	9	Cairns: Busy and prosperous port; A rich and resourceful hinterland
24.11.1923	7	Great Atherton Tableland
1.12.1923	9	Mackay: An important sugar centre; A town of banks.
8.12.1923	9	North Queensland: Four sugar centres (Lucinda, Halifax, Ayr, Ingham)

Table 8: 'The North', McMahon's series in *The Telegraph* (Brisbane)

McMahon's pictorial coverage was similar in most centres he visited. For example, in the opening feature on Innisfail, he included the main street, government offices, the post office, the hospital and the wharves on the Johnstone River. He also included the School of Arts, another iconic Australian development in suburban and rural areas. Also known as Mechanics Institutes, they had spread through the English-speaking world in the mid-nineteenth century, promoting education for the working class. Even small communities in Australia had a Mechanics Institute or School of Arts. The buildings have mostly been retained and now serve a wide range of community and commercial uses. The coverage of Innisfail was repeated for other centres. In week two of the series, McMahon depicted Kuranda in similar fashion, highlighting banks, monuments, railway stations, sugar and the timber industry.[474] These eighty-six photographs on Far North Queensland carried an important message to Brisbane readers that the north of the state was prosperous and bountiful with sugar, dairying, mining and pastoral properties.

As this series was being published, a major event was occurring in Australia with the final rails being laid for a railway linking Perth in Western Australia, via South Australia, Victoria, and New South Wales to Cairns. This was truly a massive undertaking, providing communication and access to what were still quite separate and parochial states. McMahon loved this topic, full of national rhetoric and expansion similar to his Pacific reporting over the previous ten years. His report on the new rail link was taken up and reprinted widely, for example in the *Western Mail* in Perth, in Albury on the Victorian–New South Wales border and in suburban newspapers in Sydney such as the *Circular Head Chronicle* in Manly. As a patriot with an eye for commercial

---

474   *The Telegraph*, 27.9.1923, p. 5 (with six photographs).

opportunity and economic gain, the rail link was of immediate appeal to McMahon as a story.[475]

As a journalist now employed by a city newspaper, McMahon acknowledged he needed attention-grabbing headlines, so he chose the long-running argument known as the north–south divide, declaring that northern Australia had a troubling relationship with politicians and decision-makers in Brisbane far to the south near the border with New South Wales, and even further south with the Commonwealth Parliament, then located in Melbourne, in what was still a new nation. It has been argued by historians that Australians down south ignored or knew little of the northern regions for much of the nation's history,[476] but McMahon's illustrated series contradicts this claim. Newspaper readers in the 1920s certainly knew what was happening in North Queensland, and thanks to McMahon, had visual evidence of growth and of problems.

In 1924, McMahon toured from Brisbane to the Granite Belt in the Southern Downs and NSW border districts, and this led to a series of illustrated features running through to mid-year. His reporting was thorough, and most centres scored a mention: Wallangarra for its railway depot, Glen Alpin, Ballandean, Broadwater, Thulimbah, Stanthorpe for its fruit growing and vineyards, Pikedale, Wyberba, Eukey and Killarney. This series followed the usual format with WWI monuments, hospitals, schools, churches, railways, post offices, bridges and banks, and if the timing of his visit was good, the local, annual agricultural show. The local agricultural show was a much looked-forward-to annual event in rural districts and a quintessential aspect of country life,

---

475   For example, repeated in *The Albury Banner and Wodonga Express*, 2.1.1923, p. 29.

476   See footnote 367 for references.

recreated in the capital cities with their annual city version, the Royal Brisbane, Sydney and Melbourne Shows.[477]

He published several reports on the Goomeri–Boonara district inland from Gympie, highlighting 'the rich ranges of Manumbar' and declared that the Goomeri district was 'the home of lucerne'. He depicted lucerne cultivation, bridges, the state school and prominent citizens and declared that go-ahead rural districts were well served by their civic-minded citizens and local government leaders. He declared that Goomeri–Boonara had several 'energetic public bodies'.[478]

One of his favourite towns was Thulimbah near Stanthorpe in the Southern Downs. In 1924, he published much the same article on Thulimbah in *The Queenslander*, *The Brisbane Courier*, and *The Sydney Mail*. Following his standard promotional line of reporting, this article was titled 'The rise of Thulimbah', and the eight photographs covered cabbage and bean farms, orchards and produce being carted to the railway station for shipping to Brisbane. A photograph of a young boy sorting vegetables in large baskets was repeated as a filler at the end of the year in *The Sydney Mail*, illustrating again how urban readers of illustrated newspapers were being constantly offered images of rural life and how editors gave prominence to images of rural prosperity.[479] Rural readers would have felt comforted to see that elsewhere across Australia, many others were still following the same routines of farm life.

In 1924, he also made a long trip to the 'three corner' district of Thargomindah, near the Queensland, New South Wales and South Australian borders. This series was labelled the 'Great

---

477 See Darian-Smith, Kate and Wills, Sara, *Agricultural Shows in Australia: A Survey*, Australian Centre, University of Melbourne, 1999.

478 *The Queenslander*, 25.10.1934, p. 19; 1.11.1924, p. 41 (on Goomeri).

479 *The Brisbane Courier* (Brisbane), 29.3.1924, p. 15; *The Queenslander*, 28.6.1924, p. 11 (text), p. 23 (photography); *The Sydney Mail*, 12.11.1924, p. 46 (the young boy with backets of vegetables).

Southwest'. Thargomindah was a key service town for pastoral properties and for cattle being shipped south down the Darling River to South Australia. His pictorial coverage of Thargomindah, with eight photographs in a full-page collage, included the main street, hospital, school, the town water supply (an artesian bore), the magistrate's home and a now abandoned stagecoach depot. The most poignant image was of an overladen bullock wagon heading out of town. To city audiences, this was a highly romantic view of the bush and a nostalgic reminder that, while the cities on the coast had become modern with colonnaded multistorey offices, buses, cars, trams and suburban trains, in the outback many things remained unchanged. The text had multiple headlines in the style of the day: 'Thargomindah; Busy Stock Route town; Flourishing institutions'. The text covered a classic range of rural interests and daily problems – the provision of street lighting, dust storms, dingoes and water supply – and noted the existence of original homes and buildings from an earlier era.[480]

To city readers, this was fascinating material demonstrating that some Australians continued to live in the 'bush', deep in the outback, far from city facilities and luxuries. This perhaps reinforced the city–bush divide but also endeared city audiences to rural Australia, a link promoted by AB 'Banjo' Paterson, EJ Brady, Harry 'Breaker' Morant, Will Ogilvie, Henry Lawson and other well-known literary figures. In 1925, the noted Australian author, Vance Palmer, called it 'the divide', a metaphor for the Great Dividing Range that separated the well-watered eastern coastal fringe of the continent from the vast inland, or outback. He declared that 'beyond the horizon or even the knowledge of the cities along the coast', there was a vast inland, 'the only thing after all that gives this continent meaning and a guarantee of the

---

480   *The Queenslander*, 2.2.1924, p. 25.

future'.[481] This was exactly the optimism, progress, and prosperity that McMahon was also promoting.

McMahon also visited Charleville, another major centre in the south-west. In *The Brisbane Courier*, he excelled himself with a full-page collage of eight portraits (oval-shaped head-and-shoulder) of local personalities and four general views of the town.[482] His report on Charleville two weeks later in *The Queenslander* was perhaps one of his best and was typical of the past ten years of reportage. It was a stunning example of his flowery language in text and captions, accompanied by a double-page collage of seventeen portraits and views. He began the text by drawing readers back to the old days:

> In the very early 1900s a lonely inn stood on the north bank
> of the Warrego River on the main stock route from Bourke
> in New South Wales to the west and centre of Queensland.
> This isolated hostelry was the meeting place for squatters,
> drovers, shearers and teamsters.

He then provided a detailed summary of rural community life, including the ambulance and fire brigade services, sport, aerial services, local Public Boards, the Charleville Club, post office, wines, fruit industry, churches, schools, the WWI memorial and the local *The Times* newspaper. This was a comprehensive statement about rural towns and bush life.[483]

He later reported on Chinchilla, Mitchell, Yeulba, Charters Towers and other remote centres.[484] In a full-page feature on Mitchell, between Charleville and Roma, he noted that it was a

---

481   Palmer, Vance. 'The divide', *The Bulletin*, 26.3.1925, pp. 10–11.

482   'Charleville: How a city was forged in the Great Southwest', *The Brisbane Courier*, 6.3.1925, pp. 11, 24–25.

483   *The Queenslander*, 21.3.1925, pp. 24–25 (pictorial), p. 41 (text).

484   For Mitchell, see *The Brisbane Courier*, 8.5.1925, p. 17; for Chinchilla, see *The Brisbane Courier*, 21.7.1927.

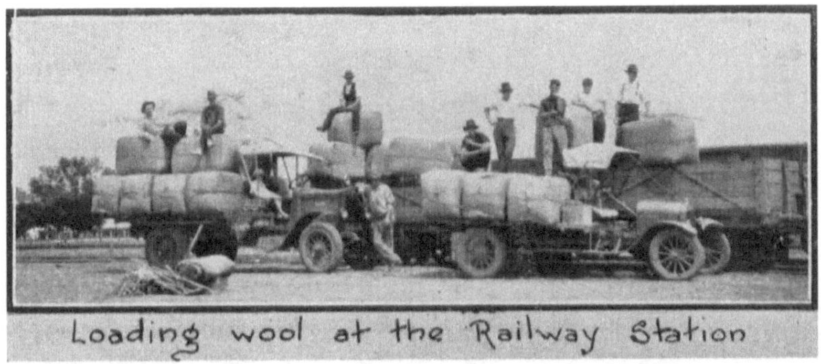

Fig. 38 'Loading wool at the railway station', 1915

prosperous centre and had well-managed public institutions. The collage on Mitchell included six views of the town and eight head-and-shoulder portraits in oval frames arranged randomly across the page.[485] This was the motif for much of his rural reporting – progress, prosperity, strong public infrastructure (railways, schools, co-ops, substantial town halls) and led by responsible pioneers and new settlers. He repeated this format later in the year in *The Brisbane Courier* when reporting on Charters Towers, claiming it was 'The dawn of a new era'.[486]

McMahon used the phrase, the 'Great Southwest', but this may have been an overuse of the superlative 'great' as he also talked about and photographed what he called the 'Great Northwest' and the 'Great Far North'. This format of boosting, panegyric adulation was the version of Queensland he presented when he travelled to Sydney in November 1924 to give a talk, with lantern slides, at the Sydney branch of the Royal Colonial Institute. The text of that talk in Sydney, and the lantern slides, have sadly not

---

485   'Mitchell: a prosperous centre; well managed public institutions', *The Brisbane Courier*, 8.5.1925, p. 17.

486   'Charters Tower', *The Brisbane Courier*, 22.12.1925, p. 11.

survived, but it probably followed the format and depiction used in *The Queenslander, The Telegraph* and *The Week*.

In 1926, he published a full-page collage in *The Queenslander* on Mount Larcom, a farming district between Rockhampton and Gladstone. These ten photographs followed the classic line-up of earlier reports with the railway, school, dairying, the town's new motor ambulance, two street scenes in the township and a portrait of an early settler.[487] In October 1926, he was still reporting on rural industries and towns like Cooyar, north of Toowoomba, and its timber and dairying resources, and the 'fruit industry of the north coast' around Palmwoods, Montville and Buderim. Two of these features appeared in the same issue of *The Queenslander*, with fourteen photographs following the same format: views of the main street; timber, dairying and pineapple farms; and the bank, the state school, the railway station and the new hotel at Cooyar.[488] He again published photographs of Cooyar in 1930, but these may have been taken during his 1926 visit. Even though now focusing mostly on the Southern Downs and Brisbane's hinterland, in 1929 he also returned to stories on the north of Queensland by presenting an impressive double-page pictorial feature on 'North of Cairns; potential asset of settlement; Slumbering isolation or splendid Daintree', with three photographs. Another feature in 1931, on Wide Bay, had thirteen photographs.[489]

Although not as prolific, throughout this period he continued to send away illustrated features to magazines. 'The Great Barrier Reef; a romance of turtle soup' appeared in *The World Today* in 1928, with eight photographs of turtles, the *MV Ethelbert* that serviced the soup factory on Northwest Island, turtle soup

---

487   *The Queenslander*, 6.3.1926, p. 28.

488   *The Queenslander*, 23.10.1926, pp. 11, 22, 24.

489   For Cairns, see *Northern Herald*, 30.10.1929, p. 23; for Wide Bay, see *The Queenslander*, 26.2.1932, pp. 12–13.

factory workers and a mysterious grave of a child on Northwest atoll. This was based on his earlier report in *The Queenslander* on the 'turtle industry of Northwest Island' which had included ten photographs, several of which were repeated in *The World Today*.[490] Typical of rural newspaper practices in the 1920s, his story from *The World Today* was picked up by a rural newspaper in Victoria and republished by *The Horsham Times* as '1000 miles of coral; The Great Barrier Reef'.[491]

In 1928, he published an article on oil drilling at Roma in *The New Nation Magazine*. This included the main street of Roma, an oil drilling rig, local motor cars and, intriguingly, a view of the gardens at the Mount Abundance pastoral property where he had been born in 1864. (He did not mention this fact in the article.) The *New Nation Magazine* article was based on a report on Roma he had published a year earlier in *The Brisbane Courier*. The drilling for oil at Roma was a regular news item at the time. He reported a year later, in 1929, on oil drilling in a large report with nine photographs on 'Longreach; The home of the merino; great progress'. The Longreach reportage was a classic McMahon depiction of commercial progress and economic growth. It included oil drilling, Longreach's main street, shire hall and offices and a portrait of a prominent citizen. He depicted the use of motor lorries to transport wool bales. He also included a photograph of the old-fashioned but continuing practice of carting wool bales by bullock wagon. To emphasise Longreach's modernity, he also photographed a Qantas plane at the local airstrip and another taking off on the Charleville–Camooweal route.[492] Two months earlier in 1925, the writer and literary critic, Vance Palmer, had

---

490 *The Queenslander*, 6.3.1926, p. 3; *The World Today*, 1926, pp. 304–310.

491 *The Horsham Times*, 11.5.1928, p. 3.

492 *The Sydney Mail*, 27.5.1925, p. 33. Qantas had only been founded five years earlier in 1920.

written in *The Bulletin* about the Charleville–Camooweal flight, declaring,

> a flash of light cuts across the sky ... flying over the western railheads, over mobs of travelling sheep, over the silver-lead fields at Mt Isa .... an amazing thing this steel-winged bird that drones over the silent reaches blotting out the sense of distance and making the very stars seem nearer.[493]

McMahon probably had read Palmer's comment in *The Bulletin* but did not note it in his own reports.

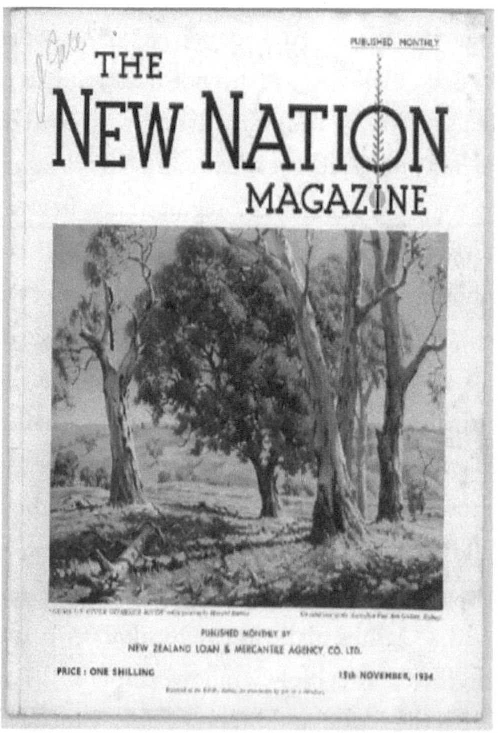

Fig. 39 Cover of *The New Nation Magazine*, November 1934

---

493   Palmer, V. 'The divide', *The Bulletin*, 26.3.1925, pp. 10–11.

Running parallel to McMahon's reporting on rural districts, *The Queenslander* also commissioned a photojournalist to travel around Queensland in a small van and report with photographs on rural topics. This series, called 'Caravanning through Queensland' (and later, 'Caravan Tales'), was written in the form of a literary travelogue popular at the time and ran weekly from May 1928 through to May 1934. It included a short text in the body of the newspaper with a full page or double page of photographs in the 'Pictorial' section. The photographer was never identified. I thought at first that it must have been McMahon as the style of writing and the framing and subject matter of the photographs were familiar. A blurry photograph in 1928 of *The Brisbane Courier*'s caravanning photojournalist proved not to be McMahon.[494]

Judged on the regularity with which he continued to report on the Granite Belt, this must have been his favourite destination once he settled in as *The Brisbane Courier*'s back-country reporter. He ran a long series of reports in *The Brisbane Courier* and *The Queenslander* beginning with a report on soldier settlers from February to November 1924 and six years later, January–February 1930, he was still photographing the grape and fruit industries and the annual Stanthorpe Agricultural Show. From 1930 to 1932, he reported twelve times on the grape- and fruit-growing industries, with thirty photographs of the region's fruit and grapes and also local attempts to diversify into arsenic mining, tobacco and hickory.[495] The importance of the Granite Belt to Queensland's rural economy, and as a matter of general interest, was indicated by the choice of McMahon's staged portrait of 'The Fruit pickers' for

---

494   *The Brisbane Courier* became *The Brisbane Courier-Mail* just after McMahon died in August 1933.

495   'Granite Belt Fruit, Tobacco and minerals; Interesting experiments', *The Brisbane Courier*, 20.1.1932, p. 12.

the cover of the 'Pictorial' section of *The Queenslander* in March 1931.[496]

Italians in Queensland

In 1919, he caused a small controversy after an article he published in London in the current affairs magazine, *The Outlook*, was republished in *The Bundaberg Mail*. McMahon had adopted his usual boosting and patriotic stance for a British audience, extolling the commercial prospects of Queensland but then alleged that the sugar industry was being threatened by unionism and in particular by the Italian owners and labourers who now dominated the industry after the departure of South Sea Islander (*kanaka*) labour in 1906. He unfairly criticised Italians in the sugar industry in racist terms, claiming that Britishers could not obtain work, that there were towns where 'not one word of English can be heard' and that towns like Halifax had become Italianised.[497] This controversy arose again after McMahon published a feature headlined 'The menace to Queensland' in *The Leader* in Melbourne. This was republished elsewhere such as in Renmark in South Australia and Launceston in Tasmania.[498] McMahon had spoken about the presence of Italians in the sugar industry in 1919 and repeated much the same argument during a talk at the Royal Colonial Institute in Sydney in November 1924. This became a minor controversy again after his report in *The Leader* was widely reprinted including the *Daily Telegraph* in Launceston, the *Murray Pioneer* in Renmark and elsewhere. McMahon's headline read, 'Italian settlers; How they are displacing Australians in the sugar industry'. In 1925, when

---

496   *The Queenslander*, 5.3.1931, p. 23.

497   *The Bundaberg Mail*, 22.12.1919, p. 4.

498   *Daily Telegraph* (Launceston), 28.11.1924, p. 7; *The Murray Pioneer and Australian River Record* (Renmark), 27.2.1925, p. 9.

Vance Palmer described them as 'sweating, sunbaked men from Milan and Tuscany', about forty-four per cent of the sugar farms in the Herbert River district, for example, were owned by Italians. It was a storm in a teacup as Italian immigration to Australia was relatively minor, only 4286 in 1924.[499] It was a controversy soon bypassed by McMahon.

Without blinking an eye, he switched to extolling the virtues of the fertile and prosperous agriculture industry in the Southern Downs without acknowledging that this success was based on the many non-British settlers in the fruit and wine industries. Readers may not have noticed these gaps and silences. In his report on Waterford near Brisbane, he noted the presence of German immigrants and photographed what he called a 'German wagon'.[500] In December 1925, he was so well-known that he was invited to submit a full-page photography collage for the annual special Christmas issue of Melbourne's *The Weekly Times*. It offered a panorama of Queensland's economic contribution to the nation – logging, cotton, wool, bark (for paper making) and farms – but oddly did not include the sugar industry. It also included a nostalgic depiction in a then-and-now format with an old mail stagecoach beside a modern motor car.[501] The page was headlined 'Through Queensland', and considering the large portfolio of Queensland images that McMahon had amassed, it was surprising for its omissions rather than what he included. The eight photographs did not include Italians or Germans.

---

499   See Moraes-Gorecki, V. '"Black Italians" in the sugar fields of north Queensland: a reflection on labour inclusion and cultural exclusion in tropical Australia,' *The Australian Journal of Anthropology*, Vol. 5, no. 3, 1994; Palmer, V. 'The divide', *The Bulletin*, 26.3.1925, pp. 10–11.

500   *The Brisbane Courier*, 20.12.1930, p. 10.

501   *The Weekly Times* (Melbourne), 19.12.1925, p. 45.

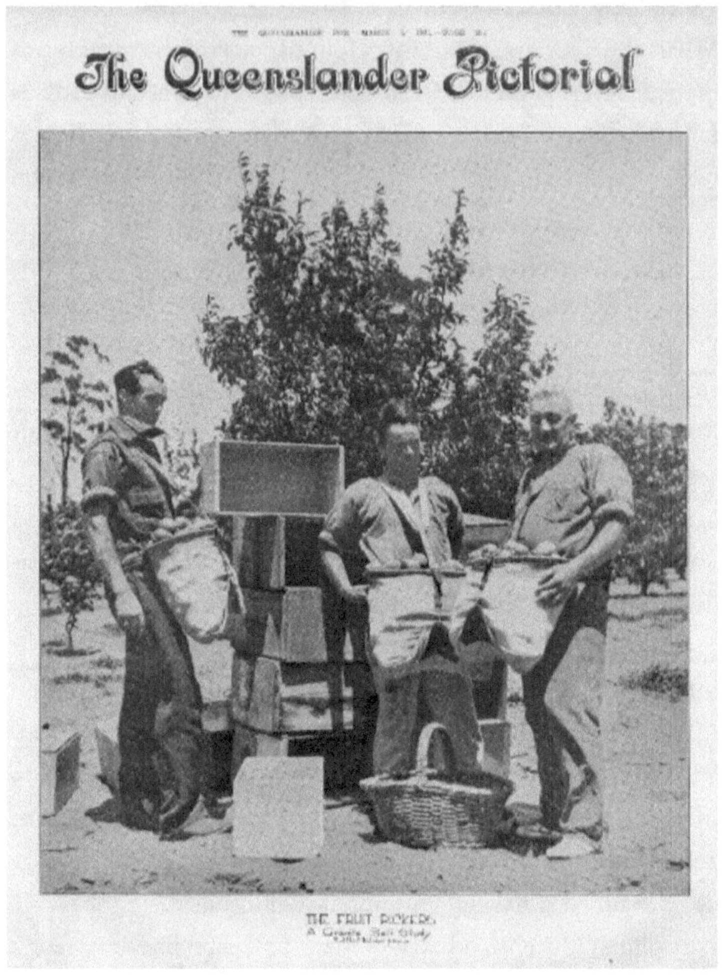

Fig. 40 'The fruit pickers', 1931

Brisbane and surrounds

In 1928, McMahon began to report on districts adjacent to Brisbane, perhaps under editorial direction by *The Brisbane Courier*, or because he had now passed sixty-five years of age and was slowing down and avoiding long coach, train or motor car journeys to the outback. After a couple of reports in 1928, he started a long run in March 1930 with ten photographs of Narangba and Cash's Crossing (now Albany Creek). He then tackled other satellite, or as we now call them, peri-urban settlements.

Publication	Date	Pics	Page	Headline
The Brisbane Courier	4.1.1928	4	21	Dunwich: A Queensland Old Folks Home
The Brisbane Courier	1.9.1928	4	11	Pine River: Agriculture and scenic beauty
The Brisbane Courier	1.3.1930	4	11	Narangba: A fertile dairying District
The Brisbane Courier	5.4.1930	6	11	Cash's Crossing: Picturesque dairying district; settlement; What ex-Diggers can do
The Brisbane Courier	13.9.1930	5	9	Highlands: Picturesque and progressive; what ex-diggers can do
The Brisbane Courier	4.10.1930	5	9	Fertile Greenbank: Land of rich hills and dales
The Brisbane Courier	25.10.1930	4	11	Woodridge: Mixed farming
The Brisbane Courier	20.12.1930	10	9	Waterford: Some old families: Prosperous rural activities

Publication	Date	Pics	Page	Headline
The Brisbane Courier	8.11.1930	9	9	Kingston: Record of steady progress: Thriving industries; Model settlement near Brisbane
The Brisbane Courier	3.1.1931	3	14	Hard work won; development of Bethania; Pioneer's hardships
The Queenslander	29.1.1931	0	14	Loganlea: The dairy; A flourishing centre
The Queenslander	19.2.1931	0	8	Jimboomba: picturesque hills and dales
The Queenslander	19.2.1931	0	14	The Dairy: Cedar Grove: Picturesque and prosperity
The Queenslander	7.5.1931	0	12	Logan Village: Rich dairying country
The Brisbane Courier	29.1.1932	1	13	Victoria point: Abundant crops

Table 9: Brisbane's peri-urban settlements, 1928–1932, in *The Queenslander* and *The Brisbane Courier*

McMahon called Kingston near Logan 'a model settlement'. It had opened its piggery two years before and was also home to the Mount Taylor gold mine and a cooperative butter factory.[502]

---

502   Now restored as the Kingston Butter Factory Cultural Precinct, a suburban performing arts, museum and entertainment centre.

McMahon also included portraits of five pioneers, even though this was stretching the definition a little, as it had just been named Kingston in 1890. Queensland was, of course, a young colony, only being proclaimed in 1859, so settlers from the 1890s were still being referred to as pioneers. Only in the later period of his back-country reporting did he emphasise portraits of prominent citizens and social occasions, such as nine photographs of people enjoying the 'Social scene at Murgon' in the Upper Burnett. He probably submitted this rare collage feature because he knew many of those depicted from his time working in the district prior to going to Papua in 1915.[503]

He referred to early settlers in these peri-urban districts, a reminder that Brisbane was a relatively new city. The proclaiming of Greater Brisbane had occurred five years earlier in 1925. In 1930, its population was 318,631. In comparison, Sydney's population of 1.2 million was four times larger and Melbourne had just passed one million. Brisbane was, as McMahon depicted, a provincial city surrounded by active agricultural districts. These districts are now suburbs of Brisbane. Thanks to Trove we can now easily access his visual record, and his reporting in the late 1920s and early 1930s and this constitutes a valuable archive of the early transformations.

McMahon's peri-urban reporting was littered with the same superlatives he had applied to back-country reporting on the north, far north, south-west and north-west – prosperity, progress, fertility and flourishing developments. Queensland was still growing, characterised by an expansionary vision and belief in growth that McMahon captured through photography. His photographs represented this prosperity through depictions of butter factories and piggeries, maize, potato, strawberries and barley, railway stations and bridges. Brisbane's rail network had already expanded

---

503   *The Queenslander*, 18.10.1924, p. 26.

to many of the hinterland districts on which McMahon reported, reaching, for example, to Bethania and Petrie in 1888, Yarraman in 1904 and Canungra in 1915. The 1920s was an exciting decade in rural Australia, and many experiments and plans were being tried, such as government-funded dentists making visits to state schools. He reported on innovations such as tobacco, turtle soup making, fruit for export, winemaking, drilling for oil and strawberry farming as well as the big industries like sugar, cattle and wool, and the soldier settlement scheme. This means we can follow several key trends in the 1920s through McMahon's photography and this makes his photography, now found in bound periodicals in libraries and digitised newspapers, a valuable archival body of evidence.

By the 1930s, when he was photographing what we now know as suburbs, they were emerging hinterland districts close to Brisbane with mining, timber, dairying, fruit and mixed farming. There were no reports of the Gold Coast now considered part of a greater conurbation with Brisbane, despite there being several small townships scattered along the coast. He did report on the hinterland district of Canungra, but that was for its cattle and timber industries.[504] He ignored the big inland mining town of Mount Isa, and never published any photography of the inner suburbs or central business district of Brisbane. He was, indeed, a back-country reporter.

Throughout the period from 1923 to 1932, McMahon sent illustrated articles to *The Sydney Mail,* usually a slightly revised version of what had already appeared in Brisbane. Some of these were of national interest, such as the completion of the Perth to Cairns railway line, and this reportage was picked up by newspapers in all states. The *Circular Head Chronicle* in Manly added its own nationalistic headline to McMahon's report, re-labelled as 'Great

---

504 'Canungra: Timber and cattle flourishing,' *The Brisbane Courier,* 7.5.1931, p. 22.

railway system; A great national undertaking'.[505] His features in *The Sydney Mail* included the cotton industry at Gayndah, arsenic mines in the Granite Belt, an old people's home at Dunwich on North Stradbroke Island off the coast of Brisbane, a reafforestation scheme on Fraser Island and the visitations of the government dentist to Queensland state schools. This gallery of back-country life brought aspects of rural Queensland to the attention of New South Wales audiences, and they probably were able to relate them to similar reportage of rural areas in their own and other states. He reported on soldier settlement schemes in a full pictorial feature in *The Sydney Mail*. It also used a photograph of the Soldiers Memorial Hall at Maryborough and one of the 'Soldier's Club' at Stanthorpe as fillers.

His last feature in *The Sydney Mail* was in 1932 when he reported on the historic property of Canning Downs, the first homestead on the Darling Downs, established in 1840. By the 1930s, it was a famous stud of 1500 acres. The four accompanying photographs depicted the original homestead, grounds, an impressive fountain in the gardens and the driveway approach to the complex of buildings, home and grounds.[506] He had published a similar full-page feature on Queensland homesteads in the Goondiwindi district in 1924 but generally refrained from depicting great mansions and homesteads.[507]

Photographing an era: an important archive

I had originally set out in this book to highlight McMahon's contribution to Pacific Island history through his prolific output

---

505   *Circular Head Chronicle* (Manly), 28.11.1923, p. 2.

506   *The Sydney Mail*, 12.10.1932, p. 37.

507   *The Queenslander*, 25.10.1924, p. 22 (with five photographs). Three photographs of Callandoon station appeared as fillers in *The Telegraph* (Brisbane), 7.2.1924, p. 4. This would have been an editorial decision, not one instigated by McMahon.

of Pacific Island photographs, but I found myself engaged in another, unrelated historical field – rural Australian history. I discovered in Trove that after his Pacific career was over and a venture in Asia had failed, he returned to the field that he had begun in 1915 when he had been a back-country reporter for *The Cairns Post* and *Northern Herald*. This reportage covered the breadth of Queensland, a huge state, and included photographing the Torres Strait and the Northern Territory. I was forced to acknowledge that, historically, McMahon's fame should be not solely because of his photography and reporting on the Pacific, and that his back-country photography of Queensland's early twentieth-century history was equally as significant. (A select list of more than 500 published photographs and the associated articles on rural Queensland are listed in Appendix 2.) As the banner stated on one of the magazines in which he published, Australia was a 'new nation' and his Queensland, Torres Strait and Northern Territory photography therefore have additional value as a record of the early decades of that growth.

McMahon was determined that city readers should understand the privations of rural life, such as having one's mail delivered only twice a week to a letterbox nailed to a tree on a remote country roadside or living in a home consisting of two canopy tents abutting each other. McMahon accompanied this photograph of a woman and child standing in front of a home made from two tents by saying, 'many a brave woman leads a lonely life yet contented and happy life in a house like this'.[508] There was a sense of romanticism of the bush in these depictions, but also an awareness that there was a city–bush divide, and that city-living Australians had a limited, romantic view based on popular art and

---

508   *The Sydney Mail*, 10.12.1924, p. 62. For the car with a blowout, see *The Sydney Mail*, 23.7.1924, p. 37.

literature of what life was like in the back-country. His imagery is a body of evidence waiting to be trawled by those historians interested in the city–bush dichotomy, spatial history and cultural history. His photography is an as yet untapped resource on early twentieth-century Queensland history.

Australia was changing rapidly in the 1920s. For example, golf clubs had only been established in the 1890s and the opening of a new golf course was still special enough for the Governor of Queensland to attend an opening at Stanthorpe in 1924 and be photographed by McMahon. Golf was so new and unusual that a year later, *The Sydney Mail* used as a filler, McMahon's photograph of golfers at Stanthorpe using an umbrella as shelter from the sun.[509] McMahon also featured camp drafting, a unique Australian competitive sport involving a horse, rider and cattle which had been invented in outback Queensland and northern New South Wales in the 1880s. It was a sporting competition that featured in many of the local annual agricultural shows on which McMahon reported and continues today with benchmark events such as the Warwick Gold Cup and Triple Crown attracting thousands of competitors. Domestic tourism was another new adventure for Australians in the 1920s and at the time of McMahon's reportage on the Barrier Reef it was beginning to attract attention, as other columnists promoted potential travel and tourism in Queensland. Emphasising the scenic element was a new element in his reportage as was the promotion of tourist visits to nearby areas easily reachable by rail and coach networks. His gallery of rural photography drew the attention of city-dwellers to the closeness of pleasant environs which he now referred to as picturesque.

He had adopted a policy of photographing railway stations and new railway lines, and this is a central aspect of rural Australian

---

509   For golf, see *The Sydney Mail*, 16.7.1924, p. 32; 20.5.1925, p. 22.

history, as the spider web tentacles of railways stretched out from the coast to mining, pastoral and agricultural districts. This great technological advance and associated social transformation had begun in the nineteenth century and was continuing in the 1920s. For example, the Brisbane Valley line to Toogoolawah opened in 1904, the east coast railway line reached Cairns in 1924 and out to Winton in central western Queensland in 1928 and Mount Isa in 1929. He also documented the moment when horse-drawn and bullock wagons were being replaced by motor lorries, and he photographed a pioneering Qantas flight at Longreach. He did note, on a single photograph of a broken-down car in 1924, that motor cars were becoming popular but getting a blowout in the far west was a problem.

McMahon photographed state schools and these feature in nearly all his reports on rural towns and districts. This transformation had been dramatic with the number of state schools in Queensland rising from 900 in 1900 to 1059 in 1909, although some townships were still undergoing this change when he visited, such as at Waterford where he noted the town hall also served as the school.[510] This was an era when the local 'co-op', butter factory, piggery and timber mill were often the central focus of work and life in a locality, and there were still original settlers who could be posed for individual or family group portraits, with occasionally an abandoned original homestead to be photographed. By the 1930s, McMahon could include photographs he had taken fifteen years earlier when starting his career as a back-country reporter, but he seems to have used this technique rarely. He did reuse earlier photographs of Yeulba near Roma[511] and a photograph of the popular vessel, *Maid of Sker*, a passenger ferry that had run

---

510   *The Brisbane Courier*, 20.12, 1930, p. 9.

511   *The Brisbane Courier*, 22.6.1929, p. 13.

for forty years between Brisbane and Southport,[512] but McMahon tended to refrain from looking back to the 'good old days'. Instead, he preferred future development, new growth and the boosting of enterprise and progress, new crops and innovations, shown in his constant use of the term prosperity in by-lines and captions.

His mundane, rather prosaic role as an outback roving newspaper photographer must have brought a wry smile to McMahon's face when, for example, he photographed a prize-winning pig at a show at Kingston,[513] a subject far removed from a few years earlier when he had been photographing costumed dancers in Nauru, three-metre tall slit-gong drums in Vanuatu, elaborately carved and decorated canoe prows in the Solomon Islands, phosphate mining on Ocean Island, sisal plantations in Papua and suit-wearing indigenous Fijians acting as a *Roko Tui* for the British colonial administration. It was indeed a huge change of role.

McMahon's reporting ended in 1932 after a series of columns with photographs on the fruit and grape industries of the Granite Belt and a few features without photographs on Loganlea, Logan and Canungra, settled districts quite close to Brisbane. Nine months later, his last appearance was the use by *The Brisbane Courier* of two of his photographs of the Stanthorpe Agricultural Show used as fillers in May 1932. Despite still being on the staff of *The Brisbane Courier*, nothing more was published in late 1932 and early 1933.

He died in August 1933 after returning home from *The Brisbane Courier* offices to have lunch at his home in the nearby suburb of New Farm. He collapsed and passed away after a stroke that afternoon. It was a disconcerting end for a career that had

---

512   *The Brisbane Courier*, 19.10.1927, p. 8 (This appeared as a single photograph or filler.)
513   *The Brisbane Courier*, 8.11.1930, p. 9.

been so prodigious and prolific with thousands of published photographs and associated essays. After 1915, he seemed to be constantly travelling around the Pacific, and after 1922, he seemed to be everywhere in Queensland – the far north, the south-west, the Upper Burnett, Charters Towers, the Granite Belt, the hinterland of Brisbane and the Georgina district.[514] His short career as a Pacific expert from 1915 to 1922 and then as a back-country photographer and reporter from 1923 to 1933 had come to an end.

Sadly, there are few traces today of TJ (Tom) McMahon – photographer, patriot and journalist – but I hope this chapter brings his published photography to the attention of Queensland and Australian historians and the wider public.[515]

---

514   The Georgina District, in the Channel Country near the Northern Territory border and Boulia, was named after Queensland Governor Bowen's wife, Georgina.

515   An appendix details his published work on back-country Queensland in the hope that future researchers will pursue his career recording outback life more thoroughly.

Chapter **14**

A visual legacy

Of the thousands of published photographs by McMahon, the scene in Fig. 41 in the Solomon Islands is my favourite. It was only used once. It is of poor quality, but it captures the moment that McMahon looked up and saw a scene framed by trees and an offshore island, with 'natives' carrying on their normal day-to-day activities without any visible involvement by Europeans. It seems to be a preparation for a presentation or trade in fish and food between those just arrived on the canoe and those onshore gathered around the pandanus leaf baskets of produce laid out on display. Unlike other McMahon photographs, this is not posed.[516] McMahon used it to open an article with fourteen photographs in *World's Markets* in 1920 on 'Cocoanut cultivation in the South Seas', despite the image not being a depiction of aspects of the copra industry. In the Solomon Islands where this was taken, McMahon had focused on plantations, shipping, trade and colonial infrastructure and less on ethnographic evidence of people and customs. Yet, in this photograph, he has captured a quintessential event in Solomon Island relationships and custom. It has classic aesthetic and artistic compositional elements, consciously framed by McMahon who, by

---

516   McMahon, TJ. 'Cocoanut cultivation in the South Seas', *World's Markets*, Aug. 1920, pp. 27–31. This photograph appeared with an incorrect caption as, 'Making copra in the Solomon Islands'. This mistake was probably made by the editors of the magazine, not by McMahon.

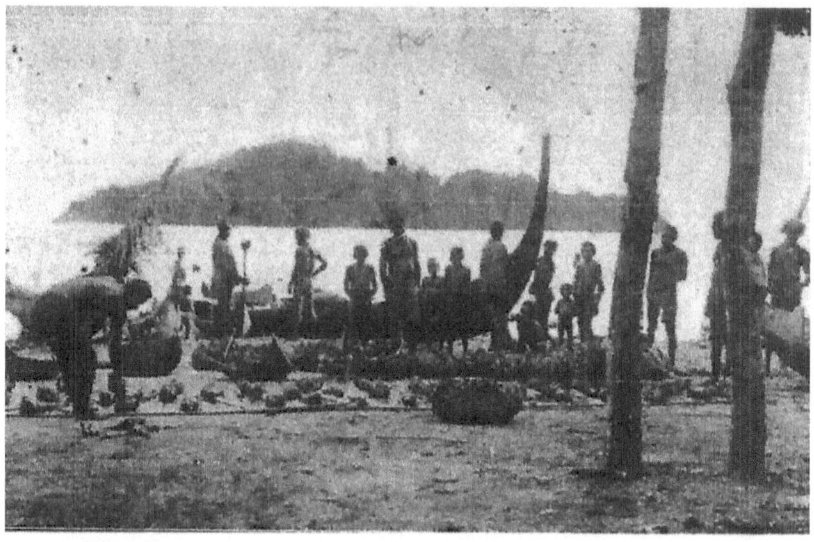

Fig. 41 'Making copra in the Solomon Islands', 1920

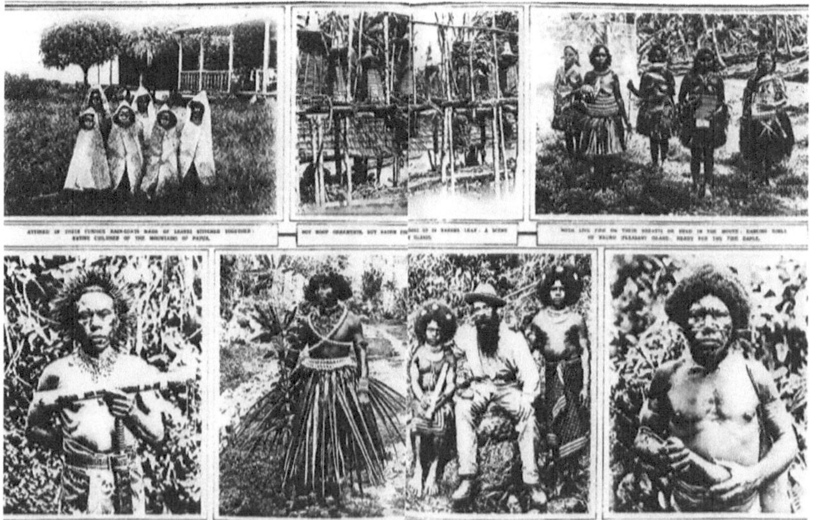

Fig. 42 Two-page layout in the *Illustrated London News*, 1919

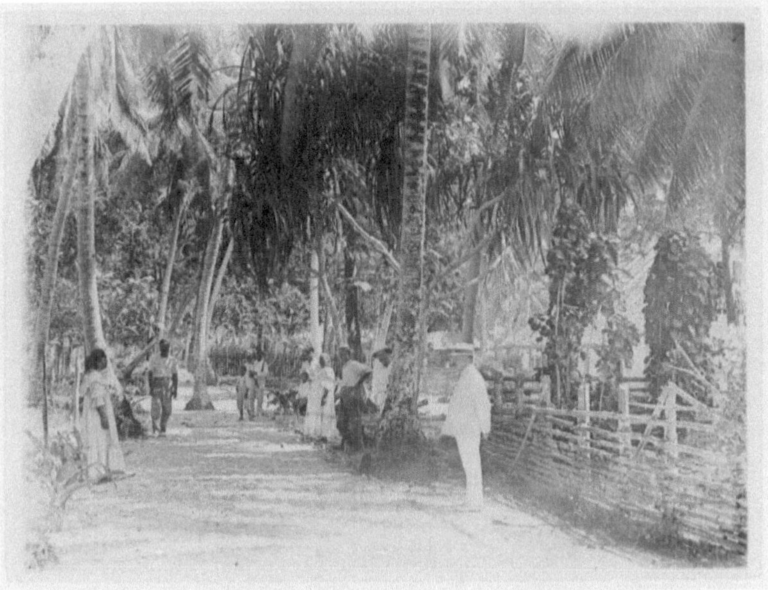

Fig. 43 A village, Marshall Islands

this time, was alert to what constituted a 'good' picture. On this fortuitous occasion, he was in his photographer mode, putting aside for the moment his journalism and booster persona. It also illustrates the ambiguity in a great many of the photographs discussed in earlier chapters, and the uncertainty of the evidence within the frame and surrounding the taking of the photograph. Why did he only use it once? Why did he include it in a gallery supposedly on coconuts and copra production? Did he take other photographs at the same place and time? Did he ask the Solomon Islanders to pose or at least stand still? The answers to these questions can only be surmises and guesses as McMahon left no record of his photography practice.

I chose this as my favourite McMahon photograph, despite the overwhelming preference he demonstrated for commercially motivated photographs of plantations, mines and shipping, because it reveals McMahon the photographer, ready to capture a scene that was not necessarily a boosting, propaganda image. His career was clearly focused on reportage of commercial opportunity, but as indicated in this Solomon Island scene and in others in the *Illustrated London News* (Fig. 42), he was also fascinated by the Islanders he saw and thought that readers far from the Pacific might find the people, their customs, culture, dress and performance of interest.

I was so immersed in McMahon's prolific output in Australia that I often forgot he also published extensively around the world, in London, the USA and New Zealand. For example, his two double-page collages in the *Illustrated London News* in 1919, shown above, included his photography from Papua, the Solomon Islands, Ocean Island and Nauru. These images gave English audiences an intimate and varied view of the Islands, their 'strange ... wondrous peoples', architecture, costumes and decoration. McMahon was making a dramatic contribution to this new visual platform for learning-by-looking about worlds far away.

The widespread and repeated publication of McMahon's photography suggests that English, Australian, American and New Zealand audiences were aware of the Islands due to being constantly updated with images, and that this visibility makes McMahon a major contributor to the early twentieth century knowing of the Pacific. It also calls for a new scholarly reading of journalism and of the impact of photography on readers. This is a new area of research, led by Thierry Gervais, Jason Hill and Vanessa Schwartz.[517] McMahon's published photography and commentary, easily accessible through Trove, makes a

---

517   Gervais, T. *The making of the news: A history of photography in the press*, London, Bloomsbury Press, 2017; Hill, J. and Schwartz, VR., eds. *Getting the picture: The visual culture of the news*, London, Bloomsbury Press, 2015.

significant contribution to our understanding of the link between photography and journalism in the early twentieth century. His flurry of publications, illustrated and not illustrated over a twenty-year period, reminds us of how important print news – as newspapers, illustrated newspapers and illustrated magazines – was to audiences. For Australia and the Pacific, there is still much to be done.

A new nation

The published material by McMahon presented in this book appears mostly in metropolitan publications in Brisbane, Sydney and Melbourne and in major provincial centres along the Queensland coast, so we can argue on this evidence that city audiences had access to a considerable body of print and photographic commentary on the Pacific, and in his later career, access to reportage on rural or back-country Queensland. This visual and text reportage was comprehensive in detailing events as they unfolded but also played a boosting role, suggesting prosperity and good fortune lay ahead as Australia developed as a nation.

The standard format for a column appearing in newspapers at the time embodied both these elements, shown for example in McMahon's three-line heading for a report on the Upper Burnett region:

UPPER BURNETT

DEVELOPMENT AND PROGRESS

DESCRIPTION OF WORK ON DEVELOPMENT FARMS[518]

---

518   McMahon, TJ. 'Upper Burnett', *Maryborough Chronicle, Wide Bay and Burnett Advertiser*, 20.6.1917, p. 3. This was followed seven months later by 'A trip through the Burnett cotton fields. Sensational developments', *Maryborough Chronicle, Wide Bay and Burnett Advertiser*, 25.1.1923, p. 6.

After a visit to the Northern Territory in 1917, he headlined his report on the land of the 'never-never', using the same multiple-heading format:

ACROSS THE GULF OF CARPENTARIA
FROM TORRES STRAIT TO THE ROPER RIVER
A GLANCE AT THE NEVER NEVER
THE TRAGEDY OF THE HALF-CASTE

Terms like development, prosperity and progress resonated with city readers but equally with rural readers who were keen for information about expansion, issues and problems in back-country districts and in other states and territories.

I began to appreciate late in my research that McMahon had made a significant contribution to reportage on rural Australia. For example, after his visit to the Northern Territory, his photographs and commentaries appeared in *The Leader* and *The Herald* in Melbourne and were then reprinted widely across all states, including the *Maryborough Chronicle, Wide Bay and Burnett Advertiser, The Queenslander, The Cairns Post, Northern Herald* and *Gympie Times and Mary River Mining Gazette*, in Victoria in *The Courier* (Ballarat) and *Weekly Times* (Melbourne) and in New South Wales in the *Murrumbidgee Irrigator* and many other small local newspapers. This means that McMahon had both city and provincial readers and that both his visual evidence and commentary were being shared by a wide range of Australians. This level of access to visual material broke down the rigid divide between city and the bush (that had been a stock phrase) and suggests that both city, and rural and remote readers had access to a comprehensive understanding of events far from home. As we can see in McMahon's reportage on the Northern Territory, for example, his views and photographic evidence were being read widely and were contributing to a shared experience of being Australian.

I also began to appreciate how significant the travelling speaker and lantern slide presenter was in both city and rural areas. For example, in May 1917, McMahon addressed the Church Missionary Association in Sydney[519] and the Australian Natives Association at Fitzroy in Melbourne and later spoke in Brisbane, Adelaide, Cairns and Townsville. The importance of lantern slides in making McMahon's talks so popular was commented on at the time and it is a tragedy that none of his lantern slides shows survived.[520] The visiting 'expert' at the local hall talking on one of a myriad of aspects of early Australian life and certainly invites further research.[521] McMahon was always referred to as a lively speaker, able to refer to his own experiences, and always supported by photographs that captured the audience's attention.

Commentator and photographer

Although he abandoned his Pacific career in 1922, McMahon's photographs of the Islands continued to be published throughout the 1920s. For example, a feature on Papua, that he had first visited in 1915, appeared in *The Sydney Mail* in 1921. 'With a camera in Papua' included five photographs, including some that he had not previously published, such as sisal bales waiting on the wharves, a panorama of Port Moresby and Fairfax Harbour, McMahon posing on a raft on the Laloki River and a large group

---

519   *Daily Telegraph* (Sydney), 12.5.1917, p. 14.

520   For lantern slides, see Jolly, M. and de Courcey, E, eds. *The magic lantern at work: Witnessing, persuading and experiencing and connecting*, London, Routledge, 2020.

521   The travelling speaker and lantern slide presenter was the subject of the movie set in the USA, '*News of the world*', in 2022 but is a phenomenon that in Australia has not attracted scholarly attention.

of school children holding their slates.[522] On the basis of his visits in 1915, 1917 and 1921, he also published an account in 1922 of the Australian military expedition in 1914 to capture Rabaul and German New Guinea.[523] Other features by McMahon also appeared overseas well after he had changed careers away from the Pacific, often unattributed but this may have been caused by editorial and publishing delays. [524]

In an interesting diversion, McMahon took several self-portraits to record his presence with a particular group or person. These are important as they tell us, in the absence of his diaries or field notes, what it was like to be a travelling photographer, the equipment used and the moments they thought significant enough to be included within the frame. On his first trip to the Islands, to Papua and German New Guinea in 1915, he posed several portraits of himself with administration officials and on patrol with the governor in the Papuan gulf. [525] He also posed with a group of Papuans from Mafula Mission, captioned as 'Civilization is starting'.[526] Later during his trip to the central Pacific, he also posed with fish-adorned female dancers on Nauru and with a row of officials on Banaba backed by a row of male dancers in full costume.[527] In the Solomon Islands, he posed with a large group

---

522   McMahon, TJ. 'With a camera in Papua', *The Sydney Mail*, 6.7.1921, p. 15.

523   McMahon, TJ. 'German New Guinea: Incident of the Australian occupation', *The Telegraph* (Brisbane), 12.8.1922, p. 11 (with three previously published photographs).

524   McMahon's photographs appeared attributed and unattributed; for example, in *The Lone Hand*, 1.11.1918, p. 508; in serial encyclopedias such as Moncrieff, ARH, ed. *The New World of Today*, London. 1922; Hammerton, JA, ed. *Peoples of All Nations*, London, 1923; and Hammerton, JA, ed. *Countries of the World*, London, 1925.

525   With Papuan officials: *The Telegraph* (Brisbane), 1.12.1917.

526   For the Mafula Mission portrait, see *Northern Herald*, 3.12.1915, p. 35; *Illustrated London News*, 15.11.1919, p. 776; *The Wide World*, Jan. 1917, p. 379; and in several other publications.

527   For dancers on Nauru, see *Sunset: the Pacific Monthly*, Mar. 1921, p. 39; *Pacific Ports*, Aug. 1919, p. 87. For officials and dancers on Banaba, see *The Wide World*, June 1919, p. 56.

of labourers, local men, overseers and planters, sitting on a pile of coconuts. In this composition, he was not only saying 'I was there', but also hinting at the supply of labour and the prosperity of a planter's life in the Islands.[528] A self-portrait with the master and crew of the local vessel, the *Rogeia*, also hinted at an ease of travel and shipping around the Islands.[529] In the Marshalls, he posed with Japanese naval officers. In the Northern Territory, he posed with his camera crew of four Torres Strait Islanders, which provides a rare opportunity to see the labour involved in being a travelling photographer in the early part of the century. These self-portraits appeared regularly enough to suggest that McMahon was alert to the need to remind audiences that the photographs they were viewing were taken by someone who could claim 'I was there'.

McMahon was not the first to photograph the Pacific Islands and send his prints to newspaper and magazine editors hoping to get them published, and he certainly would have perused the many photographs published in his local newspapers, the *Northern Herald* and *The Cairns Post*, prior to his first trip to New Guinea in 1915. On this visit in 1915, he was competing as a photographer with Australian soldiers on the expeditionary force that had captured Rabaul and who sent back thirty photographs to the *Northern Herald*; for example, Private Brooks, Lance Corporal AR Wooley and CF Buderus. The photographs by the soldiers have a close similarity in composition and framing with photographs taken slightly after by McMahon and published over the next decade. Indeed, McMahon was probably copying the framing of the many photographs of the Islands that he had already seen published between the 1890s and 1915. The soldiers

---

528 'A group at Lia-Pari Plantation, British Solomons', *The Queenslander*, 12.1.1818, p. 28; *Trans-Pacific*, Mar. 1912, p. 77; *PLA Monthly*, Mar. 1928, p. 154.

529 For the *Rogeia*, see *The Queenslander*, 22.12.1917, p. 21; *The Wide World*, Mar. 1919, p. 350.

focused relatively more on the indigenous New Guineans and published more portraits than McMahon, not unexpectedly as they were an occupation force confronting indigenous Pacific Island peoples for the first time, whereas McMahon arrived as a journalist seeking visual evidence for Australian commercial expansion and opportunities.

McMahon's Pacific Island photography and his Queensland material were not always replications or merely the copying of framing and composition in previously published photography. McMahon certainly copied from earlier photographers, but he also sought out new angles, framing and composition, new material and new approaches to already well-trodden sites. He was a good photographer. He developed several favourite styles and compositions during his trips. By the time he made the 'islands run' in 1918, he had developed the technique of a vista down a path or 'street' with locals posing. The example from the Marshall Islands (Fig. 43) could have multiple captions – a pleasant scene, a native village, atoll life, a street, housing, fencing, Islander clothing and 'I was there' with McMahon standing to one side. Like much of McMahon's photography, this type of framing suggested multiple purposes as reportage, or documentary and ethnographic photography or as entertainment – views or the picturesque.

McMahon never achieved fame as a photographer. His commercially motivated documentation of the Islands and the outback never approached the quality of photographers like Jack Cato, John Kauffmann, Harold Cazneaux, John Beattie, Frank Hurley, Cecil Bostok, George Wilkins and others in the early decades of the century.[530] McMahon was, of course, not seeking

---

530   For the early 1900s, see Newton, Gael. *Shades of light: Photography and Australia 1839–1988*, Canberra, Australian National Gallery, 1988; Davies, Alan. *An eye for photograph: The camera in Australia*, Sydney, State Library of NSW, 2000. Neither mentions McMahon. For a recent study, see Maddern, Peter. *The eye of Wilkins: The complete photographic retrospective of George Hubert Wilkins*, Sydney, Peacock, 2021.

fame as a photographer. Photography for him was merely the means to an end, providing the 'I was there' evidence to attract acknowledgement and fame as an Islands expert, commentator, journalist, Australian patriot and Imperialist. When realization of that dream faded in the early 1920s, he did become a professional photographer, it was not in the aesthetic and art worlds of photographic societies, salons and galleries where pictorialism and modernism were debated and on show, but in the prosaic world of back-country newspaper reporting of country shows, bridges, railways and monuments.

McMahon had three careers, beginning as a tutor to rural pastoral families. After 1915, his career falls into two distinct but often overlapping careers. From 1915 to 1922, he went as an independent traveller and photographer in search of fame and acknowledgement as a Pacific Islands expert, and concurrently between 1915 and 1933, he was employed as a back-country reporter and photographer, at first freelancing and then employed with a city newspaper. As we have seen in the later chapters, these fields overlapped, especially in the earlier period when he juggled trips to the Islands with a back-country reporter role to raise funds for the trips.

In the 1920s, he continued to send Pacific Island material to New Zealand, another instance historically of the parallel histories of Australia and New Zealand.[531] In the illustrated newspapers, *Auckland Weekly News* and *Otago Witness*, McMahon provided nearly thirty per cent of the Pacific photographs between 1916 and 1923. He would have noticed others in New Zealand who were submitting photographs and stories about the Islands. For example, alongside McMahon's contributions, there were eighty-eight

---

531   See Mein Smith, Philippa, Hempenstall, Peter, and Goldfinch, Shaun. *Remaking the Tasman World*, Christchurch, University of Canterbury Press, 2008.

photographically illustrated feature articles in *Otago Witness* and *Auckland Weekly News* on the Pacific between 1914 and 1923, featuring Nauru, Ocean Island, Papua, the New Hebrides and Fiji.[532]

Even after he joined *The Brisbane Courier* in 1923, he continued to send away illustrated articles on the Pacific at the same time as photographing and reporting on country towns and districts across Queensland. I make this point because McMahon must have had a rigid commitment to time management and the setting of priorities as he juggled the printing of negatives, writing of captions and articles and posting to editors, with travelling around rural districts photographing and writing reports, while at the same time planning long voyages to nearby islands and in 1919 to Europe. He was a single man, determined to succeed, and had a strong sense of purpose and achievable goals, and this perhaps explains why he dedicated most waking hours to these tasks.

McMahon was referred to as a 'ceaseless contributor to professional and upper-class journals', and was often labelled as an indefatigable traveller, usually with the superlative 'well-known' added. In 1917, *The Sydney Mail* called him a 'traveller and observer', *The Cairns Post* called him an 'experienced pressman' and *The Herald* in Melbourne noted that 'he describes himself as a roving journalist'. He was also labelled a publicist and an explorer. The pursuit of the elusive FRGS was a driving motivation. As he wanted acknowledgement in Australia as an expert on the Islands world and Australia's future relationships with the region. He aimed higher than being merely a traveller with a camera. It was ironic that he spent his last ten years in a more mundane salaried role as a back-country reporter and photographer. Sadly,

---

532   This substantial archive has not attracted the attention of New Zealand historians. I thank the staff at the Hocken Library, Dunedin, for assistance during my own brief search there for McMahon material.

his obituaries in 1933 focused more on his travels to the Orient and subsequent book rather than his prolific contribution of photography on the Pacific Islands or on his career photographing rural Queensland. *The Queenslander*'s obituary merely noted he had been a 'well-known figure as a rover of the South Seas ... and became a close acquaintance of almost every captain on the South Sea route'.[533] He never visited New Caledonia, Samoa, Niue, Tuvalu, the Cook Islands or Tonga. None of his obituaries mentioned that he was a photographer. I hope the selection offered in this book does him justice.

His publishing record was impressive, and researchers looking at the early decades of the twentieth century in the Pacific and Queensland, thanks to McMahon, have a rich archive of historically important, expansive and occasionally divergent visual evidence. Pacific Islanders searching for what it was like in the old days a century ago and never having seen McMahon's published photographs at the time or since also have, thanks to Trove, an invaluable record of their ancestors' costume, dance, housing, villages, canoes and bodies, and involvement in introduced European commercial and industrial activity.

Few of McMahon's original prints or lantern slides have survived other than a few prints in the RGS in London and Queensland and a small collection of glass plates in private hands. The Mitchell Library of New South Wales holds several hundred prints, now digitised but wrongly catalogued under 'Maslyn Williams'.[534] But McMahon does live on in the bound periodical

---

533 *The Queenslander*, 17.8.1933, p. 9.

534 The catalogue entry for the Maslyn Williams collection at the Mitchell Library acknowledges the Marshall Island photographs were taken by McMahon (Mitchell Library; PXB293, Vol. 3). Maslyn Williams was a journalist, filmmaker and writer and perhaps collected copies of McMahon's photographs of Nauru, Ocean Island and the Gilbert Islands from a private collector when he co-authored a book on the phosphate industry in the 1980s.

sections of libraries where thousands of photographs sit in the printed pages of serial pictorial encyclopedias, magazines and journals and in the newsprint pages of weekend illustrated editions of city newspapers, which, again, thanks to Trove, can easily be accessed. His life story adds to the wider history of publishing, especially the global phenomenon of photographically illustrated publications like pictorial encyclopedias and illustrated weekend editions of daily newspapers.

Thank you, Tom McMahon, for leaving that wonderful visual legacy for future generations to wonder at and ponder its meaning.

Appendix 1

Pictorially illustrated publications in which McMahon's photographs appeared

Blue Peter, the magazine of the shipping line, P&O

Boys Own Paper, (London, 1879–1967), for teenage Christian boys

Chamber's Journal (Edinburgh, 1832–1956), originally titled *Chamber's Journal of Popular Literature, Science, and Art*

Daily newspapers:

- *The Cairns Post*
- *Northern Herald* (Cairns)
- *Sydney Morning Herald*
- *The Age* (Melbourne)
- *The Argus* (Melbourne)
- *The Brisbane Courier*
- *Sunday Times* (Sydney, 1885–1930)
- *The Telegraph* (Brisbane, 1872–1988), an evening newspaper noted for its pictorial coverage

Dun's Review (New York, 1893–1933), monthly magazine of business, commerce and economic conditions

Empire Review (London, 1901–1942), a monthly journal

The Far Eastern Review, initially published in the Philippines, later in China

Geografisk Tidskrift, the Danish Journal of Geography
Illustrated weekend editions of daily newspapers:

- *Auckland Weekly News* (Auckland, 1919–1925) of the *New Zealand Herald*
- *Otago Witness* (Dunedin, New Zealand, 1851–1932)
- *The Australasian* (Melbourne, 1864–1946) of *The Argus*
- *The Queenslander* (Brisbane) of *The Brisbane Courier*
- *The Sydney Mail* (1860–1938) of the *Sydney Morning Herald*
- *The Week* (Brisbane, 1874–1934), 'a journal of commerce, farming, mining and general information and amusement' of *The Telegraph* (Brisbane)
- *Town and Country Journal* (Sydney) of the *Sydney Evening News*

Illustrated London News (London, 1842–2003), the world's first illustrated weekly news magazine

Importers and Exporters Journal of Australasia (Sydney, 1920–), 'A weekly journal devoted to the development of Australia's and New Zealand's overseas trade and commerce in the interests of our importers, exporters and manufacturers desiring British and foreign trade'

The Lone Hand (Sydney, 1907–1928), 'A monthly magazine of literature and poetry as a sister magazine to *The Bulletin*'

Mid-Pacific Travel and Tourism (Honolulu, 1911–1954), the bulletin of the Pan-Pacific Union

Munsey's Magazine, (US,1889–1929), had monthly sales of 700,000 but by 1918, numbers had fallen below 100,000. It closed and merged with *Argosy* magazine in 1929

The New Nation Magazine (Sydney, 1925–1935), published monthly by the New Zealand Loan and Mercantile Agency

The Outlook (London, 1898–1927), 'The Outlook: In Politics, Life, Letters, and the Arts'

Penny Pictorial Magazine (England, 1899–1922)

Pictorial, serial, illustrated encyclopedias (in monthly instalments, also sold as sets of bound volumes):

- *Countries of the World* (6 volumes)
- *Lands and Peoples* (7 volumes)
- *Peoples of All Nations* (7 volumes)
- *The Book of Knowledge* (8 volumes)
- *The New World of Today* (8 volumes)
- *Women of the World* (2 volumes)

PLA Monthly, the magazine of the Port of London Authority

Sea Land Air (Sydney, 1918–1934), 'A monthly magazine of general interest'

Sunset: the Pacific Monthly (San Francisco, 1898–), originally a railway magazine to promote the American West

The Quiver (London, 1861–1956), a weekly magazine on 'defence and promotion of biblical truth and the advance of religion in the homes of the people'

The Wide World Magazine, later as *The Wide World* (London, 1898–1965), whose banner read, 'Truth is Stranger than Fiction; An Illustrated Monthly of True Narrative Adventure Travel Customs and Sport; *The Wide World Magazine* may safely be trusted to carry into every home, by means of the infallible camera and the responsible traveller, the almost incredible wonders of the Wide World'

The World's Work (New York, 1900–1932), a monthly business and national affairs magazine with circulation of 100,000

Select list of McMahon's publications on Queensland, 1916–1933

1916

The Queenslander, 'Mareeba: A northern town that is 'smartening up', 19.2.1916, p. 26, 4 illustrations

The Queenslander, 'Mapoon Aboriginal Mission', 16.12.1916, (text on p. 8), pp. 22–23, 9 illustrations

1917

The Sydney Mail, 'Cooktown', 3.5.1917, p. 11, 4 illustrations

The Cairns Post, 'Paper Pulp and Dye making', 21.6.1917, p. 8

Evening Telegraph, (Charters Towers), 'Paper and Pulp making', 29.6.1917, p. 3

Weekly Times (Melbourne), 'North Queensland and the Islands (TSI)', 30.6.1917, p. 25, 4 illustrations

The Australasian (Melbourne), repeat 'Paper and Pulp making', 7.7.1917, p. 25, 5 illustrations

Northern Herald, repeat 'Mapoon Aboriginal Mission', 10.8.1917, p. 27, 2 illustrations

The Queenslander, 'The tip-top of Queensland I', 10.11.1917, p. 23, 6 illustrations

The Queenslander, 'The tip-top of Queensland II' (some

used in his book, *The Orient I Found*), 17.11.1917, p. 23, 6
illustrations

1918

The Queenslander, 'Storm swept places: Innisfail', 23.3.1918, p.
23, 5 illustrations

1919

Bundaberg Mail, 'A moral for Queensland' on McMahon's
report on sugar, in *Outlook* (London), 22.12.1919, p. 4
Northern Herald, Views of Cairns (but includes one from
Solomon Islands), 29.5.1919, pp. 30–31, 11 illustrations
Northern Herald, 'Mining and Wolfram District news; a rich
centre in Queensland', 27.8.1919, pp. 36–37, 11 illustrations
Northern Herald, 'The North' (mostly Cairns plus one from
Solomon Islands), 29.5.1919, pp. 30–31, 11 illustrations

1921

Townsville Daily Bulletin, notes McMahon's return from Papua
on the *Marsina* on 12 May, 14.5.1921, p. 2

1922

The Telegraph, 'The Burnett scheme: some of its defects',
9.6.1922, p. 3
The Week, repeat 'The Burnett scheme: some of its defects',
16.6.1922, p. 25
The Telegraph, 'The Burnett district', 17.6.1922, p. 11, 3
illustrations
The Week, 'The Burnett District: Depression in the cattle
industry', 23.6.1922, p. 25, 3 illustrations

The Week, 'Boring for water, Upper Burnett', 24.6.1922, p. 11, 1 illustration

The Week, 'In the Southwest' (notes the visit of McMahon), 8.7.1922, p. 6

The Week, 'The solar eclipse: Preparations at Goondawindi', 15.7.1922, p. 11

The Week, 'The great sheep industry: Its progress, enterprise … troubles and taxation', 22.7.1922, p. 15, 4 illustrations

The Geraldton Express, repeat 'The Pearl Fishers of the Torres Strait Islands' (in *Chambers Journal*), 26.7.1922, p. 1

The Telegraph, 'The Great Southwest: Progress of the famous sheep runs', 29.7.1922, p. 11, 4 illustrations

The Brisbane Courier, 'Chinchilla: A progressive western town', 30.8.1922

The Week, repeat 'The Great Southwest: Progress of the famous sheep runs', 4.8.1922, p. 5

The Week, 'Malanda: The heart of the tableland', 25.10.1922, pp. 42–44

The Week, (noted that McMahon gave a talk in Sydney), 21.11.1922, p. 6

1923

The Telegraph, 'Gayndah: The cotton metropolis of Queensland (Nth Burnett)', 28.4.1923, p. 11, 1 illustration

The Week, repeat 'Gayndah: The cotton metropolis of Queensland (Nth Burnett)', 4.5.1923, p. 25

The Telegraph, 'Nambour: Rich and beautiful district', 9.6.1923, p. 11, 3 illustrations

The Telegraph, 'Progressive Sydney: City of gaiety and enterprise', 14.7.1923, p. 11, 6 illustrations

The Telegraph, 'Townsville Show: Resources of the Great North', 28.7.1923, p. 27, 1 illustration

The Telegraph, (reports McMahon back from two-month tour of North Queensland,) 11.9.1923, p. 10

The Week, (repeat reports McMahon back from two-month tour of North Queensland) 14.9.1923, p. 4–5

The Telegraph, (editorial refers to 'The empty North' and McMahon's forthcoming reports), 11.9.1923, p. 8

Bundaberg Mail, 'Developing the North', 14.9.1923, p. 2

Beaudesert Times, repeat 'Developing the North', 21.9.1923, p. 3

The Week, 'What the North needs' (announcing McMahon's series on 'The North', repeated for two weeks), 21.9.1923, p. 3

The Week, 21.9.1923, pp.12, 14, 1 illustration of Innisfail

The Telegraph, 'Innisfail: The Gold land; surpassing fertility and beauty', 22.9.1923, p. 11, 6 illustrations

The Telegraph, 'North Queensland: Richest and most resourceful portion of the Commonwealth', 27.9.1923, p. 5, 6 illustrations

The Week, repeat 'North Queensland: Richest and most resourceful portion of the Commonwealth', 28.9.1923, p. 15

The Week, 'Disabilities of settlement: Commercial relationships of Nth Qld to Southern States', 5.10.1923, pp. 22, 28, 6 illustrations

The Telegraph, 'The North: Go ahead Townsville; the capital of the north', 13.10.1923, p. 11, 6 illustrations

The Telegraph, 'Chillagoe and district: The Mining smelters', 20.10.1923, p. 11. 5 illustrations

Western Mail (Perth), 'The iron trail: From Cairns to Perth', 11.10.1923, p. 30

The Cairns Post, 'New state for Queensland and why', 22.10.1923, p. 9

Northern Herald, repeat 'New state for Queensland and why', 28.10.1923, p. 29

The Telegraph, 'Bowen; Its resourceful district, Rich coal fields of Collinsville, Beautiful sugar lands of Proserpine', 27.10.1923, p. 16, 6 illustrations

The Sydney Mail, 'Sydney to Townsville by Rail; Innisfail Jubilee', 31.10.1923, p. 26, 8 illustrations

The Albury Banner, 'Perth to Cairns Railway', 2.11.1923, p. 29

The Telegraph, 'El Arish: Successful soldier settlement in North Queensland', 3.11.1923, p. 11, 5 illustrations

The Sydney Mail, repeat 'El Arish: Successful soldier settlement in North Queensland', 28.11.1923, p. 29, 5 illustrations

The Week, repeat 'El Arish: Successful soldier settlement in North Queensland', 2.11.1923, p. 3

The Week, 'Babinda: A rich sugar district', 9.11.1923, p. 15

The Telegraph, repeat of 'Babinda: A rich sugar district', 10.11.1923, p. 11, 7 illustrations

The Telegraph, 'Cairns: Busy and prosperous Port; A rich and resourceful hinterland', 17.11.1923, p. 11, 9 illustrations

The Telegraph, 'Great Atherton Tableland', 24.11.1923, p. 11, 7 illustrations

Circular Head Chronicle, 'Great railway system; a great national undertaking', 28.11.1923, p. 2

The Telegraph, 'Mackay: An important sugar centre; A town of banks', 1.12.1923, p. 13, 9 illustrations

The Telegraph, 'North Queensland: Four sugar centres (Lucinda Point, Halifax, Ayr, Ingham)', 8.12.1923, p. 13, 9 illustrations

1924

The Sydney Mail, anonymous response to 'El Arish: Successful soldier settlement in North Queensland', 9.1.1924, p. 30

The Brisbane Courier, 'Wallangara Rail Centre', 24.1.1924, p. 10

The Queenslander, 'Thargomindah: Busy stock route town', 2.2.1924, p. 25, 11 illustrations

The Brisbane Courier, 'Granite Belt: Soldier settlers', 9.2.1924, p. 11

The Brisbane Courier, 'Glen Alpin', 23.2.1924, p. 15

The Brisbane Courier, 'Pikedale, Wybera and Eukey', 8.3.1924, p. 15

The Brisbane Courier, 'Granite Belt Orchardists', 15.3.1924, p. 15

The Brisbane Courier, 'Ballandean orchards and Grapes', 22.3.1924, p. 15

The Brisbane Courier, 'Killarney Show: Some Impressions', 22.3.1924, p. 6

The Brisbane Courier, 'Thulimbah', 29.3.1924, p. 11

The Queenslander, repeat 'Thulimbah', 28.6.1924, p. 11

The Queenslander, 'Ballandean wines', 12.4.1924, p. 11

The Brisbane Courier, 'Stanthorpe', 26.4.1924, p. 20

The Sydney Mail, 'Gayndah: Cotton metropolis of Queensland', 7.5.1924, p. 3, 2 illustrations

The Sydney Mail, 'Mailbox in the trees at Mondure, Burnett District', 14.5.1924, p. 23, 1 illustration

The Sydney Mail, 'Pile of chain wire netting for the 150-mile-long rabbit and dog fence', 11.6.1924, p. 27, 2 illustrations

The Sydney Mail, 'Qld Governor opening Stanthorpe Golf Club', 16.7.1924, p. 32, 1 illustration

The Sydney Mail, 'Motor car with a blow out in the far west', 23.7.1924, p. 37, 1 illustration

The Queenslander, 'Broadwater: Granite Belt', 26.7.1924, p. 11

The Sydney Mail, 'Soldier's Memorial Hall, Maryborough', 6.8.1924, p. 38, 1 illustration

The Sydney Mail, ' Entrance to the "Soldier's Club" at Stanthorpe', 24.9.1924, p. 43, 1 illustration

The Sun (Sydney), notes McMahon talk at Royal Colonial Institute with lantern slides on Queensland, 3.11.1924, p. 12

The Sydney Mail, 'The wonderful arsenic mines of Queensland' (Granite Belt), 26.11.1924, p. 19, 6 illustrations

Daily Telegraph, 'Menace to Queensland, (Launceston)', 28.11.1924, p. 7

The Brisbane Courier, 'Magnetic Island: Its wonderful climate; an ocean paradise; Townsville's holiday resort', 3.12.1924, p. 6, 4 illustrations

The Sydney Mail, 'Two tents forming a settler's home in the "back blocks" of Queensland', 10.12.1924, p. 62, 1 illustration

The Sydney Mail, 'Carting hay at Goomerai, "The Mudgee of the northern state"', 17.12.1924, p. 35, 1 illustration

The Sydney Mail, 'Muckadilla Sanitorium and Hot Springs', Queensland, 17.12.1924, p. 25, 1 illustration

1925

The Sydney Mail, 'A western Queensland (artesian) bore', 7.1.1925, p. 29, 1 illustration

The Sydney Mail, 'The homestead at Norley Station (a Kidman property)', 14.1.1925, p. 27, 1 illustration

Western Mail (Perth), 'Perth to Cairns linked by rail', 15.1.1925, p. 26

The Brisbane Courier, 'The Georgina Country: A fine pastoral area', 23.1.1925, p. 15, 4 illustrations

The Leader (Perth) citing *The Leader* (Melbourne), 'The fruit industry in Queensland: Amazing possibilities', 6.2.1925, p. 6

The Sydney Mail, 'St Catherine's Church of England College for Girls' (Stanthorpe), 25.2.1925, p. 23, 1 illustration

Murray Pioneer, 'An Australian River Record', repeat 'Italian
  settlement in Queensland' (from The Leader), 27.2.1925, p. 9
The Brisbane Courier, 'Charleville: How a city was forged in the
  great Southwest', 6.3.1925, p. 11, 12 illustrations
The Brisbane Courier, 'Stanthorpe', 11.3.1925, p. 3
The Queenslander, 'Charleville; western commercial centre',
  21.3.1925, p. 24, 41, 8 illustrations
The Sydney Mail, 'Main street of Dalby', 1.4.1925, p. 19, 1
  illustration
The Brisbane Courier, 'The Oakey District: Rich area of the
  Darling Downs', 2.5.1925, p. 15, 5 illustrations
The Sydney Mail, 'QANTAS flight about to take off
  (Charleville to Camooweal)', 7.5.1925,
p. 33, 1 illustration
The Brisbane Courier, 'Mitchell: A prosperous centre; Well-
  managed public institutions', 8.5.1925, p. 17, 14 illustrations
The Sydney Mail, Golfers under an umbrella, probably at
  Stanthorpe, 20.5.1925, p. 22, 1 illustration
The Sydney Mail, 'Bullock wagons piled high and lambs being
  branded (Longreach)',
1.7.1925, p. 31, 2 illustrations
The Queenslander, 'In the Upper Burnett: (Ceradotus railway
  construction)', 18.7.1925, p. 26, 6 illustrations
The Telegraph, repeat 'Disabilities of settlement: Commercial
  relationships of Nth Qld to Southern States', (on Collinsville,
  Bowen, Townsville, and Lucinda Point), 6.10.1925, p. 11, 28
Weekly Times (Melbourne) *Xmas Annual*, 'Through
  Queensland' (full-page collage), 19.12.1925, p. 4, 58
  illustrations
The Brisbane Courier, 'Charters Towers: The dawn of a new era',
  22.12.1925, p. 11, 18 illustrations (12 portraits and 6 pics)

1926

The Sydney Mail, 213 cm high man on pastoral property (Barkly Tableland), 3.3.1926, p. 35, 1 illustration

The Queenslander, 'The turtle shell industry of Northwest Island', 6.3.1926, p. 23, 10 illustrations

The Queenslander, 'Development of Mount Larcom', 6.3.1926, p. 28, 10 illustrations

The Queenslander, 'A family of pioneers: the Creeds of Langmorn Station', 20.3.1926, p. 40

The Queenslander, 'Cooyar: Timber and dairying resources', 23.10.1926, pp. 11, 24, 8 illustrations

The Sydney Mail, review of *The Orient I Found*, 26.10.1926, p. 13

1927

The Sydney Mail, single illustration, three children canoeing on Youngerman Creek near Surat, 4.5.1927, p. 30, 1 illustration

The Brisbane Courier, single illustration, *The Maid of Sker* (the Brisbane-Southport ferry), 19.10.1927, p. 18, 1 illustration

The Brisbane Courier, 'Oil prospects: Activity at Roma; A profitable field', 5.11.1927, p. 9

1928

The Sydney Mail, 'Dunwich: A Queensland Old Folks Home', 4.1.1928, p. 21, 4 illustrations

The Sydney Mail, 'A Reafforestation scheme; Fraser Island, Queensland', 15.2.1928, p. 19, 5 illustrations

New Nation Magazine, 'Oil prospects: A visit to Roma', March 1928, pp. 39–40, 4 illustrations

The Sydney Mail, 'The Dentist at a Queensland school', 10.5.1928, p. 43, 6 illustrations

The Horsham Times, '1000 miles of coral: The Great Barrier

Reef' (reprinted from *The World Today*, January 1928),
11.5.1928, p. 3

The Brisbane Courier, 'Pine Rivers district: Agriculture and
scenic beauty', 1.9.1928, p. 11, 4 illustrations

The Cairns Post, notes that McMahon is visiting Cairns and the
Malanda Agricultural Show, 22.9.1928, p. 4

1929

The Brisbane Courier, 'Fletcher (near Ballandean)', 2.3.1929, p. 11

The Brisbane Courier, 'Yeulba: A fertile district', 22.6.1929, p.
13, 3 illustrations

The Brisbane Courier, 'Longreach: Home of the merino; Great
progress', 23.10.1929, pp. 12–13, 9 illustrations

Northern Herald, 'North of Cairns: Potential assets to
settlement; Slumbering isolation or splendid Daintree and
Mosman Area', 30.10.1929, p. 23, 3 illustrations

1930

The Brisbane Courier, 'Granite Belt: Enterprising orchardists',
25.1.1930, p. 10, 5 illustrations

The Brisbane Courier, 'Granite Belt: Progress of the Grape
Industry', 22.2.1930, p. 11, 4 illustrations

The Brisbane Courier, 'Narangba: A fertile dairying district',
1.3.1930, p. 11, 4 illustrations

The Brisbane Courier, 'Dalby District: Dairying progress',
22.3.1930, p. 11, 8 illustrations

The Brisbane Courier, 'Cash's Crossing: Picturesque dairying
district', 5.4.1930, p. 11, 6 illustrations

The Brisbane Courier, 'The Highlands: Picturesque and
progressive settlement; what ex-diggers can do', 13.9.1930, p.
9, 5 illustrations

The Brisbane Courier, 'Fertile Greenbank: land of rich hills and dales; Kyogle line stimulus', 4.10.1930, p. 9, 5 illustrations

The Brisbane Courier, 'Woodridge: Mixed farming', 25.10.1930, p. 11, 4 illustrations

The Brisbane Courier, 'Kingston: Record of steady progress; Thriving industries; model settlement near Brisbane', 8.11.1930, p. 9, 10 illustrations

The Brisbane Courier, 'Waterford: Some old families; Prosperous rural activities', 20.12.1930, p. 9, 9 illustrations

The Brisbane Courier, 'Granite Belt', 22.12.1930, p. 11

1931

The Brisbane Courier, 'Hard work won: Development of Bethania; Pioneers and hardships', 3.1.1931, p. 14, 3 illustrations

The Queenslander, 'Diary: Loganlea; A Flourishing Centre', 29.1.1931, p. 14

The Queenslander, 'Jimboomba: Picturesque hills and dales', 19.2.1931, p. 8

The Queenslander, 'Warra district: A record of progress', 19.2.1931, p. 10

The Queenslander, 'The Diary: Cedar Grove; Picturesque and prosperity', 19.2.1931, p.14

The Brisbane Courier, 'Granite Belt: Fruit Growing', 21.2.1931, p. 9

The Queenslander, 'The Farm: The Granite Belt Fruit for Overseas markets', 26.2.1931, p. 9

The Queenslander, 'Wide Bay' (double page spread), 26.2.1931, pp. 12–13, 13 illustrations

The Queenslander, 'The Fruit Pickers: A Granite Belt study' (cover of the *Pictorial*), 5.3.1931, p. 23, 1 illustration

The Brisbane Courier, 'Granite Belt Wine', 7.3.1931, p. 8

The Queenslander, 'The Granite Belt: Progress of Grape Growing', 12.3.1931, pp. 12–13

The Queenslander, 'Logan Village: Rich dairying', 7.5.1931, p. 12

The Queenslander, 'Canungra: Timber and Grazing; flourishing dairy centre', p. 22

1932

The Brisbane Courier, 'Granite Belt: Fruit, Tobacco and Minerals: Interesting experiments', 20.1.1932, p. 12, 3 illustrations

The Brisbane Courier, 'Activities at Wallangara: Surprising fertility', 8.2.1932, p. 15, 3 illustrations

The Queenslander, Stanthorpe Show (champion hack and kangaroo products display), 18.2.1932, p. 28, 2 illustrations

The Brisbane Courier, 'Mixed farming – Pinkenba-Myrtletown: Fructivity of Soil', 7.4.1932, p. 7, 1 illustration

The Brisbane Courier, 'Mixed farming: Growth of Greenbank area', 6.9.1932, p. 17, 1 illustration

The Brisbane Courier, 'Victoria Point: Abundant crops', 21.9.1932, p. 13, 1 illustration

The Sydney Mail, 'Historic Canning Downs: A beautiful station home', 12.10.1932, p. 37, 4 illustrations

Appendix 3

Illustration credits and endnotes

Cover Unpublished print held in the archives of the Royal Geographical Society (Queensland).

Fig. 1 *The Queenslander*, 1.4.1916, p. 24. An accompanying story was published separately in the 'Sketcher' column.

Fig. 2 McMahon photograph, coloured, used as the cover for edition 37 of *Countries of the World* (London 1923); Sir Basil Thompson, 'South Sea islands; Palm fringed Edens of Oceania', *Countries of the World*, Vol. 6, p. 3755.

Fig. 3 'A noted authority on South Pacific questions,' *The Sydney Mail*, 14.1.1920, p. 10; *The Trade Promoter of Australia and New Zealand*, 1920, p. 38.

Fig. 4 *The Sydney Mail*, 27.2.1918, p. 9. This was one of McMahon's most circulated images.

Fig. 5 *The Queenslander*, April 1916.

Fig. 6 *The Lone Hand*, 1.7.1916, p. 83; *Illustrated London News*, 15.11.1919, p. 780.

Fig. 7 *The Sydney Mail*, 16.1.1918, p. 26.

Fig. 8 *The Lone Hand*, 1.3.1918, p. 159. Used widely, including *Pacific Islands Monthly*, 16.8.1930, p. 8. Variously said by McMahon to have been owned by Queen Emma or Dr Moulton, a survivor of the ill-fated Marquis de Rays scheme.

Fig. 9   *The Queenslander*, 11 May 1918, p. 25. Typical format in the 'Pictorial' supplement of *The Queenslander*.

Fig. 10   *The Queenslander*, 12.1.1918, p. 21.

Fig. 11   *Countries of the World*, London, 1923, p. 3755 (in colour).

Fig. 12   *The Queenslander*, 12.1.1918. State Library of Queensland, http://onesearch.slq.qld.gov.au/permalink/f/1oppkg1/ slq_digitool864900. This was the second of his ten-part series on the British Solomon Islands.

Fig. 13   *The Queenslander*, 11.5.1918, p. 25. McMahon used this pair of photographs of Bougainville islanders many times from 1918–1920 to argue that Islanders could become an effective labour force. Readers were told the men on the left were 'wild' and recently recruited while the men on the right were reliable, steady, trained labourers.

Fig. 14   *Countries of the World*, Vol. 6, 1923, p. 3756 (colourised). Reproduced in black-and-white in Ellis, A. *Ocean Island and Nauru*, 1935, p. 68.

Fig. 15   Archives of the Royal Geographical Society (Queensland). Published in *The Leader* (Melbourne) 11.1.1919, p. 20.

Fig. 16   *Dun's International Review*, June 1919, p. 1333; *Trans-Pacific Magazine*, Nov 1920, p. 56; in *Geografisk Tidskrift* (the *Danish Journal of Geography*) 1920, p. 224.

Fig. 17   *Peoples of All Nations*, 1922, p. 922. McMahon published nine photographs of these dancers.

Fig. 18   *Pacific Ports*, August 1919, p. 85. Note the same group of men in the previous photograph. (Digital copy held by Mitchell Library; PXB 293 (v.5/1-169); FL15849676)

Fig. 19   *World's Work*, 1920, p. 147. State Library of NSW,   https://digital.sl.nsw.gov.au/delivery/

DeliveryManagerServlet?dps_pid=FL979859&embedded=true&toolbar=false

Fig. 20 Basil Thompson, 'South Sea Islands: Palm-fringed Edens of paradise', *Countries of the World*, Vol. 6, 1923, p. 3787.

Fig. 21 *The Sydney Mail*, 1.1.19, p. 9. State Library of NSW, https://collection.sl.nsw.gov.au/record/9arpErXn/AGewKJWak4jDR. The headline continues with '...the extensive lagoon is nowadays invariably full of Japanese shipping'.

Fig. 22 No. 1, State Library of NSW, https://collection.sl.nsw.gov.au/record/9PQyjRln.

Fig. 23 No. 40, State Library of NSW, https://collection.sl.nsw.gov.au/record/9arpErXn/2wqVXbEkBWzZy

Fig. 24 No. 51, State Library of NSW, https://collection.sl.nsw.gov.au/record/9arpErXn/GdBo2eXVk2y0B

Fig. 25 *Illustrated London News,* 1.10.1921, p. 444.

Fig. 26 *The Sydney Mail*, 1919.

Fig. 27 *Countries of the World*, 1923.

Fig. 28 *The Sydney Mail*, 1921.

Fig. 29 *Countries of the World,* Vol. 6, p. 3754 (colourised).

Fig. 30 *New World of Today*, 1928.

Fig. 31 *The Sydney Mail*, 1922.

Fig. 32 *The Wide World*, 1923.

Fig. 33 *The Australasian* (Melbourne), 21.4.1917. p. 5.

Fig. 34 *The Australasian* and *The Sydney Mail* 1917; *The Queenslander*, 1919; *Auckland Weekly News*, 1920. Print held by State Library of Queensland, https://digital.slq.qld.gov.au/cantaloupe/iiif/2/IE1451987:FL1453455.jpg/full/1000,719/0/default.jpg

Appendix 4

Bibliography

Previous publications on Thomas J McMahon by the author

Quanchi, M. 1994, 'A trip through the islands in 1918; the photography of TJ McMahon', *Meanjin*, Vol. 53, 4, pp. 714–22.

Quanchi, M. 1995, 'TJ McMahon; photographer, essayist and patriot in colonial Australia, the Pacific and empire' in *Messy Entanglements*, edited by Talu, Alaima and Quanchi, Max. Brisbane, Pacific History Association, pp. 49–62.

Quanchi, M. 1997, 'Thomas McMahon; photography as propaganda in the Pacific Islands', *History of Photography*. Vol. 21, no. 1, pp. 42–53.

Quanchi, M. 2000, 'Thomas McMahon' in *The Encyclopedia of the Pacific Islands*, edited by Lal, Brij and Fortune, Kate. Honolulu, University of Hawaii Press, 2000, p. 163.

Quanchi, M. 2011, 'A Collector of Images: The Pacific Archive of Photographer Thomas McMahon' in *Hunting the Collector: Pacific Collections in Australian Museums, Art Galleries and Archives*, edited by Cochrane, Susan and Quanchi, Max. Newcastle, Cambridge Scholars Press, pp. 147–66.

Quanchi, Max. 2015, 'Thomas McMahon's Pacific neighbours; an early Australian photojournalist' in *Shifting focus: colonial Australian photography 1860–1920*, edited by Maxwell, Ann and Croci, Josephine. Melbourne, Australian Scholarly Publishing, pp. 218–229.

Select bibliography of secondary works

Ahrens, P, ed. *Tour of paradise: An American soldier in the South Pacific.* Carlton, The Vulgar Press, 2006.

Albers, P. and James, WR. 'Travel photography; a methodological approach', *Annals of Tourism Research.* Vol. 15, pp. 134–58, 1988.

Andrews, CF. and Pearson, WW. *Indian indentured labour in Fiji.* Star Printing Works, Calcutta, 1916.

Antsapouva, T. and Maidment, E. 'Pacific focus: Bringing knowledge about Photographic Collections in Australia to Pacific Communities', *Hunting the collectors: Pacific collections in Australian Museums, Art Galleries and Archives*, edited by Cochrane, Susan and Quanchi, Max. Newcastle, Cambridge Scholars Publishing, pp. 377–394, 2011.

Barrar, W. *Fields of vision: Photography, phosphate, and landscape from a Pacific History.* unpublished, Master of Design, Massey University, 1995.

Bell, J. 'Sugar Plant Hunting by Airplane in New Guinea A Cinematic Narrative of Scientific Triumph and Discovery in the 'Remote Jungles', Journal of Pacific History, Vol. 45, no. 1, pp. 37–56, 2010.

Bennett, J. *Wealth of the Solomons: a history of a Pacific archipelago 1800–1978.* Honolulu, University of Hawaii Press, 1987.

Bevan, S. *Battles Lines: Australian artists at war.* Milson Point, NSW, Random, 2004.

Bloembergen, M. *Colonial Spectacles: The Netherlands and the Dutch East Indies at the World Exhibitions 1810–1930.* Singapore, Singapore University Press, 2006.

Brady, EJ. *Australia Unlimited.* Melbourne, Robertson, 1918.

Broomhead, R. *Living on the edge of paradise,* Buddina, Qld, Joshua Books, 2014.

Buckingham, J. 'Indenture and the Indian Experience of Leprosy on Makogai Island, Fiji', *Journal of Pacific History,* Vol. 52, no. 3, pp. 325–42, 2017.

Buckley, K. and Klugman, K. *The Australian Presence in the Pacific: Burns Philp 1914–16.* Sydney, George Allen and Unwin, 1983.

Burns, A. *Fiji.* London, HMSO, 1963.

Cayrol-Baudrillart, F. *Arthur Lavine's Pacific Inspiration: Early photographs of New Caledonia.* Noumea, Èditions de musée de Nouvelle-Calédonie, 2008.

Clyde, PH. *Japan's Pacific Mandate.* New York, Macmillan, 1935.

Cochrane, Susan, and Quanchi, Max, eds. *Hunting the collectors: Pacific collections in Australian Museums, Art Galleries and Archive.* Newcastle, UK, Cambridge Scholars Publishing, 2007.

Coffee, Frank. *Forty years in the Pacific.* Sydney, Oceanic Publishing Company, 1925.

Cole, T. *Hell west and crooked.* Sydney, Angus and Robertson, 1988.

Colley, AC. *Robert Louis Stevenson and the colonial imagination.* London, Routledge, 2004.

Colquhoun, AR. *The Mastery of the Pacific.* New York, Macmillan, 1902.

D'Arcy, P, ed. *The Cambridge History of the Pacific Islands.* Cambridge, CUP, 2022.

Darian-Smith, K. and Wills, Sara. Agricultural Shows in Australia: A Survey. Australian Centre, University of Melbourne, 1999.

Davies, A. *An eye for photography; The camera in Australia.* Sydney, State Library of NSW, 2000.

Denoon, D, Mein-Smith, Philippa and Wyndham, Marivic. *A History of Australia, New Zealand and the Pacific.* Blackwell Publishing, Oxford 2000.

Dixon, Robert. *Prosthetic Gods; Travel, representation and colonial governance.* St Lucia, Qld, University of Queensland Press, 2001.

Douglas, N. *They came for savages; 100 years of tourism in Melanesia.* Astonville, Southern Cross University Press, 1996.

Dowling, P. 'Destined not to survive: the illustrated newspapers of colonial Australia,' Vol. 3, nos 1–2, pp. 85–98, Francis & Taylor Online, https://www.tandfonline.com/doi/abs/10.1080/13688809509357919, 1995.

Edgeworth-David, Mrs. *Funafuti, or Three Months on a Coral Island; an Unscientific Account of a Scientific Expedition.* London, John Murray, 1899.

Eggleston, FW. 'Australia's View of Pacific Problems', *Pacific Affairs*, Vancouver, University of British Colombia, Vol. 3, 1930.

––– 'The British Empire, Australia and the Pacific', *Australian Quarterly.* Vol. 4, 1936.

Eggleston, FW, ed. *The Australian Mandate in New Guinea.* Melbourne, Macmillan, 1928.

Ellis, A. *Ocean Island and Nauru: Their Story.* Sydney, Angus and Robertson, 1935.

Evans, R, Moore, Clive, Saunders, Kay and Jamison, Brian, eds. *1901: Our Future's Past: documenting Australia's federation.* Sydney, Pan Macmillan,1997.

Firth, S. 'The Germans in New Guinea', in May, RJ and Nelson, H, eds. *Melanesia beyond diversity.* Canberra, ANU Press, 1982.

–––'German firms in the Western Pacific Islands 1857–1914'. *Journal of Pacific History*, Vol. 8, pp. 10–28, 1973.

———'The transformation of the labour trade in German New Guinea 1899–1914'. *Journal of Pacific History,* 11, 1, pp. 51–65, 1976.

Fitzhardinge, LF. 'Australia, Japan and Great Britain 1914-18', *Historical Studies.* Vol. 14, no. 54, pp. 250–9, 1970.

Forman, CW. 'Missions and colonialism: the case of the New Hebrides in the Twentieth Century', *Journal of Church Studies.* Vol. 14.1.1, pp. 75–92, 1972.

Garnham, F. *A report on the social and moral condition of Indians in Fiji, being the outcome of an investigation set on foot by the combined women's organizations of Australasia.* Sydney, Kingston Press, 1918.

Gervais, T. *The making of the news: A history of photography in the press.* London, Bloomsbury Press, 2017.

Gesimar, H, and Herle, A. *Moving images; John Layard, fieldwork and photography on Malakula since 1914.* Honolulu, University of Hawaii Press, 2010.

Greenwood, G, and Grimshaw, Charles, eds. *Documents on Australia's International Affairs 1901–1918.* Sydney, Thomas Nelson, 1977.

Hall, E. *The Territory; The classic saga of Australia's far north.* Sydney, Angus and Robertson, 1951.

Halter, N. *Australian travellers in the South Seas.* Canberra, ANU Press, 2021.

Halter, N, and Quanchi, M. 'Boosting the Frontier: Australian Settler Colonialism in the Pacific 1860s–1900s', *Australian Historical Studies.* Vol. 53, no. 3, pp. 415–32, 2022.

Hayes, M. 'Photography and the emergence of the Pacific cruise', *Colonialist Photography: Imag(in)ing race and place,* edited by Hight, EM and Sampson, GD. London, Routledge, pp. 172–87, 2002.

Hempenstall, P. *Pacific Islanders under German rule: a study in the meaning of resistance.* Canberra, ANU Press, 1978.

Hezel, F. *Strangers in their own land; a century of colonial rule in the Caroline and Marshall Islands.* Honolulu, University of Hawaii Press, 1995.

Hiery, H. *The neglected war: the German South Pacific and the influence of World War I.* Honolulu, University of Hawaii Press, 1995.

Hight, EM, and Sampson, GD, eds. *Colonialist photography: imag(in)ing race and place.* London, Routledge, 2002.

Hilder, B. *Navigator in the South Sea.* London, Percival and Marshall, 1961.

Hill, J, and Schwartz, VR, eds. *Getting the picture: The visual culture of the news.* London, Bloomsbury Press, 2015.

Hore, J. *Visions of nature; How landscape photography shaped settler colonialism.* Oakland, University of California Press, 2022.

Hudson, WJ. *New Guinea Empire. Australia's Colonial Experience.* Melbourne, Cassell, 1974.

Hughes, W. 'Australia and the Pacific', *United Empire.* pp. 293–5, 1918.

Hughes-D'Aeth, Tony. *Paper nation; the story of the Picturesque Atlas of Australia 1886–1888.* Melbourne, MUP, 2001.

Im Thurn, E. 'The present state of the Pacific Islands', *Journal of the Royal Society of Arts.* pp. 38–45, 1918.

Inglis, K. *Sacred places; War memorials in the Australian Landscape,* Melbourne, Oxford University Press, 1998.

Jolly, M, and de Courcey, E, eds. *The magic lantern at work: Witnessing, persuading and experiencing and connecting.* London, Routledge, 2020.

Joyce, T, and Thomas, NW, eds. *Women of All Nations: A record of their characteristics, habits, manners, custom and influence.* London, Cassell and Company, 1908.

Lal, BV. *Girmityas: The origins of the Fiji Indians.* Canberra, Journal of Pacific History, 1983.

———*Broken Waves: A history of the Fiji Islands in the Twentieth Century.* Honolulu, University of Hawaii Press, 1992.

Lal, BV, and Fortune, K, eds. *The Encyclopedia of the Pacific Islands.* Honolulu, University of Hawaii Press, 2000.

Lamb, L, and Lee, C. *Moving Pictures; Repatriation, Exchange, and Colonial Legacies in the Gulf of Papua.* London, Palgrave, 2022.

Latukefu, S. *Papua New Guinea; a century of colonial impact*, Port Moresby, UPNG Press, 1992.

Lewis, D, *The plantation dream: developing British New Guinea and Papua, 1884-1942.* Canberra, JPH, 1996.

Lindstrom, L, and White, G. *Island encounters: Black-and-white Memories of the Pacific War. Washington, Smithsonian, 1990.*

Lowndes, AG. 'The sugar industry of Fiji', *South Pacific Enterprise: The Colonial Sugar Refining Company Limited*, edited by Lowndes, AG, Sydney, Angus and Robertson, pp. 67–90, 1956.

Louis, WR. 'Australia and the German colonies in the Pacific 1914–19', *Journal of Modern History.* Vol. 38, pp. 407–21, 1966.

Louis, WR. *Great Britain and Germany's Lost Colonies 1914–19.* Oxford, Clarendon Press, 1967.

Mackenzie, J. *Propaganda and Empire; the manipulation of British public opinion 1880–1960.* Manchester, Manchester University Press, 1986.

Mackenzie, SS. *The Australians at Rabaul.* Melbourne, Angus and Robertson, 1927.

McGregor, W. 'The Pacific Islands and their political settlement', *United Empire.* pp. 107–10, 1918.

———'The settlement of the Pacific', *Scottish Geographical Magazine*. pp. 161–77, 1918.

McIntyre, S. *The Oxford History of Australia: the succeeding age, 1901–1942*. Melbourne, MUP, 1986.

McLaren, AD. 'A Monroe doctrine for Australasia', *Contemporary Review*. pp. 158–63, 1918.

McKillop, R, and Firth, SG. 'Foreign Intrusion; the first fifty years', in Denoon, D, and Snowden, C, ed. *A Time to Plant and a Time to Uproot; A history of agriculture in Papua New Guinea*. Port Moresby, Institute of Papua New Guinea Studies, 1981.

McMullin, Ross. Life So Full of Promise: Further Biographies of Australia's Lost Generation. Melbourne, Scribe, 2023.

Maddern, P. *The eye of Wilkins: The complete photographic retrospective of George Hubert Wilkins*. Sydney, Peacock, 2021.

Manfredi, Carla. *Robert Louis Stevenson's Pacific impressions: Photography and travel writing*. Basingstoke, Palgrave Macmillan, 2018.

Maxwell, A, ed. *Women photographers in the Pacific world 1857-1930*. London, Routledge, 2023.

Maxwell, A. *Colonial photography and exhibitions*. London, Leicester University Press, 1999.

Mein Smith, P, Hempenstall, Peter, Goldfinch, Shaun. *Remaking the Tasman World*. Christchurch, University of Canterbury Press, 2008.

Moore, C. 'Queensland and its Coral Sea: implications of historical links between Australia and Melanesia', in Gillies, Malcolm, ed. *Northern Exposures*. pp. 79–102, Canberra, Australian Academy of the Humanities, 1997.

———*Tulagi: Pacific outpost of British Empire*. Canberra, ANU Press, 2019.

---*New Guinea: crossing boundaries and history.* Honolulu, University of Hawaii Press, 2003.

Moraes-Gorecki, V. '"Black Italians" in the sugar fields of north Queensland: a reflection on labour inclusion and cultural exclusion in tropical Australia,' *The Australian Journal of Anthropology.* Vol. 5, no. 3, pp. 306–19, 1994.

Morris, RC, ed. *Photographies East: The camera and its histories in East and Southeast Asia.* Durham, Duke University Press, 2009.

Muijzenberg, O van den. *The Philippines through European lenses: late nineteenth century photographs from the Meerkamp van Embden Collection.* Manila, Ateneo de Manila University Press, 2008.

Mullins, S. *Octopus Crow: Maritime History and the Business of Australian Pearling in its Schooner Age.* Tuscaloosa, University of Alabama Press, 2019.

Newton, G. *Garden of the East: Photography in Indonesia 1850s–1940s.* Canberra, National Gallery of Australia, 2014.

---*Shades of light: Photography and Australia 1839–1988.* Canberra, National Gallery of Australia, 1988.

Nelson, H. *Black, White and Gold: Goldmining in Papua New Guinea 1878–1930.* Canberra, ANU Press, 1976.

Odo, D. 'Asia's colonial photographs', *IIAS International Study for Asian Studies Newsletter.* Vol. 44, p. 3, 2007.

Palmer, D, and Jolly, M. *Installation View: Photography exhibitions in Australia 1848–2020.* Melbourne, Perimeter Editions, 2021.

Peattie, M. *Nan'yo: The rise and fall of the Japanese in Micronesia 1885–1945.* Honolulu, University of Hawaii Press, 1988.

Petrosian-Husa, CC-H. *The De Brum Photo Collection – Memento Mori Alele* Report 2005/1. Majuro, Marshall Island, Historic Preservation Office, 2005.

Phillips, J. *To the memory: New Zealand's war memorials*. Nelson, Potton and Burton, 2016.

Pinney, C. *Photography and Anthropology*. London, Reaktion, 2011.

Price, AG. *The history and politics of the Northern Territory*. Brisbane, University of Queensland Press, 1930.

Purcell, DC. 'The economics of exploitation', *Journal of Pacific History*. Vol. 11, nos. 3–4, pp. 198–211, 1976.

Quanchi, M. 'Pacific Island Photography; Knowledge and history in the public domain', *Spectator*. Vol. 23, no. 1, pp. 13–26, 2003.

–––'Power of Pictures; Learning by Looking at Papua in Illustrated Newspapers and Magazines', *Australian Historical Studies*. Vol. 35, no, 123, pp. 37–53, 2004.

–––'The imaging of Samoa in illustrated magazines and serial encyclopedia in the early 20th-century', *Journal of Pacific History*. Vol. 41, no. 2, pp. 207–217, 2006.

–––'Visual histories and photographic evidence', *Journal of Pacific History*. Vol. 41, no. 2, pp. 165–74, 2006.

–––'Norman H Hardy: Book Illustrator and Artist'. *The Journal of Pacific History*. Vol. 49, no. 2, pp. 214–233, 2014.

–––'Learning by looking, for example, at *Peoples of All Nations*: European education and serial encyclopedia', *Pacific Geographies*. Vol. 45, pp. 11–16, 2016.

–––'Melanesia: a region and a history' in *The Melanesian World*, edited by Hirsch, Eric, and Rollason, Will. London: Routledge, pp. 63–76, 2019.

–––'Recording of my journeys in the Coral Sea: Randolph Bedford's 1906 album of the Solomon Islands', *Journal of New Zealand and Pacific Studies*. Vol. 8, no. 1, pp. 39–56, 2020.

–––'Researching early photography of the Pacific islands: An Overview', *JNZPS*. Vol. 8, no. 1, pp. 269–81, 2021.

---*Glorious Company: The Polynesia Company in Melbourne and Fiji*. Suva, Pacific Studies Press, 2022.

Quanchi, M, and Shekleton, M. *An ideal colony and epitome of progress: Colonial Fiji in picture postcards*. Suva, USP Press, 2019.

---*Postcards from Oceania: Port Towns, Portraits and the Picturesque During the Colonial Era*, Suva, USP, 2015.

Reynolds, H. *North of Capricorn; The untold story of Australia's north*. Sydney, Allen and Unwin, 2003.

Rice, M. *Dean Worchester's fantasy islands: Photography, film and the colonial Philippines*. Ann Arbor, University of Michigan Press, 2017.

Robson, RW. *Queen Emma: The Samoan American girl who founded an empire in 19th century New Guinea* (4th ed.). Sydney, Pacific Publications, 1971.

Rowley, CD. *The Australians in German New Guinea 1914–1921*. Melbourne, Melbourne University Press, 1958.

Ryan, JR. *Picturing Empire: Photography and the Visualization of the British Empire*. Chicago, University of Chicago Press, 1997.

---*Picturing Place: Photography and the Geographical Imagination. London, Bloomsbury, 2003*.

---*Photography and Exploration*. London, Reaktion, 2013.

Scarr, D. *Kingdoms of the Reefs: the history of the Pacific Islands*. Sydney, Macmillan, 1990.

Scholefield, GH. 'Problems of reconstruction in the Pacific', *United Empire*. pp. 326–9, 1919.

---*The Pacific: Its Past and Future*. John Murray, London, 1919

Schreuder, DM, and Ward, S, eds. *Australia's Empire: The Oxford History of the British Empire*. Melbourne, OUP, 2008.

Smith, G. *Photography and travel*. London, Reaktion, 2013.

Snelling, RC. 'Peacemaking 1919: Australia, New Zealand and the

British empire delegation at Versailles', *Journal of Imperial and Commonwealth History*. Vol. 40, pp. 15–28, 1975.

Steel, F. *Oceania Under Steam: Sea transport and the cultures of colonialism, c.1870–1914*. Manchester, Manchester University Press, 2016.

Stephenson, Elsie. *Fiji's past on picture postcards*. Suva, Caines Janiff, 1997.

Tassell, Margaret, and Wood, David. *Tasmanian Photographer: From the John Watt Beattie Collection*. Melbourne, Macmillan, 1981.

Tate, M. 'The Australasian Munroe doctrine', *Political Science Quarterly*. Vol. 55, no. 4, pp. 971–79, 1961.

Thompson, RC. 'The Labor Party and Australian imperialism in the Pacific 1901–1919', *Labour History*. Vol. 23, pp. 27–37, 1972.

———'Making a Mandate: The Formation of Australia's New Guinea Policies 1919–1925', *The Journal of Pacific History*. Vol. 25, no. 1, pp. 68–84, 1990.

———*Australian imperialism in the Pacific; the expansionist era 1820–1920*. Melbourne, Melbourne University Press, 1980.

Tinker, H. *A New System of Slavery: The Export of Indian Labour Overseas 1820–1920*. London, Oxford University Press, 1974.

Vargas, B. *Displaying Filipinos: photography and colonialism in early 20th century Philippines*. Manila, University of Hawaii Press, 1995.

Waiko, JD. *A Short History of Papua New Guinea*. Melbourne, OUP, 1993.

Ward, S. *Australia and the British Embrace: The Demise of the Imperial Ideal*. Melbourne, Terra Australis, 2001.

Williams, M, and Macdonald, Barrie. *The Phosphateers: a history *of the British Phosphate Commission and the Christmas Island Phosphate Commission.* Melbourne, MUP, 1985.

Wright, C. *The echo of things: The lives of photographs in the Solomon Islands.* Durham, Duke University Press, 2013.

Young, JMR. 'Australia's Pacific frontier', *HSANZ.* Vol. 12, no. 47, pp. 373–88, 1966.

Young, JMR, ed. *Australia's Pacific frontier: Economic and cultural expansion into the Pacific 1795–1885.* Melbourne, Cassells, 1968.

Index

www.ingramcontent.com/pod-product-compliance
Lightning Source LLC
Chambersburg PA
CBHW032144050726
47591CB00001B/78